3D DESIGN STUDIO HANDBOOK

ARTS 1420 3D DESIGN

Fred Herbst

SUNY CORNING COMMUNITY COLLEGE

Published by SUNY OER Services

SUNY Office of Library and Information Services

10 N Pearl St
Albany, NY 12207
Distributed by State University of New York Press

ISBN: 978-1-64176-067-6

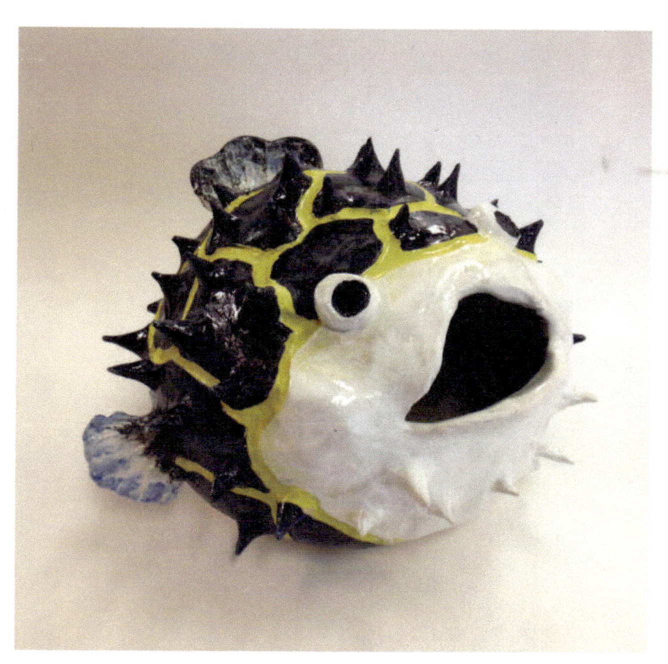
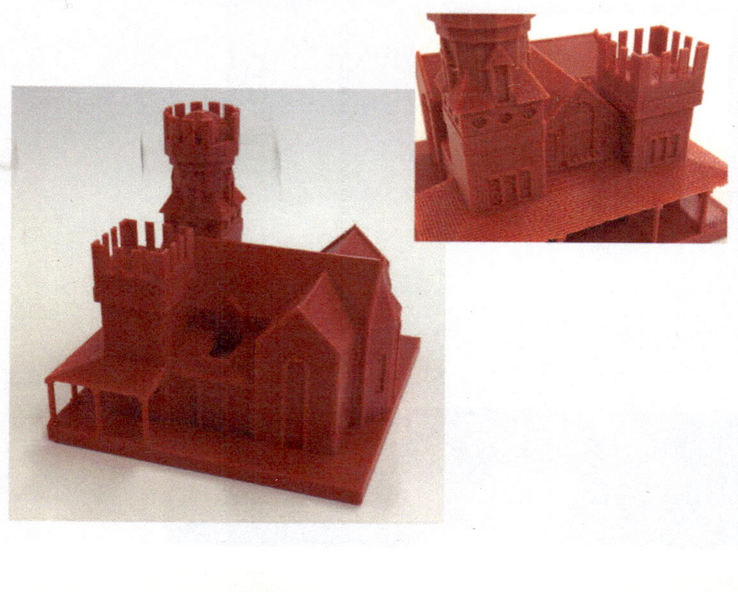
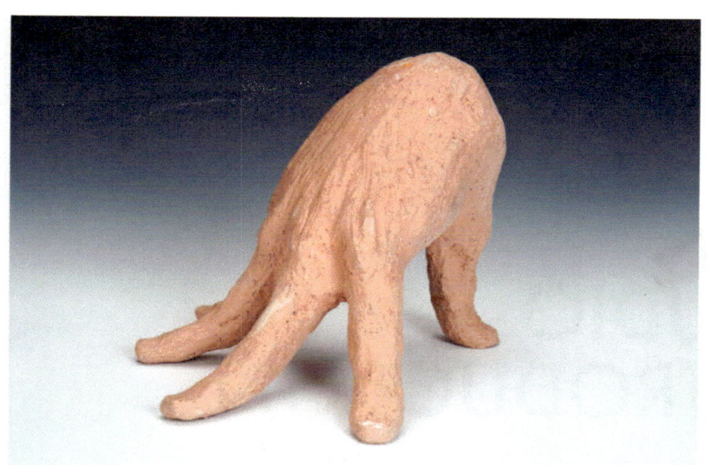
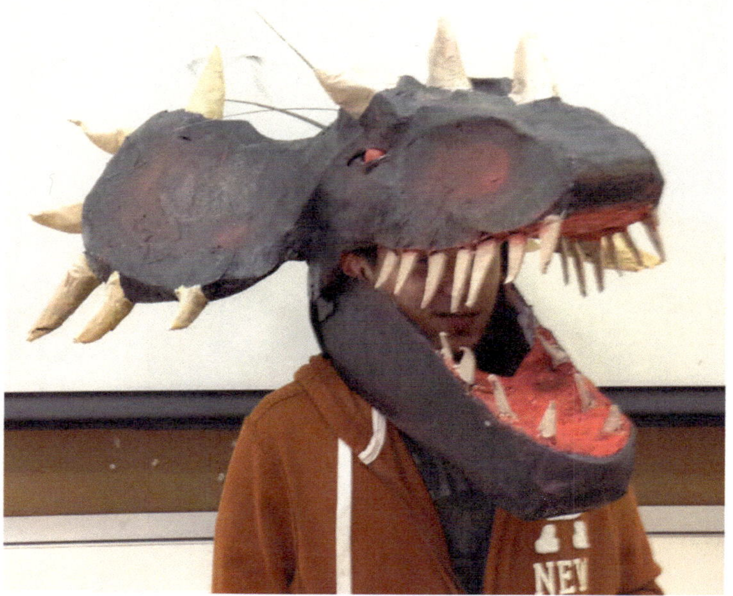

SUNY - CORNING COMMUNITY COLLEGE

3D DESIGN STUDIO HANDBOOK

ARTS 1420 3D DESIGN

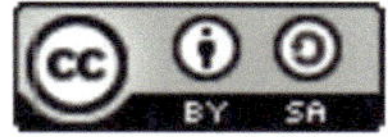

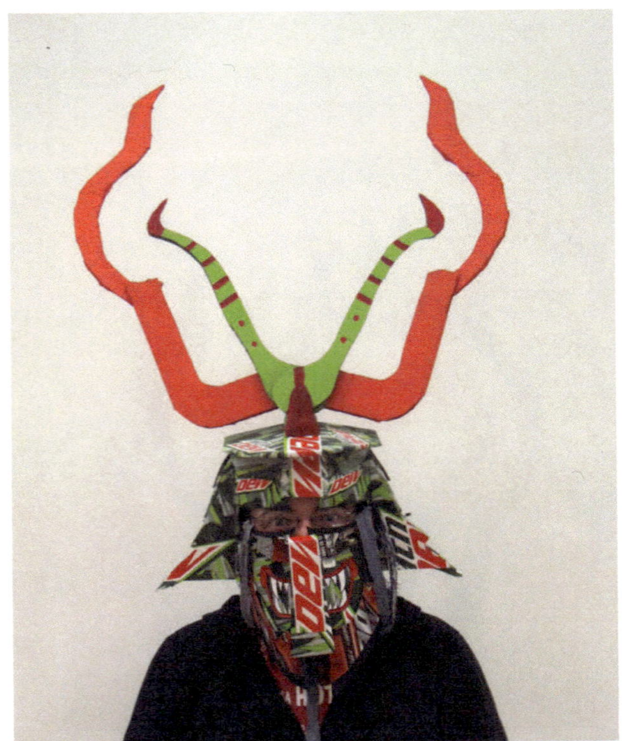

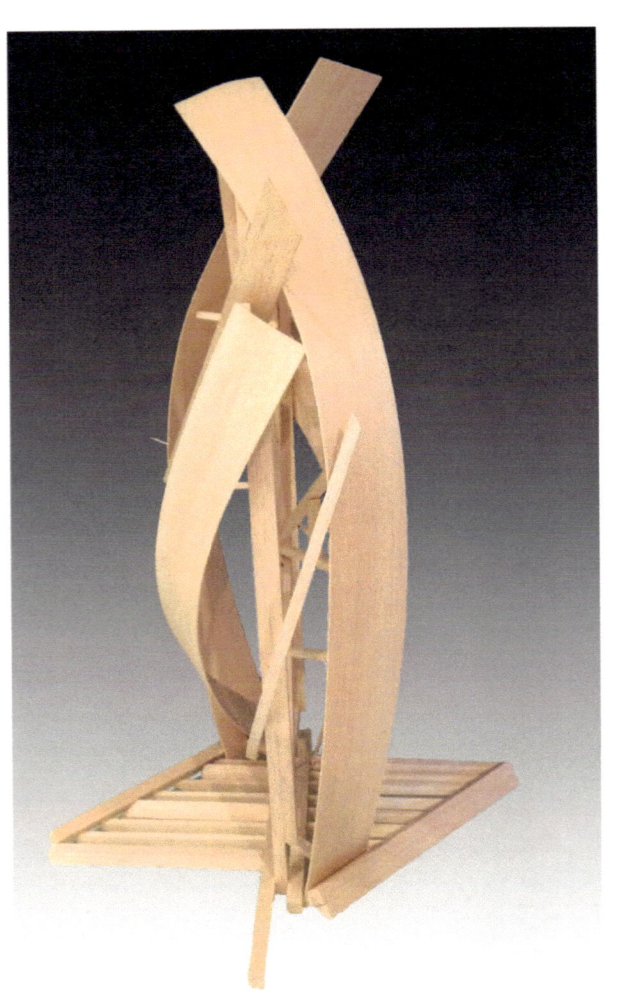

Examples of SUNY-CCC student work[1]

1

STUDIO INTRODUCTION

SUNY-CCC

Design and Ceramics Studio Policies and Procedures

Please follow these rules during your time in class and during open studio access.

1. Bring your tools and studio manual with you each class and / or work session. Some projects will fit inside assigned cabinets to store between classes but you may need to take larger pieces with you.

2. You need to clean up your own mess. You are expected to put your projects away, clean your table, tools, etc. All paper and cardboard scraps need to be recycled. Any tools, materials, or projects left out may be thrown away.

3. Always label your work so there is no confusion about who it belongs to.

4. If you are wearing ear buds or headphones, do not turn the volume up loud enough to disturb others. You should also be able to easily hear any announcements or comments from the instructor.

5. Do not cut directly on the wood table tops. Always use a cutting mat or make your own out of recyclable cardboard sheets.

4. Make sure to change blades in your Exacto knife often. Old, dull blades should be wrapped in masking tape and placed in the container next to the light table.

5. Food and drink are allowed in the studio but make sure to wash your hands before eating and be careful not to spill on your projects.

6. Open studio access will be stopped if you don't clean up your mess when working outside of class.

Safety Information

Every art making process has its own safety concerns. In 3d Design, the main issues include dust inhalation, cuts from X-acto and utility knives, and burns from hot kilns when we work in the Ceramics studio. Over time, excessive exposure to material (sawdust, clay, plaster, etc.) dusts can cause lung damage. Proper use of dust masks or respirators and good ventilation will minimize this exposure and help to ensure healthy conditions. In general, always wear a dust mask rated for at least N95 (an industrial rating for filtering particles) or a respirator with dust filtering cartridges. In the Ceramics studio, always use **wet sponges**, use a HEPA filtered vacuum, and/or wet mop. **DO NOT sweep the floor** as this causes dust to get airborne. **DO NOT brush your clay crumbs onto the floor since they will get crushed into dust that you will breathe later**.

Kilns used to fire ceramics can reach VERY high temperatures. The electric kilns in the studio are commonly firing to between 1,800 and 2,200 degrees Fahrenheit. The outside surface of all these kilns can get very hot and burn you! **NEVER** place anything on top of the electric kilns. **NEVER** stand next to a heating kiln, there are small "spy holes" in the side that can burn you or your clothes.

We will use a variety of tools and basic equipment in 3d Design. As needed, you should always wear safety glasses, ear protection, and dust masks. If have long hair, always tie it back away from tools and equipment, Always know where your hands are, what you're breathing, what's protecting your eyes and ears, and where the hot things are. Having an awareness and using logical steps toward safety will ensure a long career in art making.

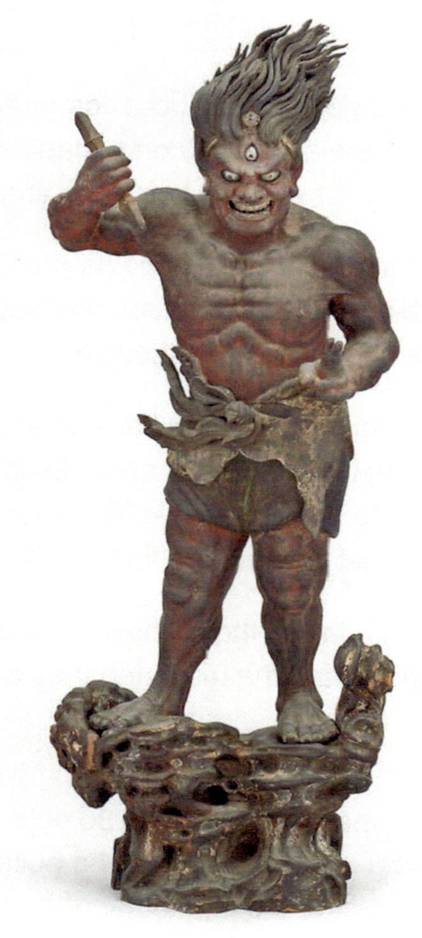

2

INTRODUCTION TO 3D ART MAKING

From the beginning of our species, humans have been object makers. The first things made were items for survival (tools, weapons, and clothing) or for spiritual use (representations of animals or gods). As human cultures evolved, the kinds of 3d objects also evolved to serve a huge range of purposes and functions. We are on that evolutionary makers continuum as we make things that are relevant to contemporary culture.

This course deals with the construction of 3d objects. One major difference between this way of working other art modes is that 3d work has actual physical depth and material texture. It doesn't need to try to create the illusion of space. These objects take up real space with the viewer often seeing multiple sides or points of view.

At its core, art and design are about communication. The goal is to communicate with the viewer or user. There are three components to any work that can be examined to see how well it communicates to the viewer. They are:

1. **Subject**- (What) this is what is being presented. Is the object meant to be representational of something, non-representational but an abstraction of something, or conceptual (where the idea becomes the subject)?

2. **Form**- (How)- this is the overall arrangement or organization of the work. This uses the elements (building blocks/words) and principles (organizing elements into relationships/sentences) of art to build the work. The arrangement is often more complex in 3d work because of our most challenging force in 3d art and design- gravity.

3. **Context**- (Why)- this is the emotional / intellectual message of the work. The context is the artist's intention and the message they are trying to get to the viewer.

The challenge of making interesting 3d objects and ideas is a complex and rewarding process. Breaking down the basics and building up an effective art making process will be discussed in the rest of the studio handbook.

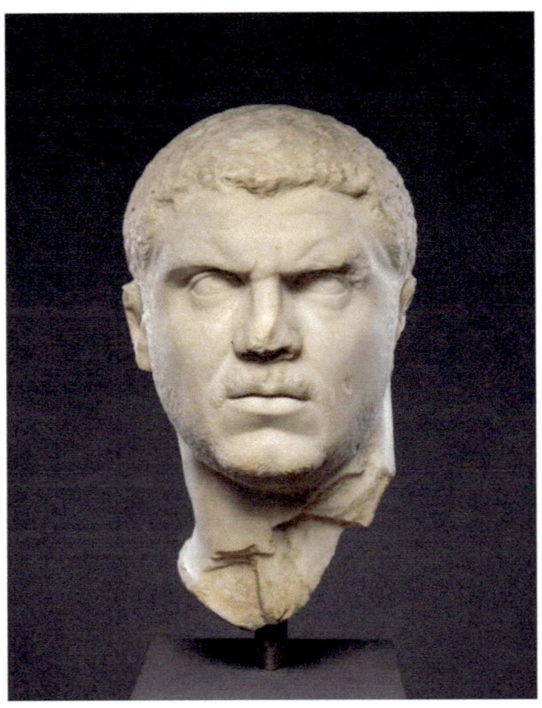

Portrait of Emperor Caracalla, carved marble, Roman , 212-217 CE[4]

CRITIQUE / CRIT

Individual and group evaluations of art works (critiques) are key to learning in the studio art environment. This experience will help you to see where your projects are successful, where they need more work, and also discuss other students' work in the same manner. The critique process should be one of constructive criticism that in the end, helps you make better decisions about your work and become a stronger visual artist. It is not a process used to give everyone a "pat on the back" just for showing up or as a way to put others down. The crit should be about the work that is being discussed separate from the maker. Every object / artwork ever made could be better somehow and the goal of the critique process is to discover how the works could be more effective and interesting.

Effectively presenting your ideas, projects, or objects to a group is a skill that matures with experience and has a great deal of value outside the college art studio. The critique process should help you develop your confidence with talking about your ideas, receiving criticism, and responding appropriately. These are skills that should serve you well in your future career, whatever that may be.

In this studio course, we will be looking at your projects and discussing a number of issues. Some of these aspects include how well your work fits the assigned criteria, how visually dynamic your solutions are, how interesting your concept is, and how well crafted your objects are. Sometimes a piece will be very strong in some of these areas but not in others. For example, a work might have a very exciting idea behind it but it is poorly constructed and is falling apart. Or another might be extremely well crafted but the idea behind the project is weak. The best works always have a balance of idea, visual interest, and careful construction. We will use critiques to help you see where your work is strong and where it needs to continue to improve.

There are a number of questions to ask when **analyzing** an art work in a studio art class.
For example, did the maker use the required materials and techniques skillfully?
Does the piece work as a successfully integrated object or are there parts that don't fit?
Did the artist use the elements and principles of art in the work effectively?
If the work is meant to be functional, does the piece make you want to pick it up and use it?

There are a number of questions to ask when **interpreting** an art work in a studio art class.
For example, what is your response to the piece?
How does it make you feel, does it make you think of anything from your own experience?
Can you tell what the artist was trying to communicate to the viewer / user?

There are a number of questions to ask when **judging** an art work in a studio art class.
For example, if you think the piece is successful, why do you feel that way?
What are the works strengths and what could be done to make it more successful?
What would the maker want to do over? What would be the next idea in a series of these kinds of pieces?

Critiques should be a valuable experience for all involved. Carefully looking at, thinking about, and discussing the works will help to make everyone a better artist. Remember, everything could be better somehow!

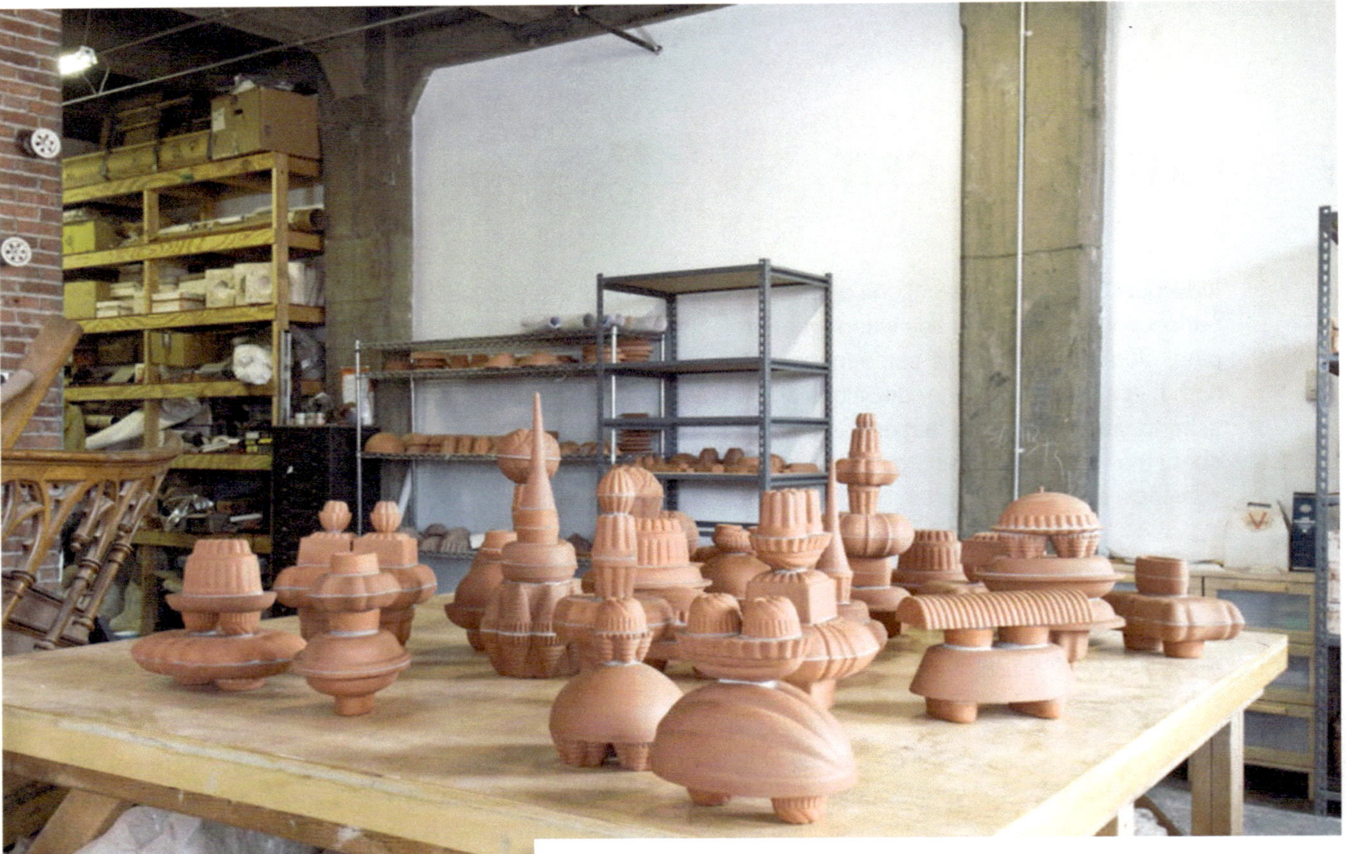
Studio view, Nicholas Kripal[2]

3

ART ELEMENTS

Elements of Art and Design as they apply to 3d artworks and objects

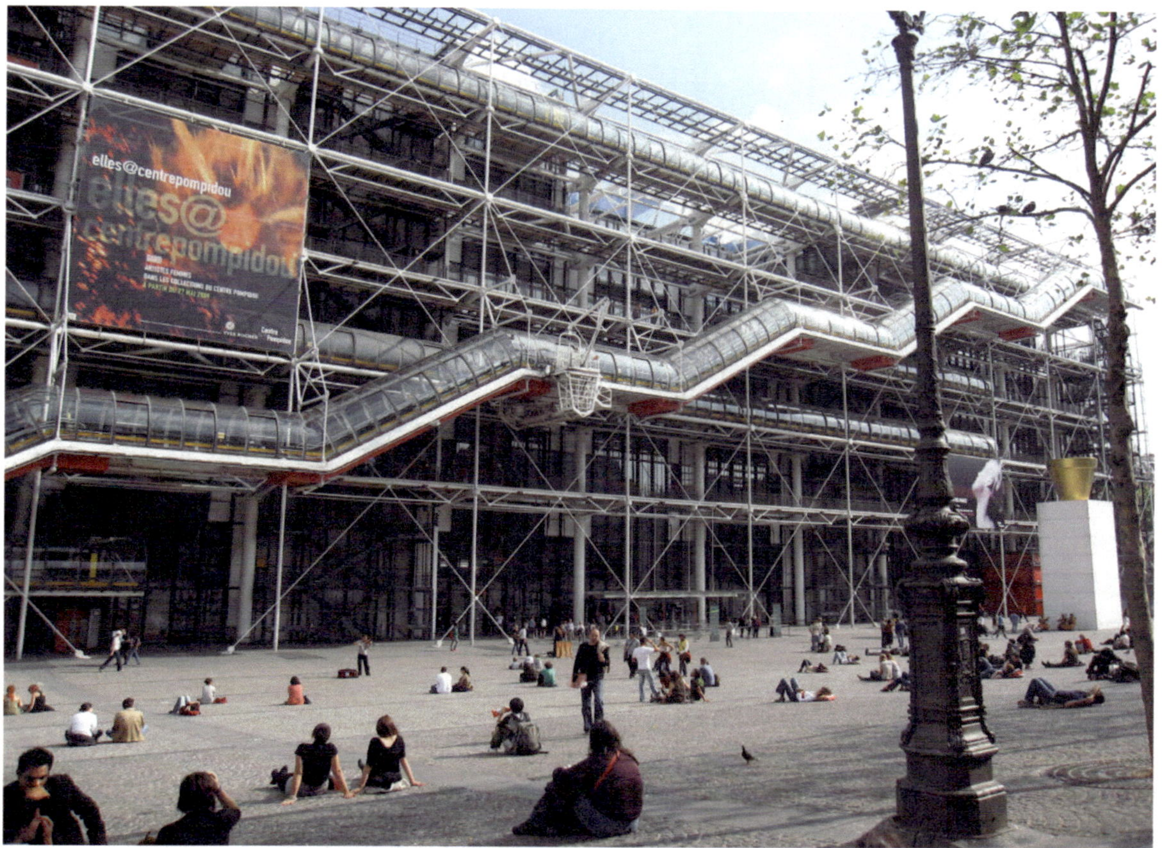

The Centre Pompidou in Paris, France has linear elements making up the exterior of the structure[1]

LINE

Line is the most familiar of art elements because it is used everyday in basic communication. Our handwritten language is made of lines and symbols created using pencil or ink. When asked to depict something by drawing, lines are used to create that image on a 2d surface. Line is essential to communication and image making on a flat surface but once you move into the 3d dimension, the use of line changes.

By definition a line is a point that has been stretched for a distance. Lines do not occur in our three dimensional reality but our eyes create the line because of differences in shape, value, texture, and other factors. This also shows how line can interact with the other elements of art to create a compelling 3d object. Linear (line like) elements often direct the viewers eye around an artwork since our eyes like to follow a "path".

As an element of art, line has a variety of characteristics that can be identified and utilized. The first is direction. These directions include horizontal, vertical, and diagonal. The direction of lines can imply feeling and meaning to the artwork. Horizontal lines suggest resting, passive or reclining forms. Vertical lines often make the object feel like they are reaching, growing up, or stretching. Diagonal lines are usually the most visually interesting. They often appear active, dynamic, and in motion.

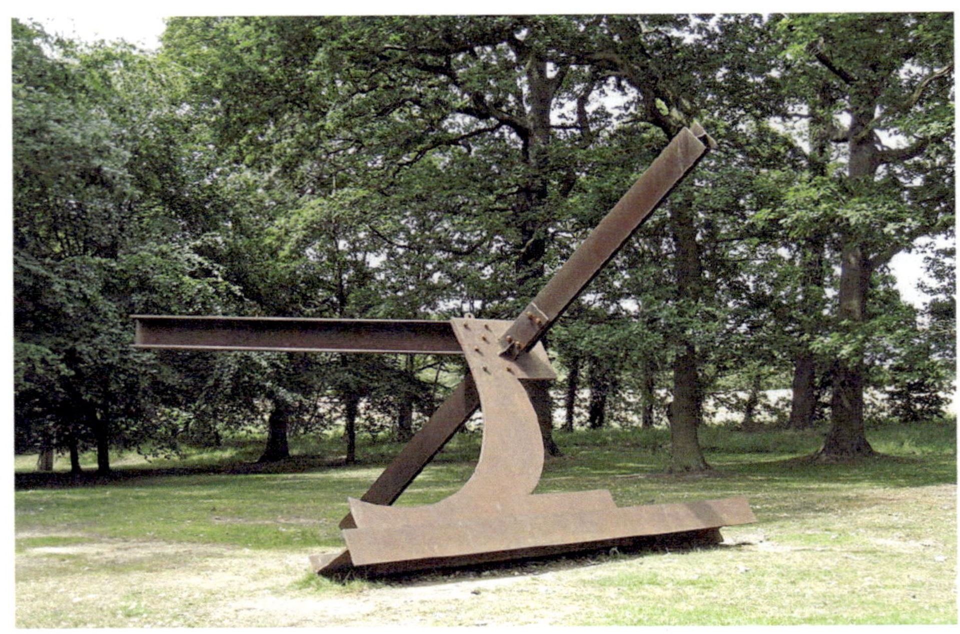

"Nelly" by Mark di Suvero, This steel sculpture contains a variety of diagonal elements that create a more dynamic structure.[19]

In addition to direction, line also has character that could include the following: straight, curved, wavy, broken, implied (your eye completes the line without it being there), angular, thick, thin. These terms are often discussed in drawing and three dimensional elements can be manipulated to create similar line character effects.

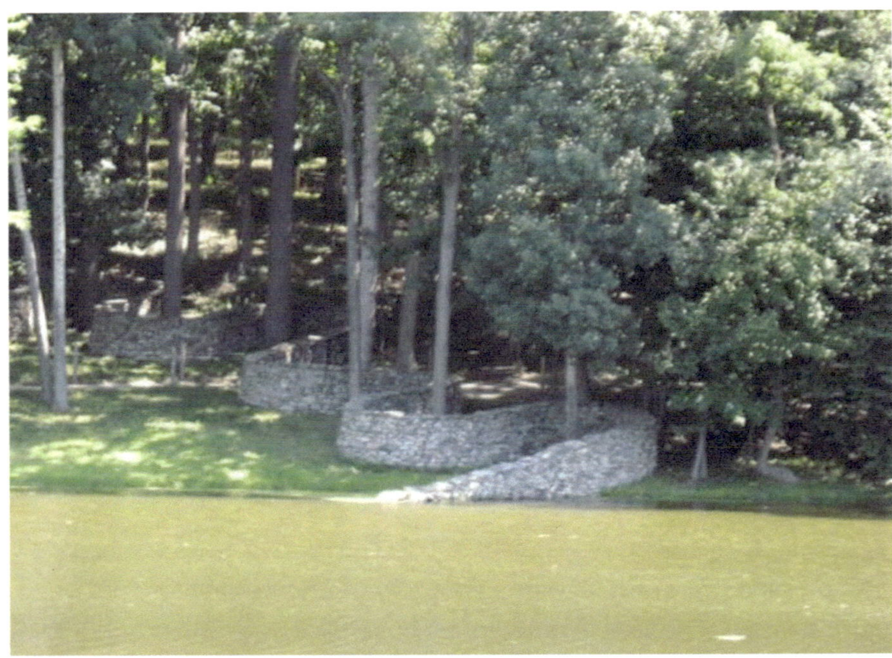

"Storm King Wall" by Andy Goldsworthy This stone wall snakes its way through the trees at Storm King Art Center.[20]

Some art making materials are extremely linear in character and lend that feeling to the finished object. This would include materials like wire, clay coils, cable, string, tubes, pipes, thin boards, balsa wood, and steel I-beams.

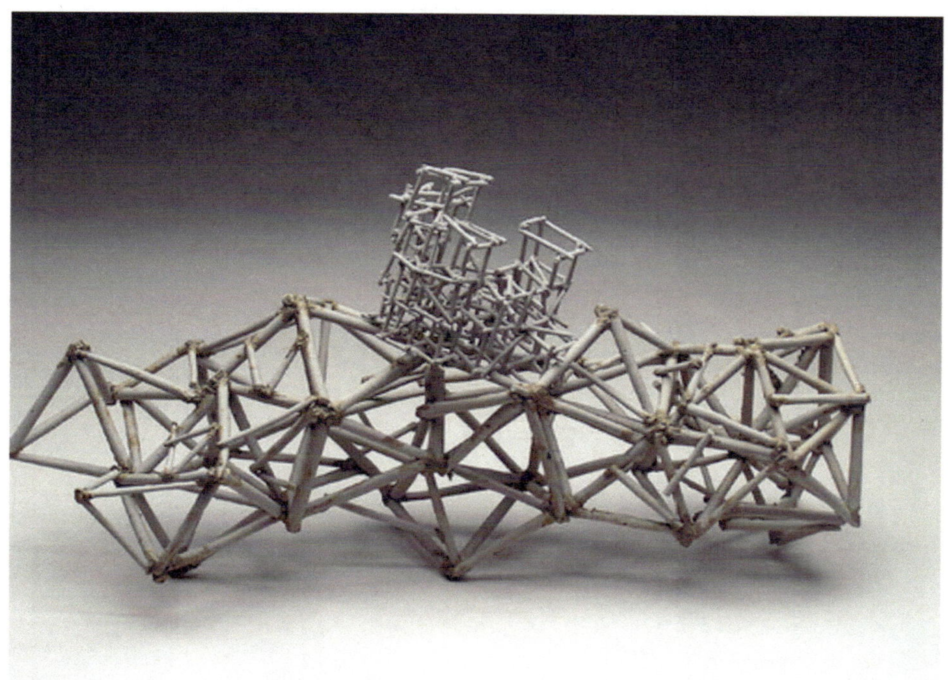

"Migration Grid 1" by Stanton Hunter, mixed media[5]

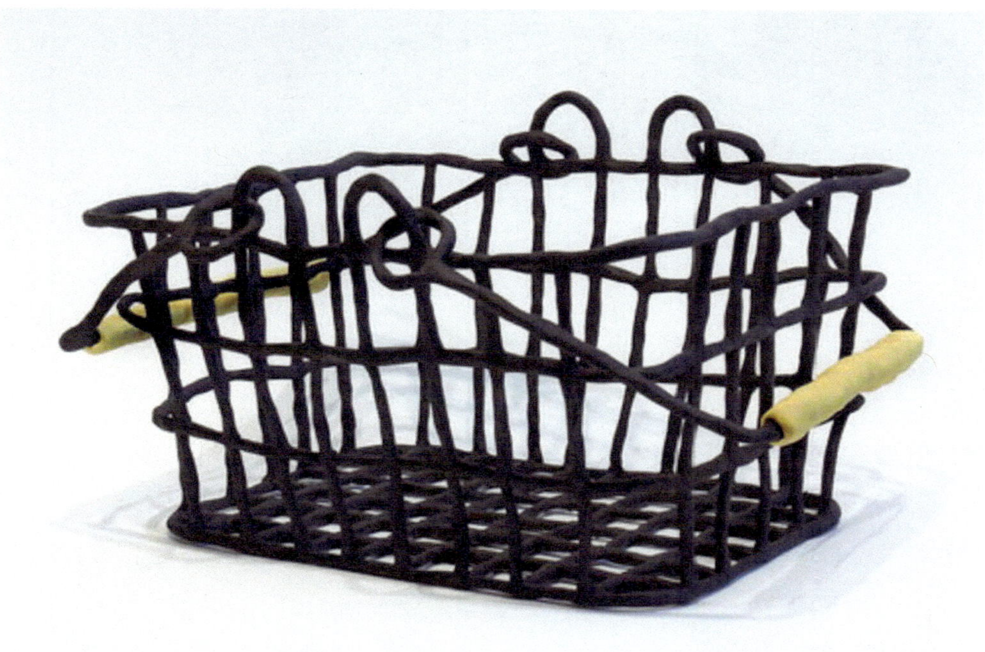

"Basket with Yellow Handles" by Priya Thoresen, ceramic and mixed media[2]

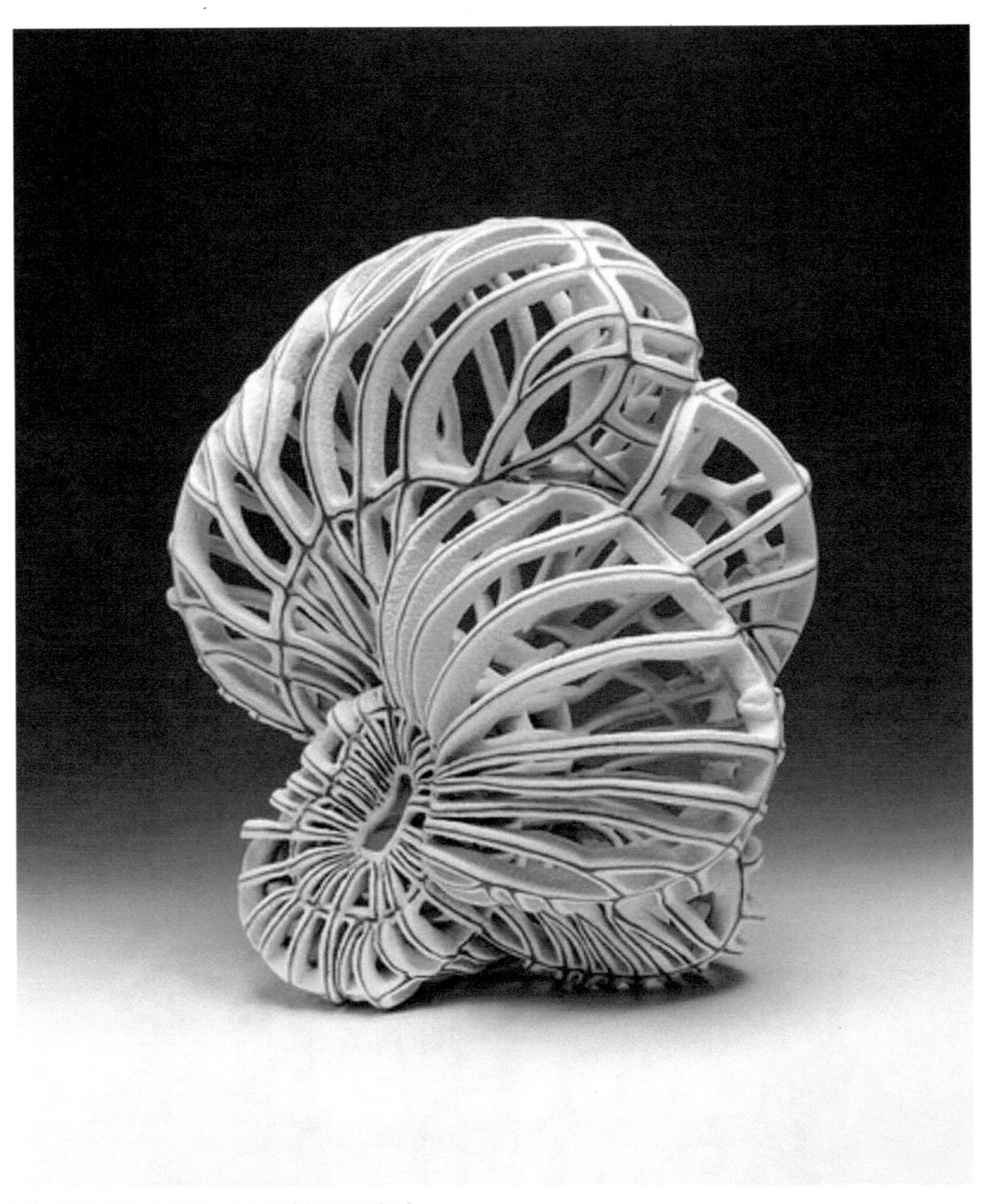

"Blue Vein 7" by Shiyuan Xu, porcelain paperclay.[3]

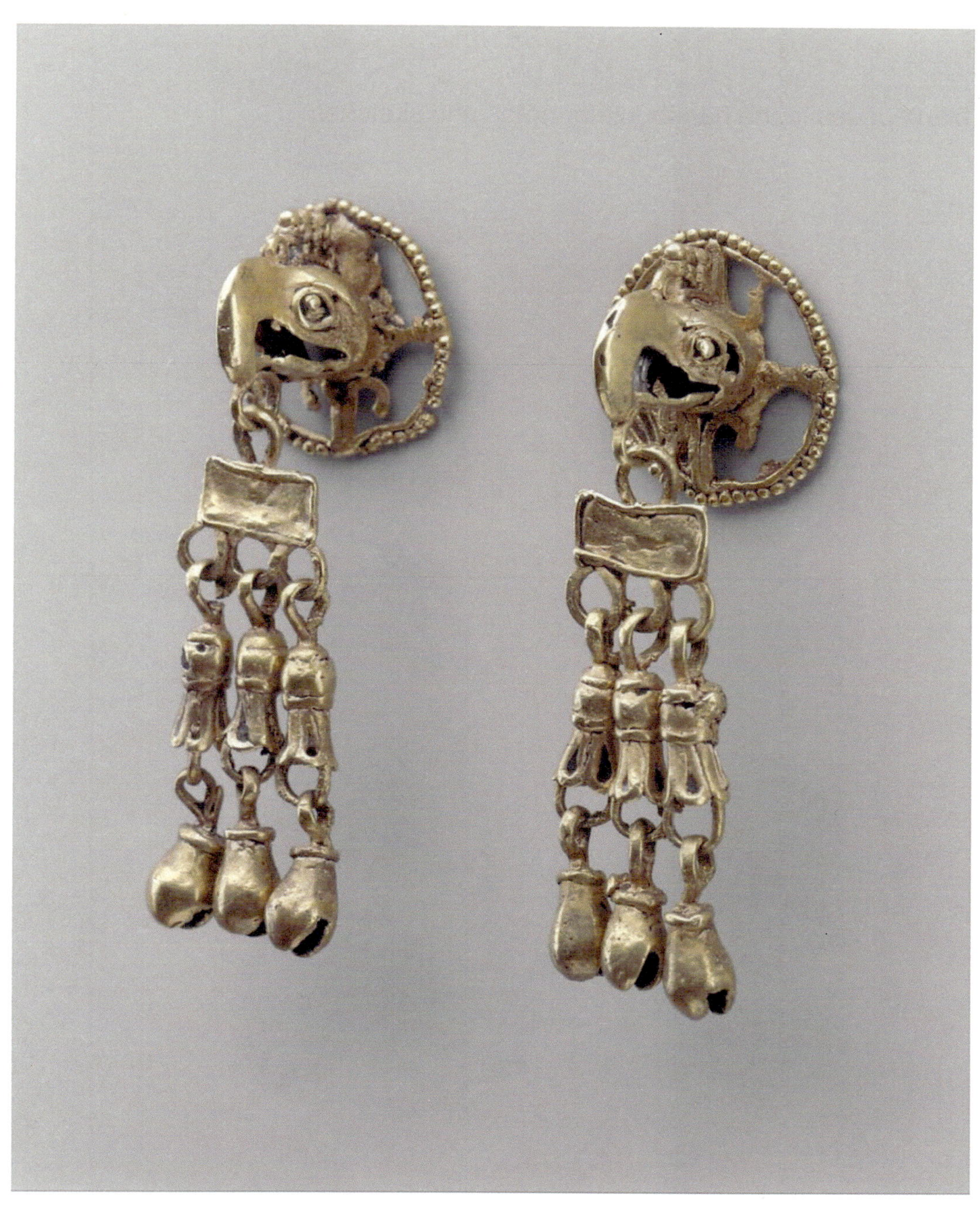

"Pair of Eagle Ear Ornaments", Aztec, 15th or 16th century, gold.[4]

Use blank pages in the handbook for notes and sketches:

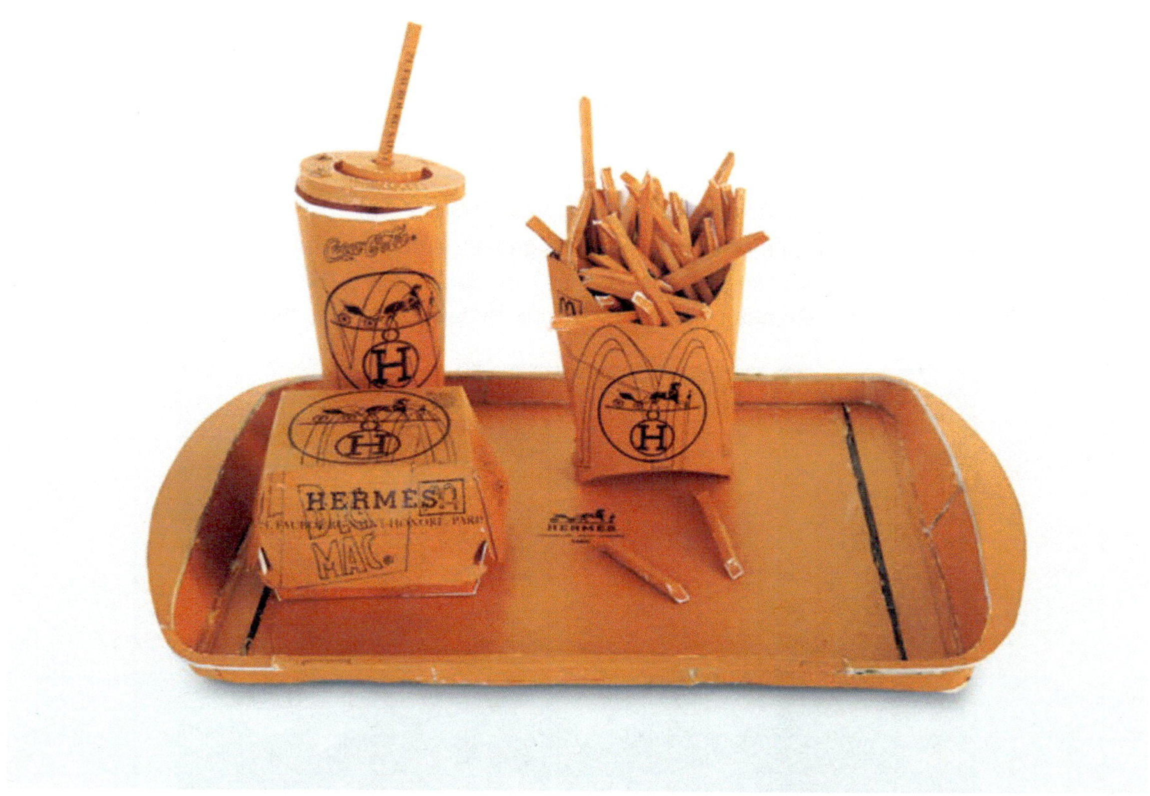

Tom Sachs "Hermes Value Meal"[15]

SHAPE

Shapes are the building blocks of 3d objects. By definition, shape is an area that stands out from the space next to or around it due to a defined or implied boundary often due to differences in value, texture, or color.

Just like line, shapes have a variety of possible characteristics. One of the most basic is the difference between being geometric or organic in nature. Geometric shapes are typically made by humans and are made up of 3d spheres, cubes, pyramids and their corresponding 2d shapes; circles, spheres, and triangles. Geometric shapes are derived from mathematics and can be curvilinear (made of curves) or rectilinear (made of straight lines).

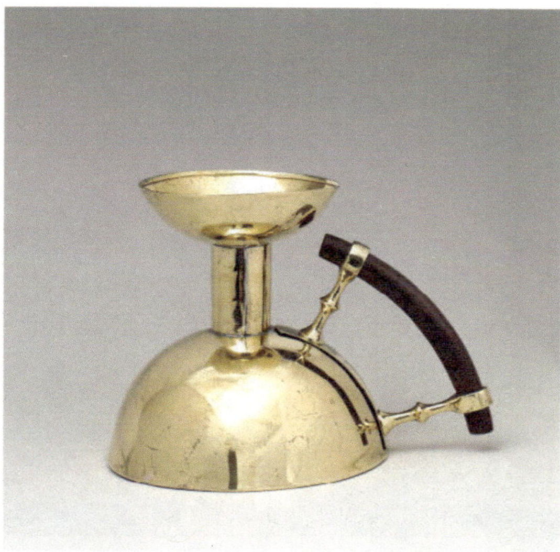

"Candlestick", by Christopher Dresser, 1883, made of metal and has a very geometric shape focus.[4]

In contrast, organic or biomorphic shapes are those generally found in nature. These shapes often have rounded, curving forms suggesting natural processes like growth, erosion, or decay. Water, wind, ice, and snow are the planet's most important and effective sculptors as they continually reform the landscape. Humans are organic shapes and have worked with natural materials to create new forms over the history of our species.

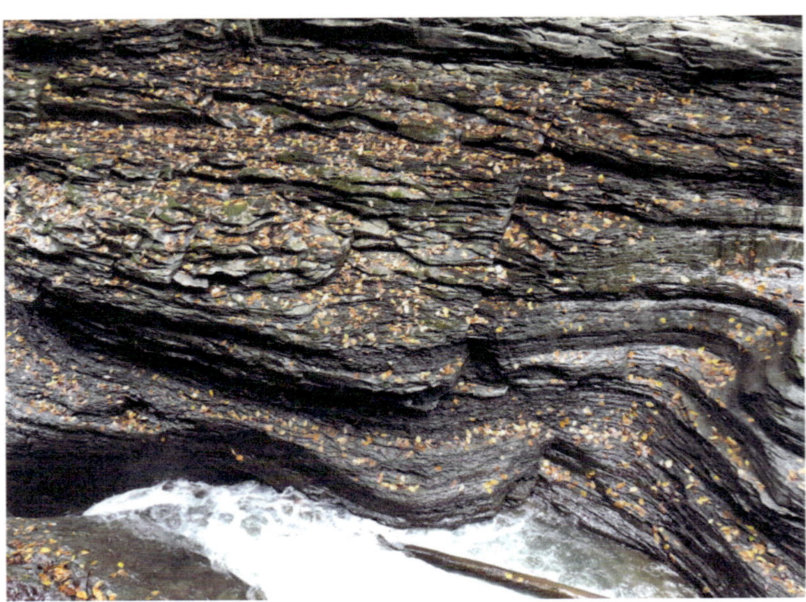

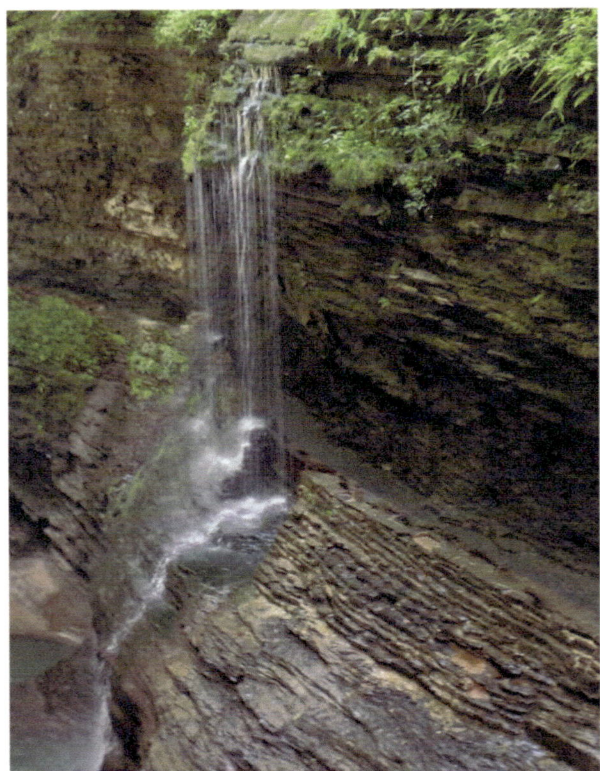

Images from Watkins Glen State Park showing the power of water as a sculptor. [1]

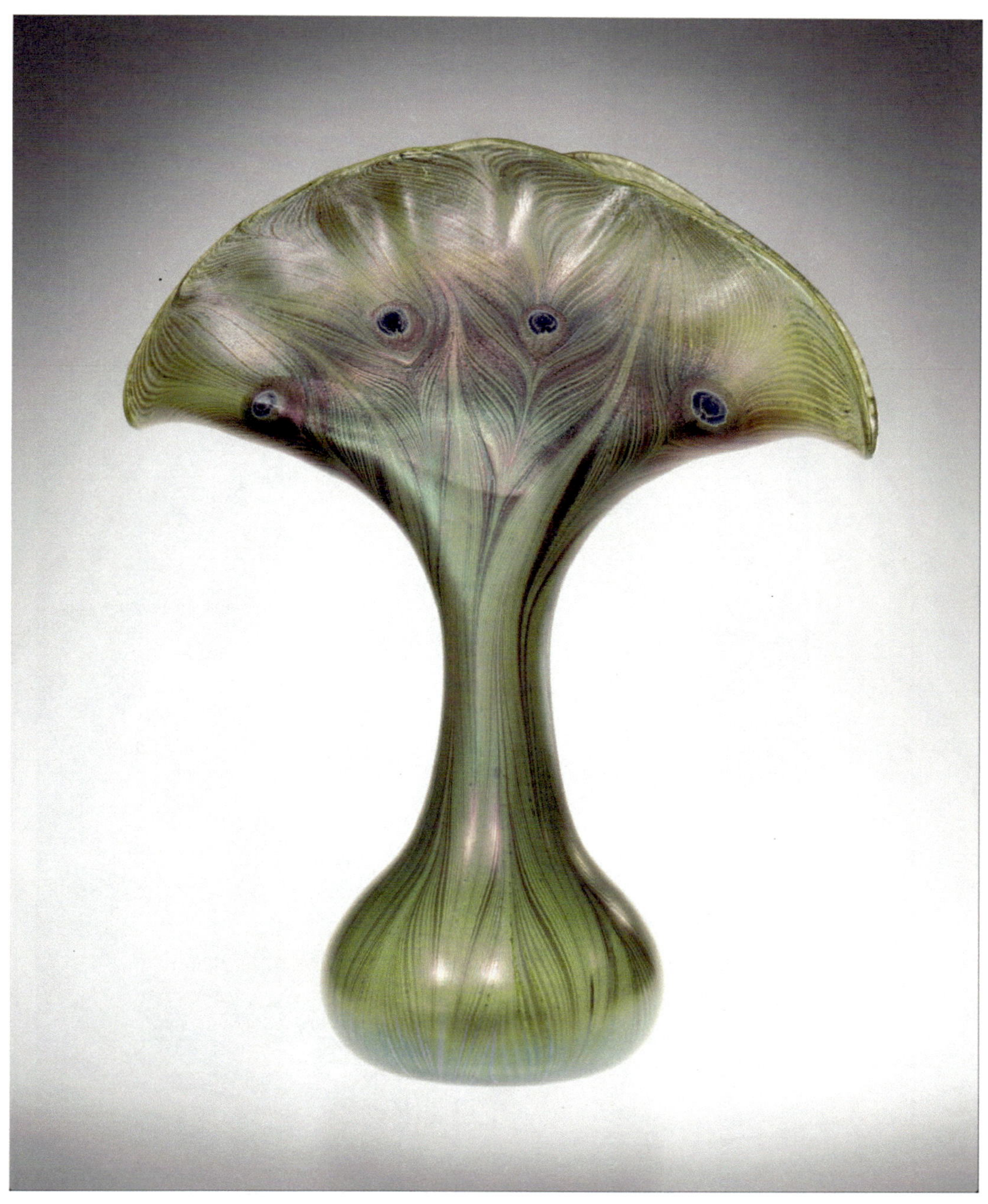

"Vase", by Louis Comfort Tiffany, 1893-96, made of blown Favrile glass. Tiffany was looking to create a very organic form in both the shape. color, and pattern in the surface of this vase.[4]

Another important characteristic when discussing shape is the difference between mass and vloume. Mass is defined as the physical weight of an object. Stone, clay, plaster, concrete, and metal objects generally appear to have a large mass.

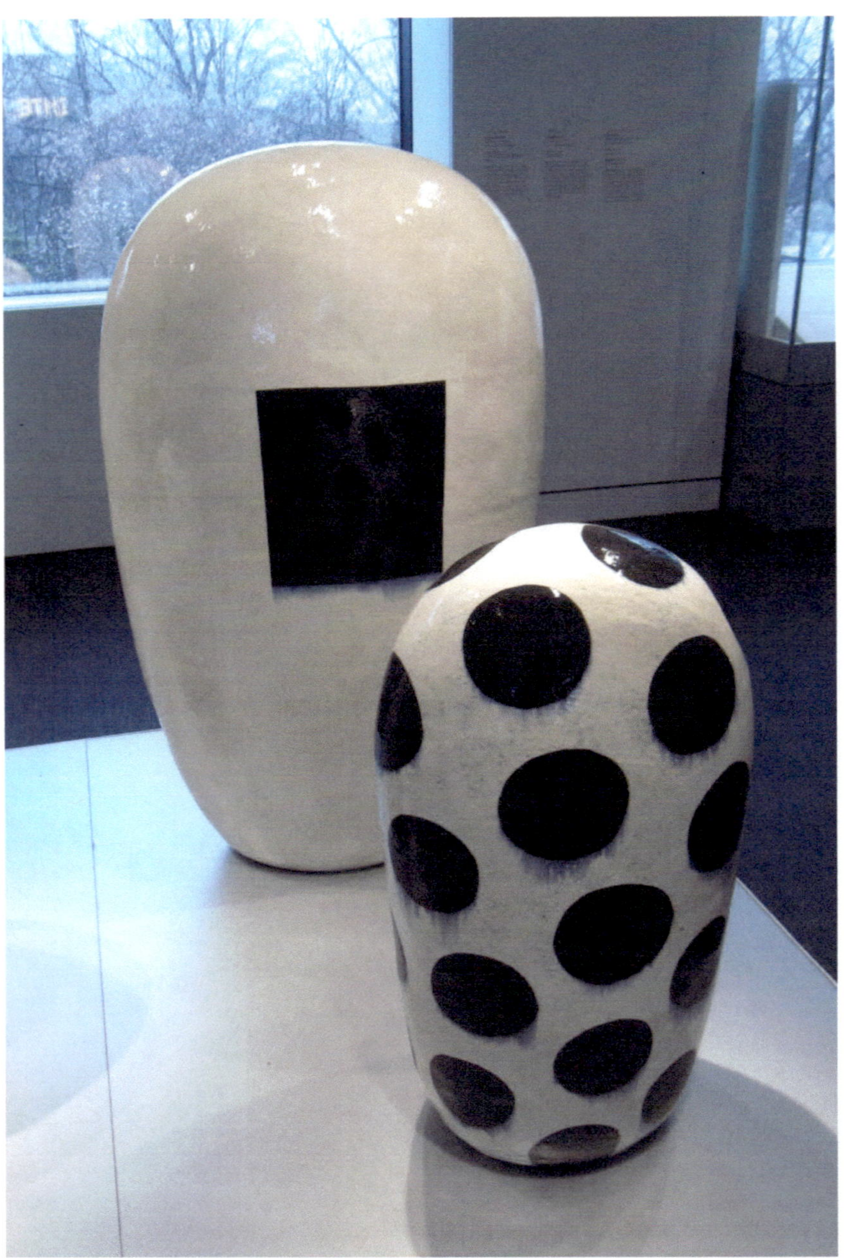

Two "Dango" sculptures by Jun Kaneko made of glazed ceramic. These pieces were constructed hollow in order to survive the kiln firing process but they still have considerable visual mass.[1]

Volume is how much space an object occupies. A massive shape generally takes up a large amount of space but a lighter object can also have the same volume and occupy the same amount of space. This concept can be simplified to: All mass has volume, but not all volume has mass.

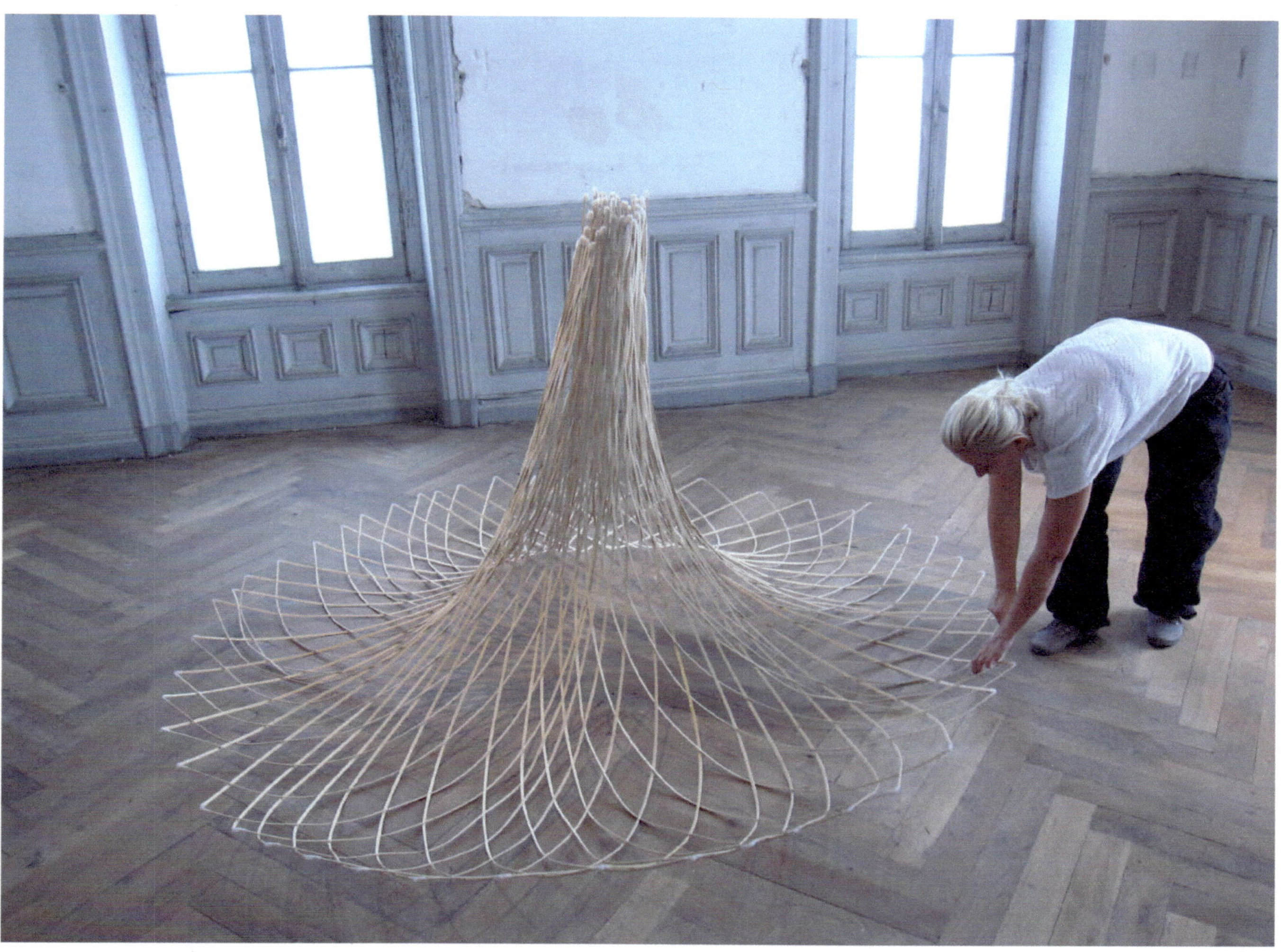

This bamboo structure has a relatively large volume but very little physical weight or mass.[1]

SPACE

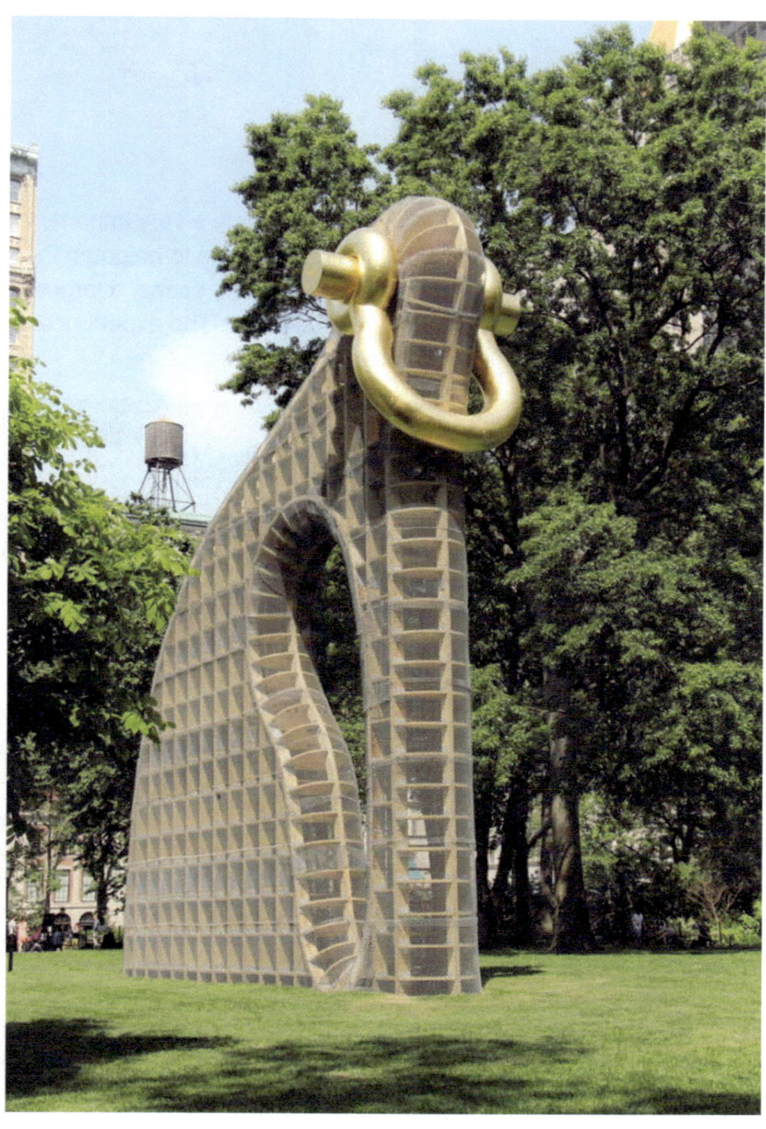

Martin Puryear, "Big Bling".[16]

Space is the interval, or measurable distance between pre-established points or objects. In 3d art and design, we are not trying to create the illusion of space on a flat surface since there is actual physical space we are constructing in. There are a few important considerations and aspects of space in the third dimension. The first is the positive / negative space relationship.

Positive space is the area that the object take up. It's the volume that the object you create fills. In contrast, negative space is the empty space around the object. The relationship between these two can create interesting visual tension as the viewer moves around and interacts with object. For example, designers will examine the negative space inside the handle of a teapot or cup to see if it works technically (it's comfortable to hold onto) and if it creates a pleasing negative space when looked at. In addition, positive / negative space relationships can happen on surface decoration adding more visual interest. Typically, darker shapes are seen as negative space shapes and lighter as viewed as positive.

In contemporary art, the installation has become a very important way to utilizing and manipulating space. The installation works inside the space to heighten the viewers awareness of the feeling of being in the space. This could be a gallery space, a larger environment, or general public spaces that get taken over to make the artwork. The experience of being in the installation is very different than just looking at an individual sculpture.

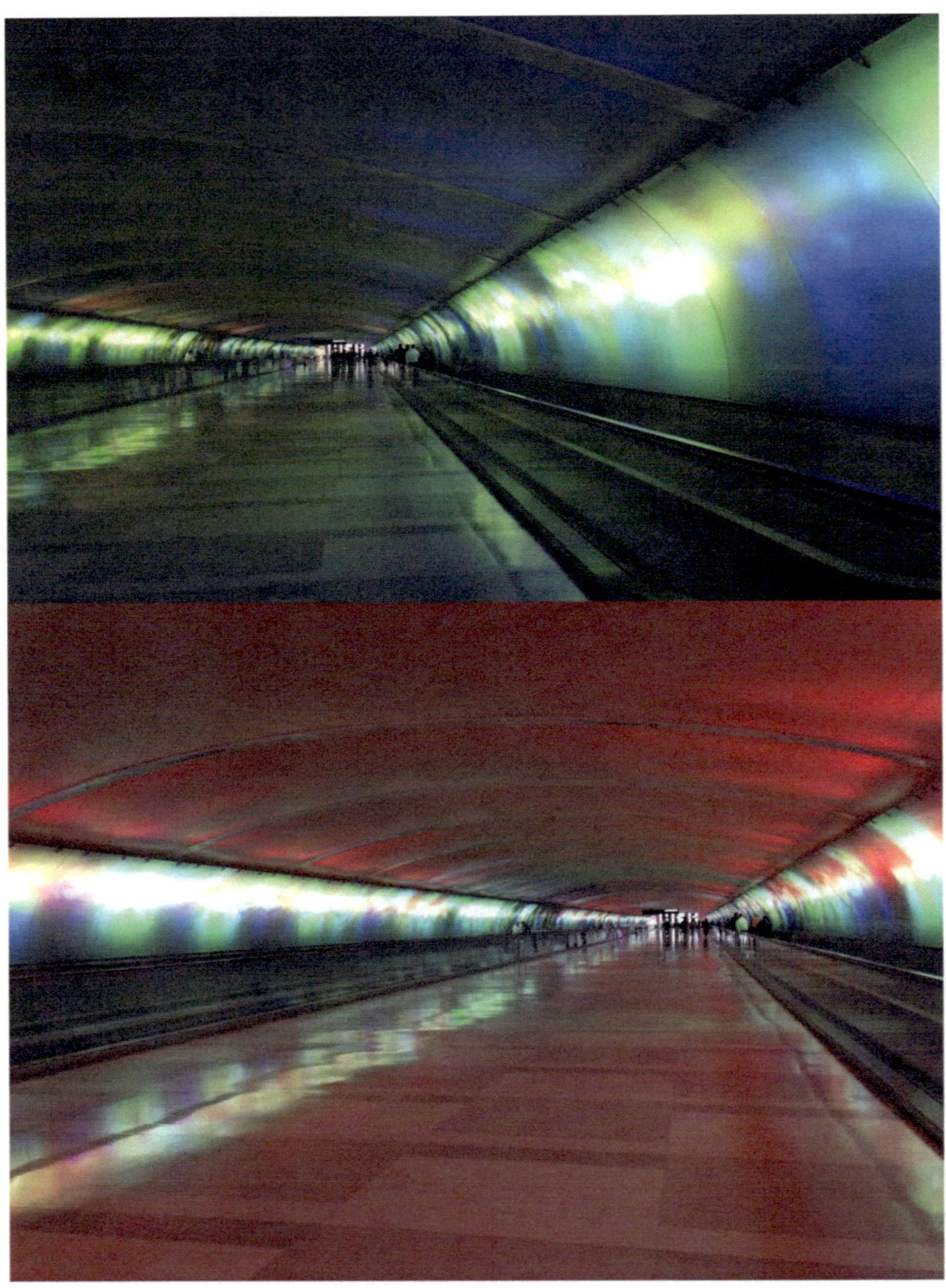

Mills James Productions, "Light Tunnel" at Detroit's airport that connects terminals. The installation is made up of sculpted glass panels, colored LED lights, and music to continually change the viewers experience of moving through a busy airport.[1]

In traditional sculpture, two terms are used to describe the space around the object when they are attached to a backing or as part of architecture. The first term is high-relief meaning a sculpted form that is cut away from the background to a high degree. The piece is almost fully sculpted and free standing but is still attached to a background. The second approach is low relief, also known as bas relief. This approach is the have the sculpted form mostly attached to the background and it does not project very far out from that surface.

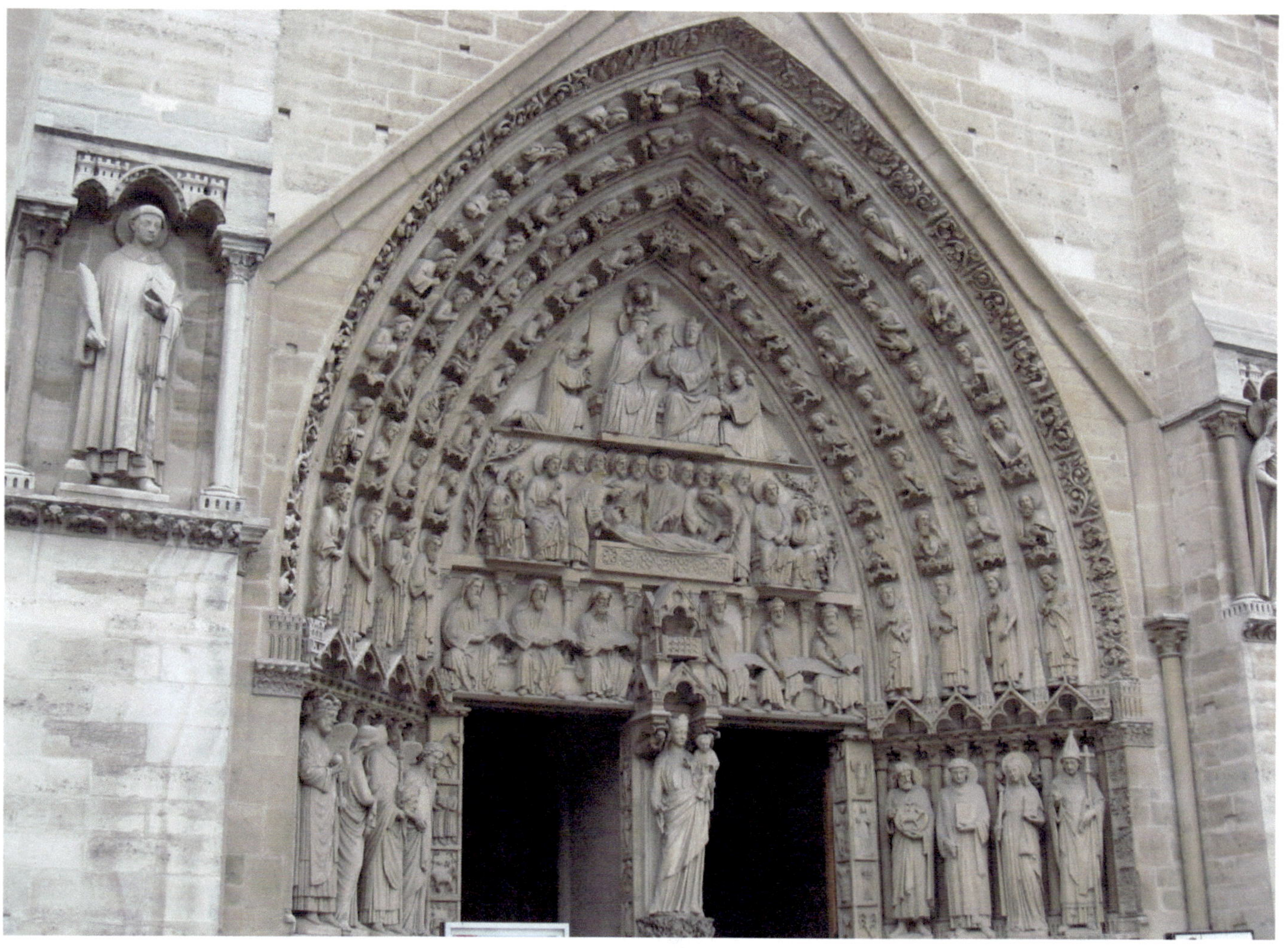

Above one of the front doors of Notre Dame Cathedral in Paris, France., The figures are carved from stone in relatively high relief.[1]

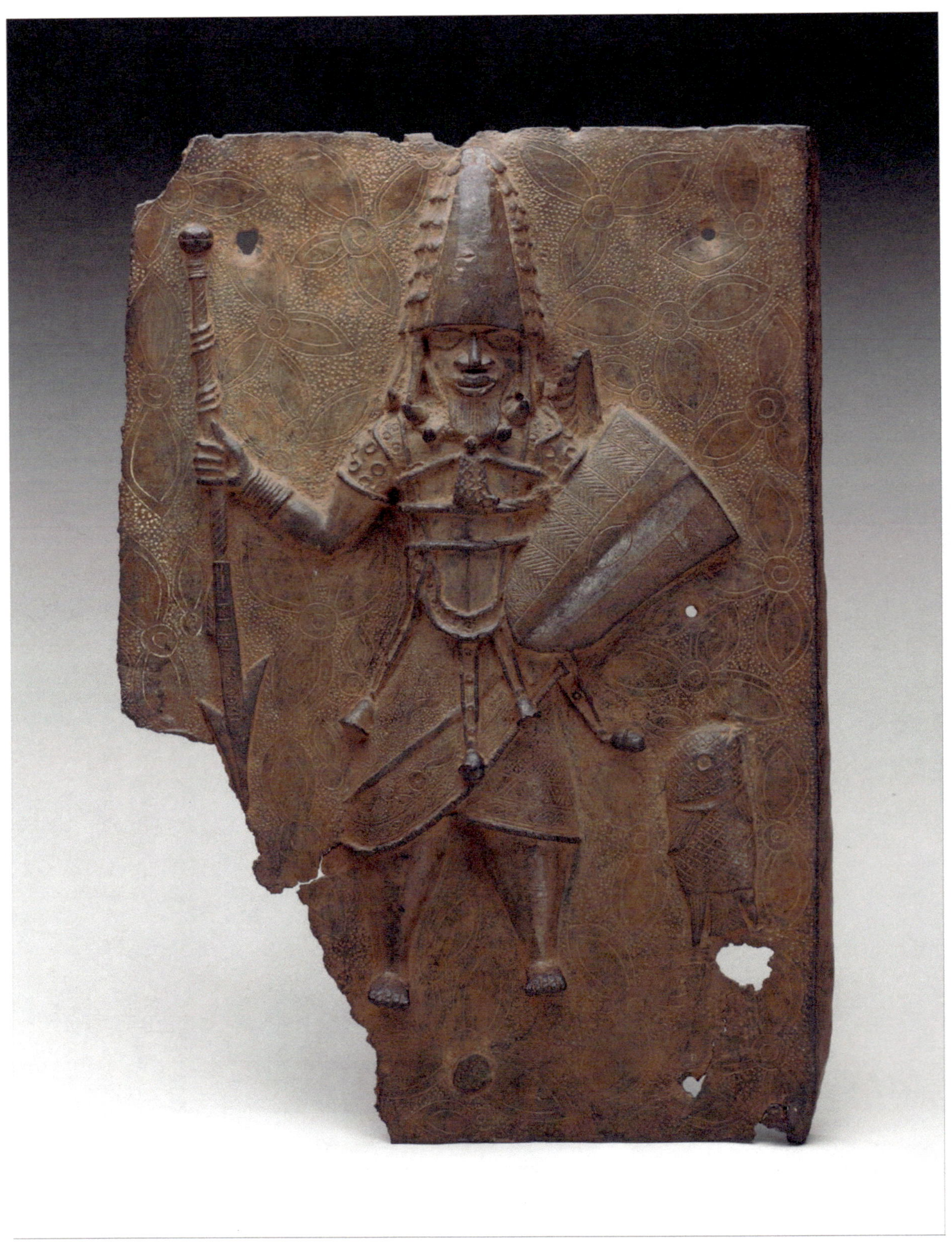

"Plaque: Warrior", Nigeria Benin Culture, brass, 16th to 17th century. This cast metal form has a warrior figure in low relief. [4]

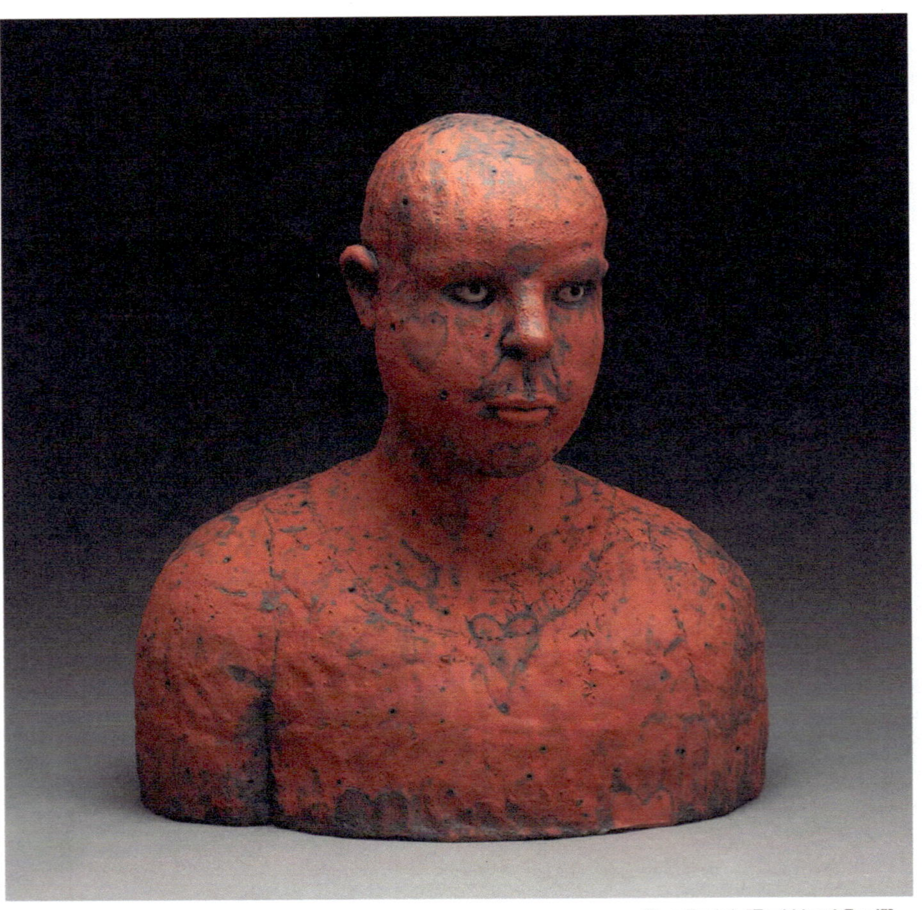

Tom Bartel, "Red Heart Bust"[3]

TEXTURE

Texture is the surface character of a material which can be experienced through touch or the illusion of touch. Surface texture can work differently depending on the purpose of the object. Functional objects (pottery, furniture, jewelry, fabrics, glass) that are meant to be handled, worn, or sat on need to have textures that be safe and appealing for the user. Textures can also be purely visual. As a result, they can be anything from the actual texture of the materials that make up the piece to totally invented textures trying to imitate something else.

In three dimensional works, the materials used to make the object have their own textures. Artists can work with those characteristics or try to hide or change them. This is a continual consideration, challenge, and opportunity for the artist and designer working in the third dimension.

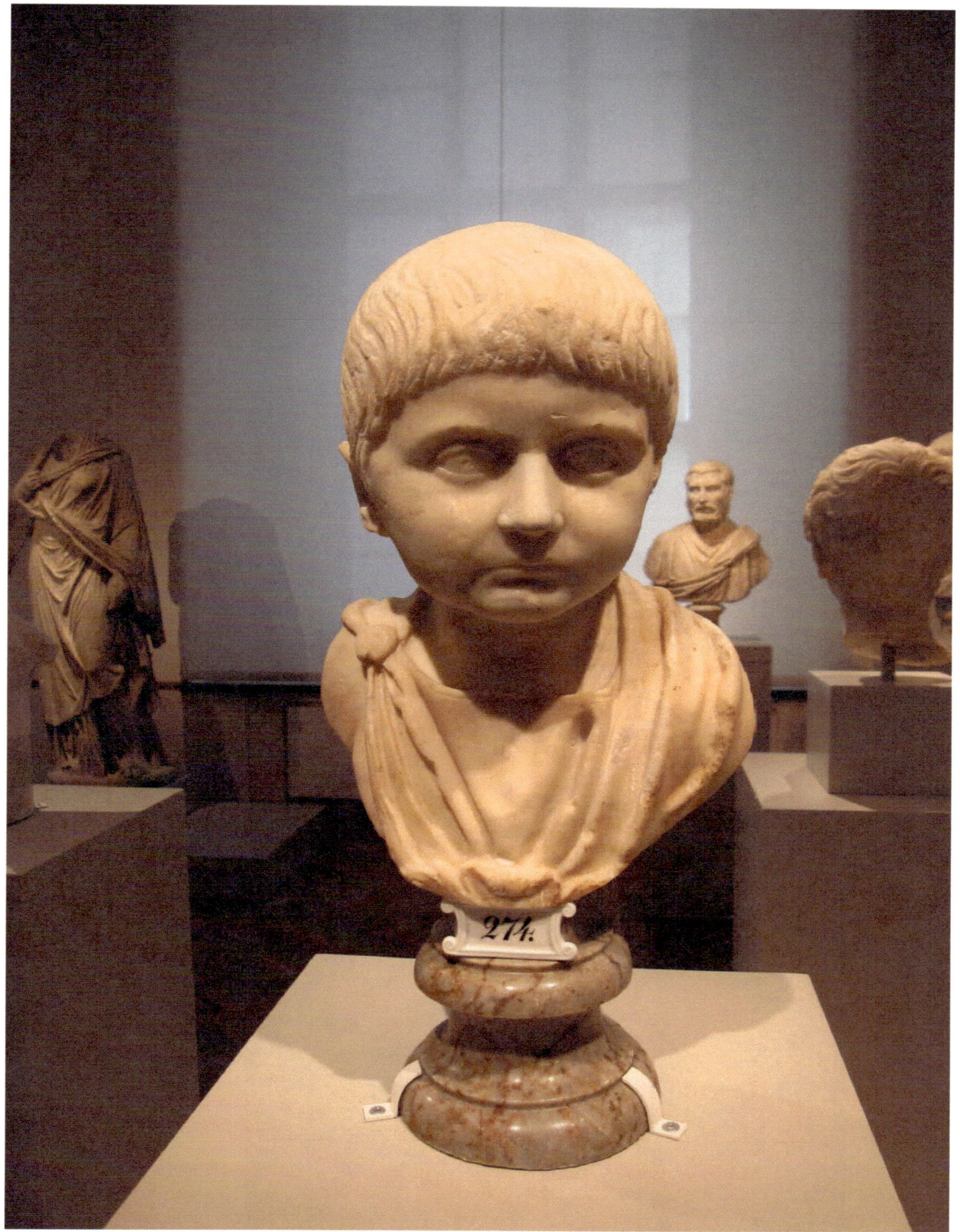

A carved stone sculpture of a young boy from an ancient cemetery. Roman sculptors were able to achieve a high degree of realism in textures like skin, hair, and cloth. Their mastery of manipulating hard stone into soft surface texture is profound and influenced countless later artists.[1]

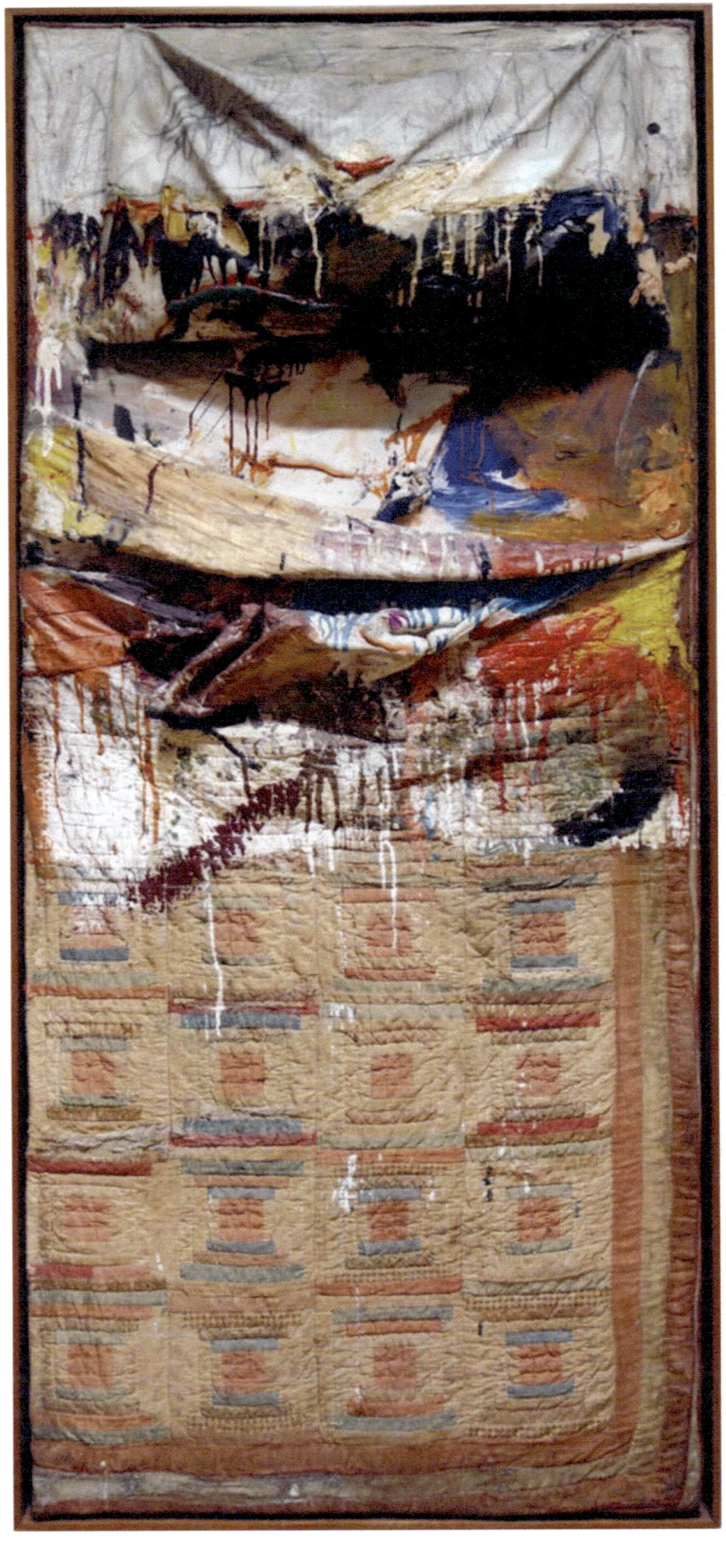

Robert Rauschenberg "Bed", 1955. This work was one of Rauschenberg's early "Combines" or assemblage mixed media sculpture / paintings. These were attached to the wall like a traditional painting but had a variety of materials incorporated to make them very dimensional. The texture of the other materials were key elements of these works.[21]

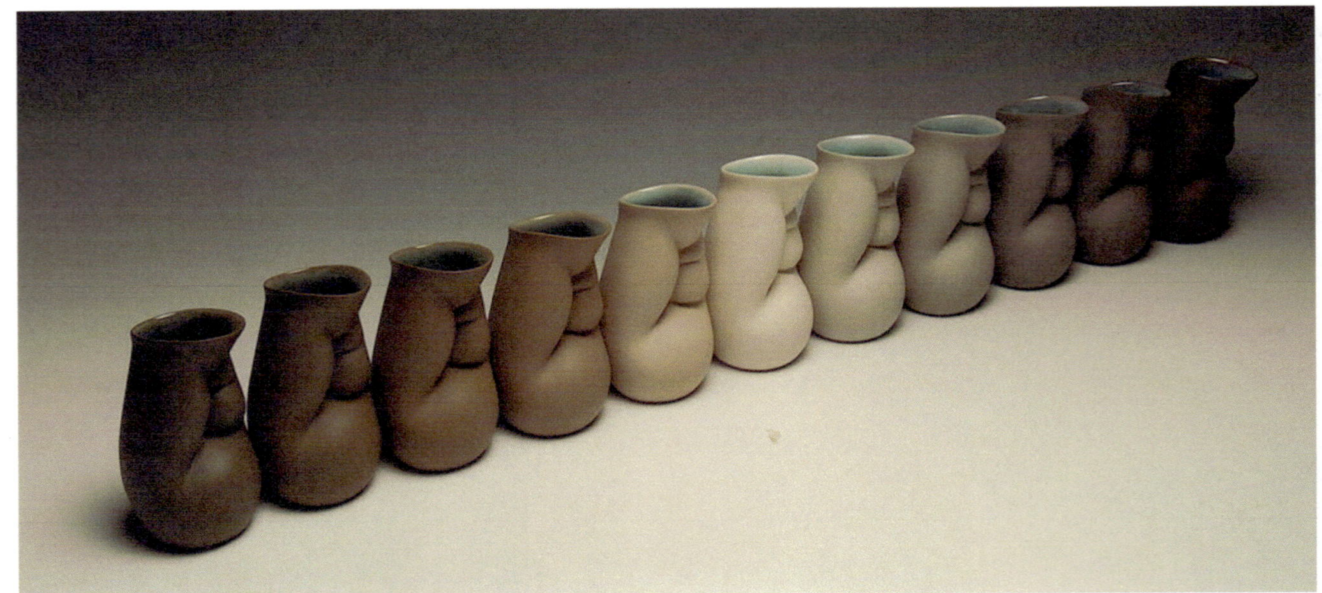

Mika Negishi Laidlaw. "All One"[2]

VALUE

Value is the relative degree of light or dark of an object. Typically it is not a major consideration for decision making like other art elements. Purposefully manipulating value is a bit more incidental to the result of light acting on an object. Gallery lighting or full sun can have a dramatic effect on how the viewer experiences the work. This also explains why objects often look more dramatic in a gallery setting as opposed to siting on the shelf in a cluttered studio.

There can be value considerations when dealing with surfaces and spaces on a work. Highly textured surfaces can be emphasized by the dramatic highlight and shadows on a piece. A matte surface will have a different value than a shiny surface of the same color. In addition, dark colors can make a large piece appear smaller and light colors can make a small piece appear larger. Projecting strong light on your work and observing cast shadows can help you understand the object in a different way from your first concept. This could lead to revisions in the overall design.

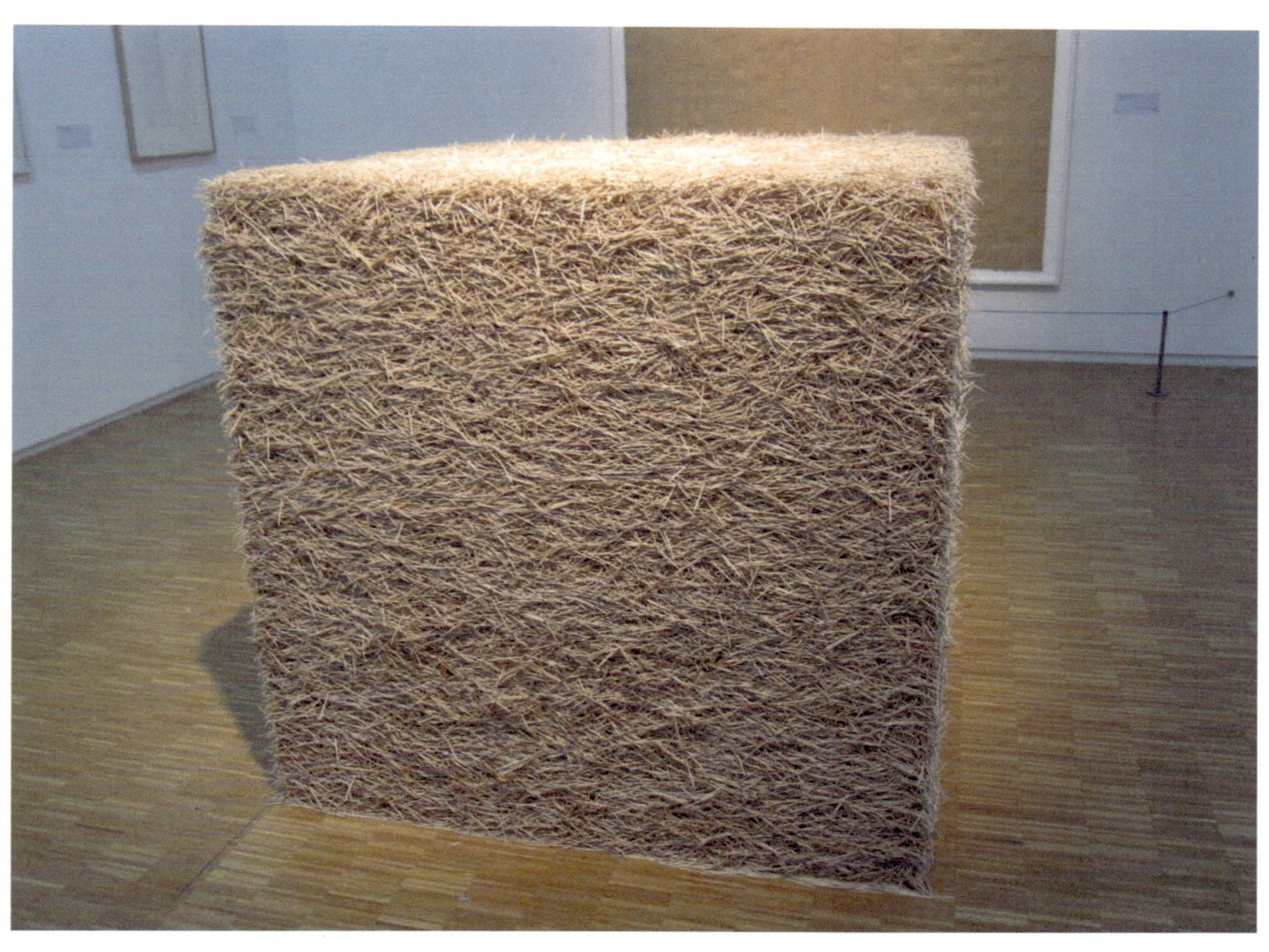

Tara Donovan, "Toothpicks", 2004. The gallery lighting emphasizes the dramatic texture of this work built entirely of toothpicks.[1]

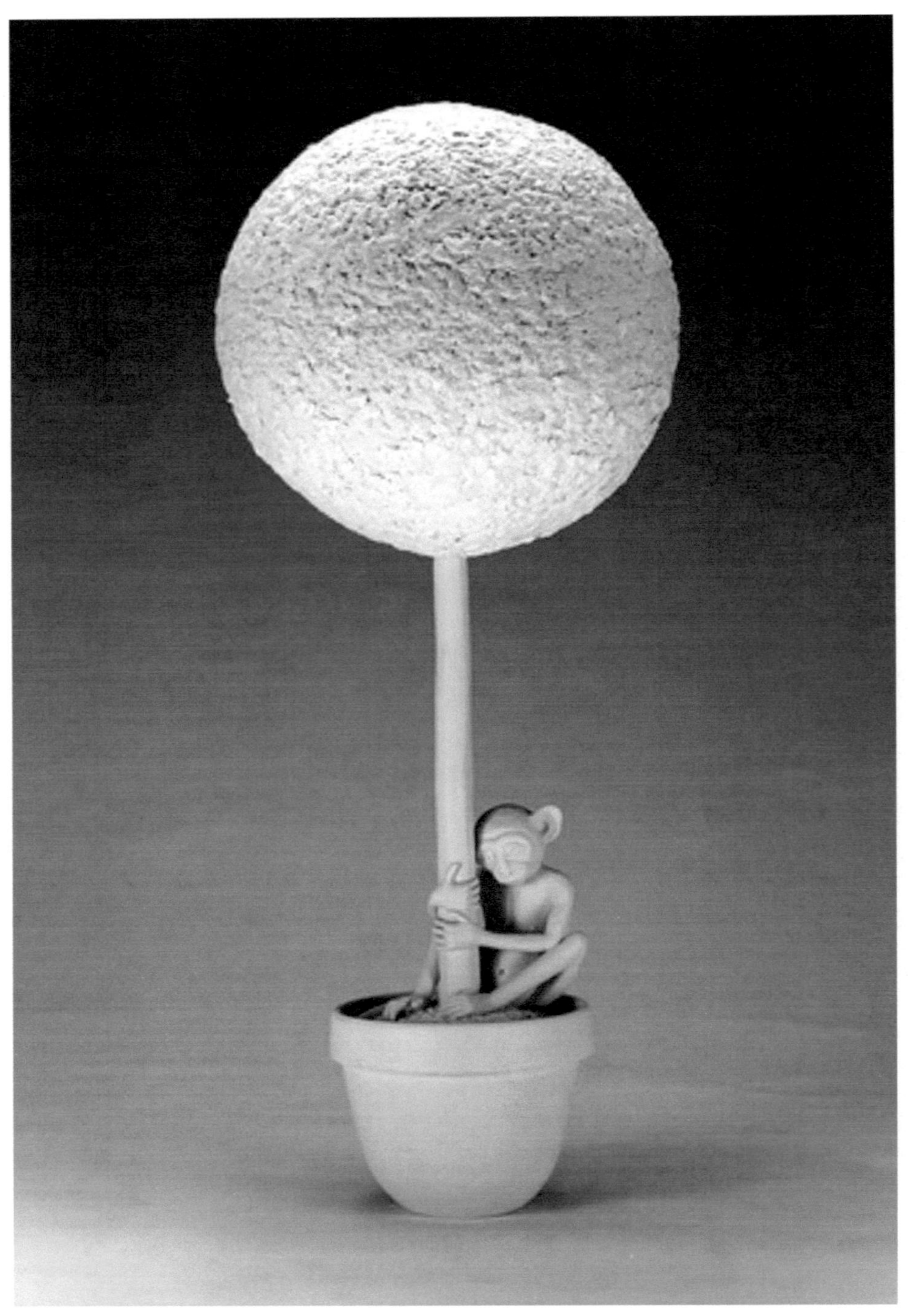

Bethany Krull, "Surrogate (Monkey / Topiary)", porcelain and paper, 2011. The choice of making this sculpture white allows highlight and shadow to add additional interest to this already powerful object .[3]

Mihrab (Prayer Niche) from Iran, 1354-5[4]

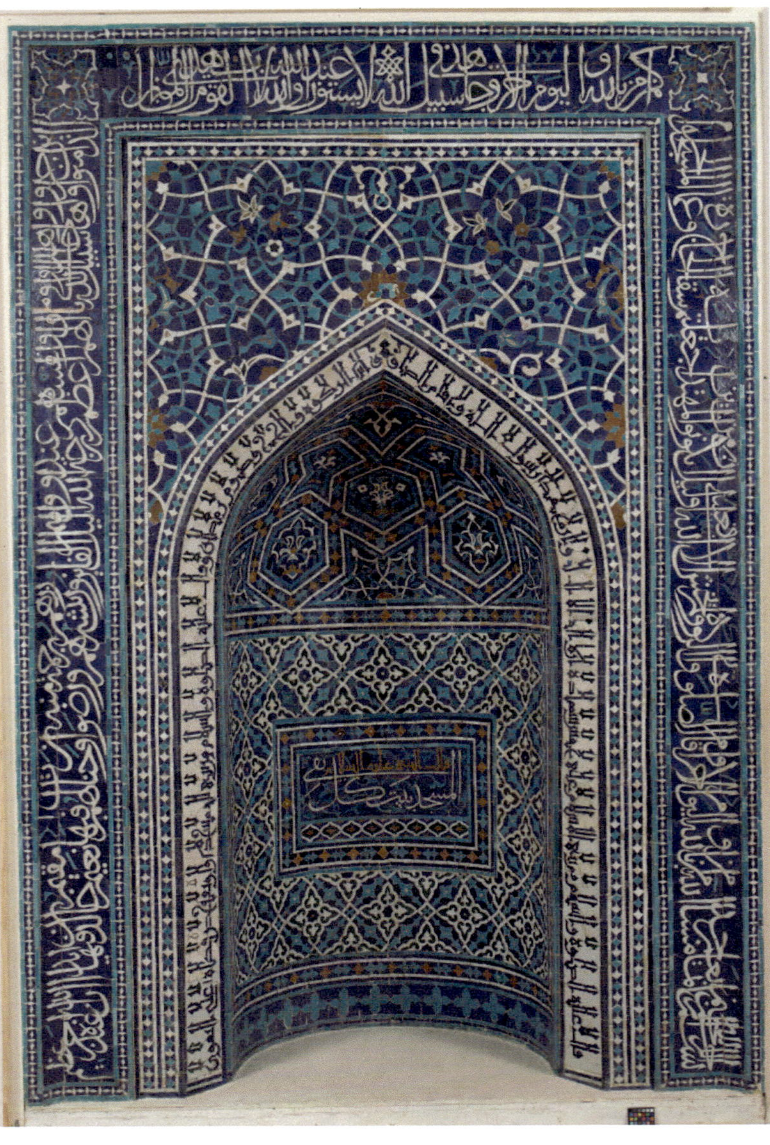

COLOR

Color is the eye's visual response to the wavelengths of light identified that can be identified as red, green, blue, and so on. Color has important physical and cultural meaning that the artist can manipulate to make their work more appealing and powerful. Color systems like color wheels were developed to help artists and designers understand and work with the relationships of colors such as primary, secondary, intermediate, complementary, and other combinations.

Color is most often dealt with extensively in 2d art making but there are important considerations for the 3d artist. For example, using one or only a few colors on a very complex shape can emphasize the complexity of that object. Using a variety of colors or complex patterns on a simple shape will do the same thing, create a more visually dynamic object. Color temperature (warm/cool) can also change how the viewer sees the work. Warmer colors (reds, yellows, oranges) seem active and closer to the viewer. Cooler colors (blues, greens, purples) are generally more subdued and recede away from the viewer. Using both kinds on one object will create interest that relates to color relationships mentioned above.

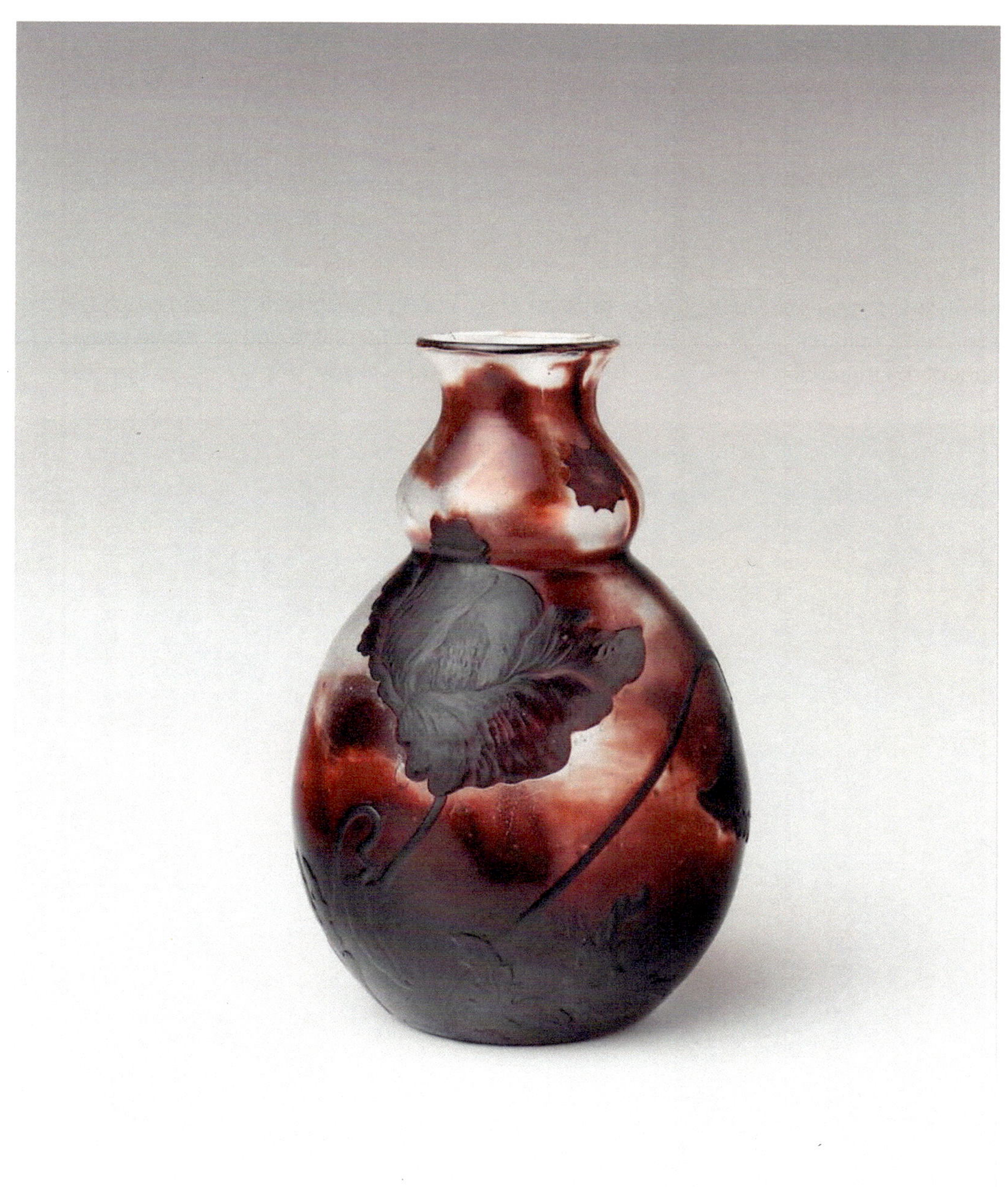

"Vase", Emile Galle', blow and carved glass. 1896. The strong red of this vase has a powerful effect on the viewer. Many colors, like red, have specific cultural connotations.[4]

Since we are working with specific actual materials to make our 3d objects, artists often emphasis the natural color and character of those materials. Wood and steel can be left natural to age or can be sealed to preserve the character of the material.

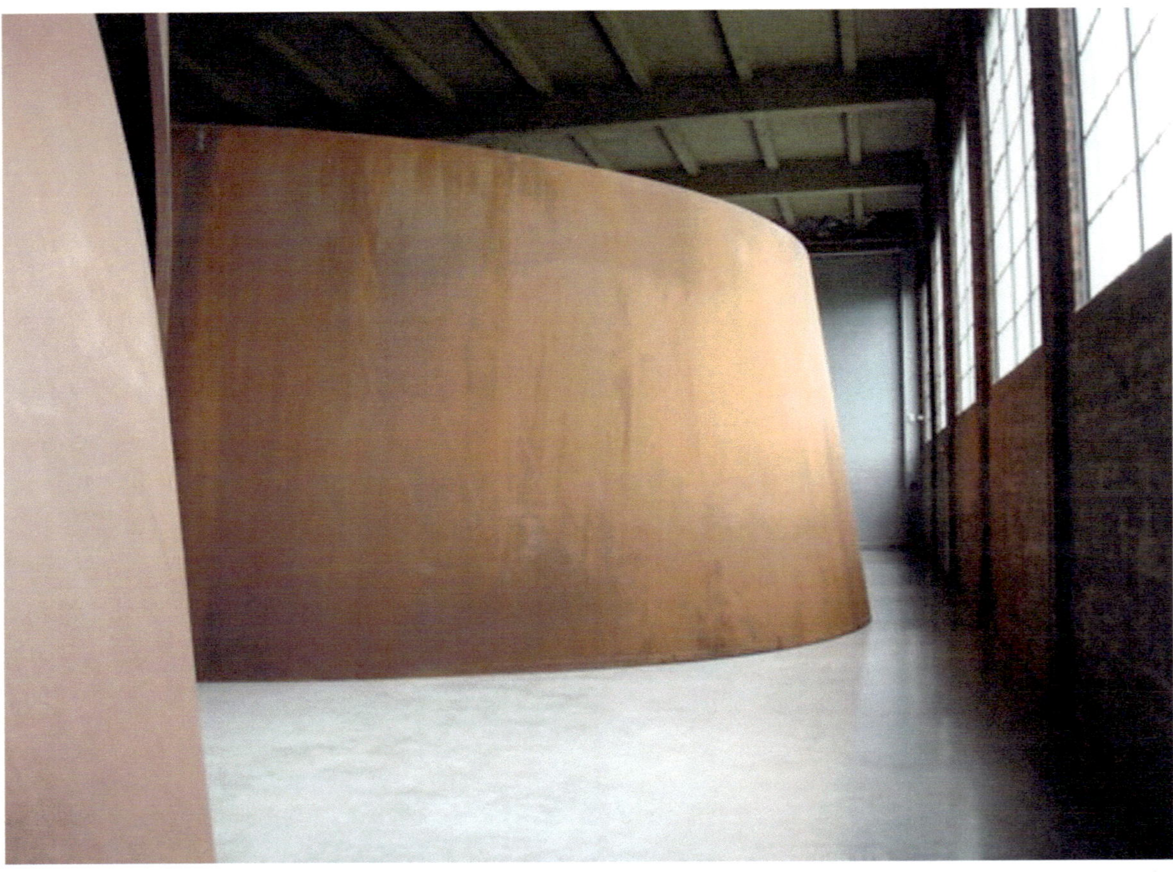

Richard Serra, "Torqued Ellipse", steel. These monumental steel shapes have the naturally rusted color of the material. They use the concept of "truth to materials" to a high degree.[22]

Paints, applied metal patinas, and ceramic glazes can also be used to change the color of the object or hide the materials being used. The color relationships then become part of the overall impact of the work.

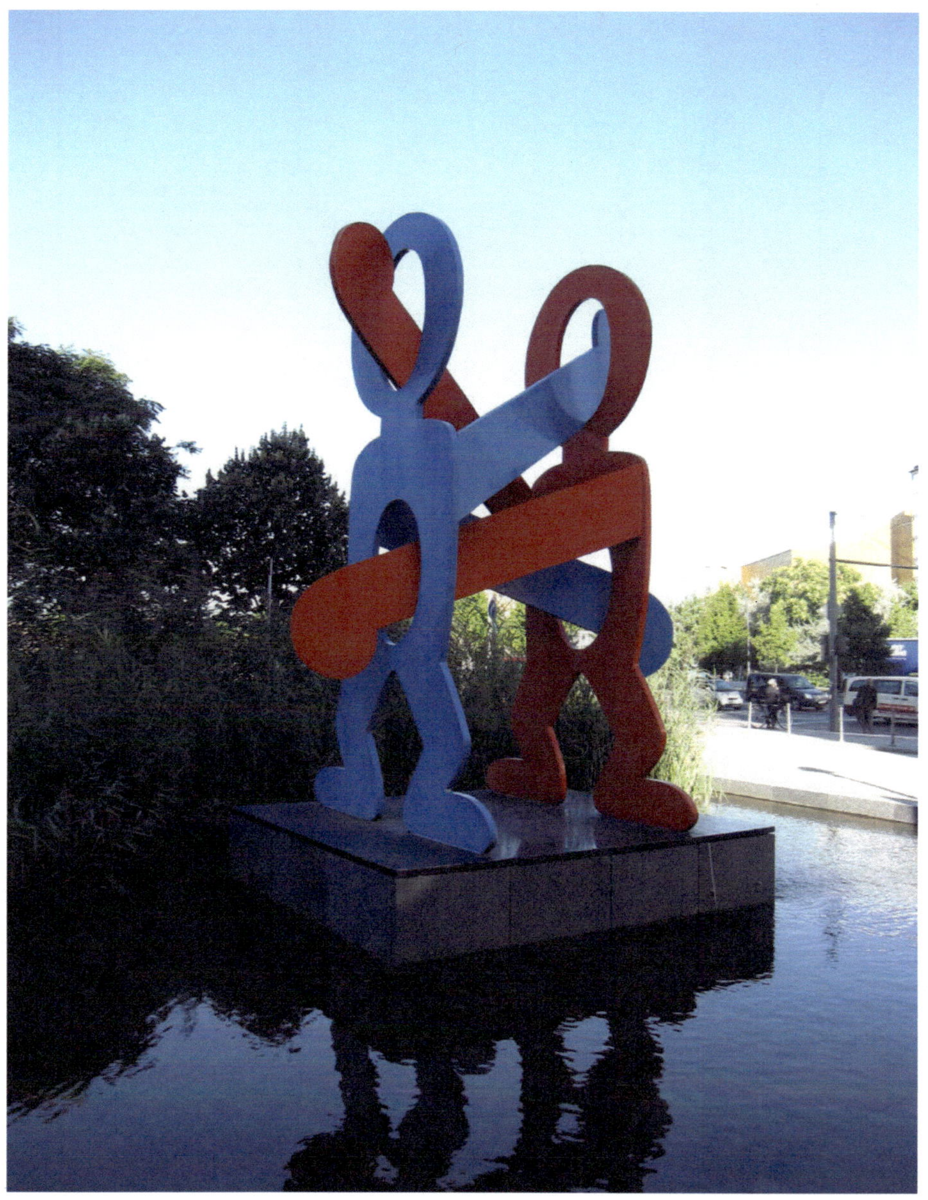

A Keith Haring sculpture made of painted steel in a Berlin public fountain. The primary red and blue colors add another layer of interest to the interaction of these abstract figures..[1]

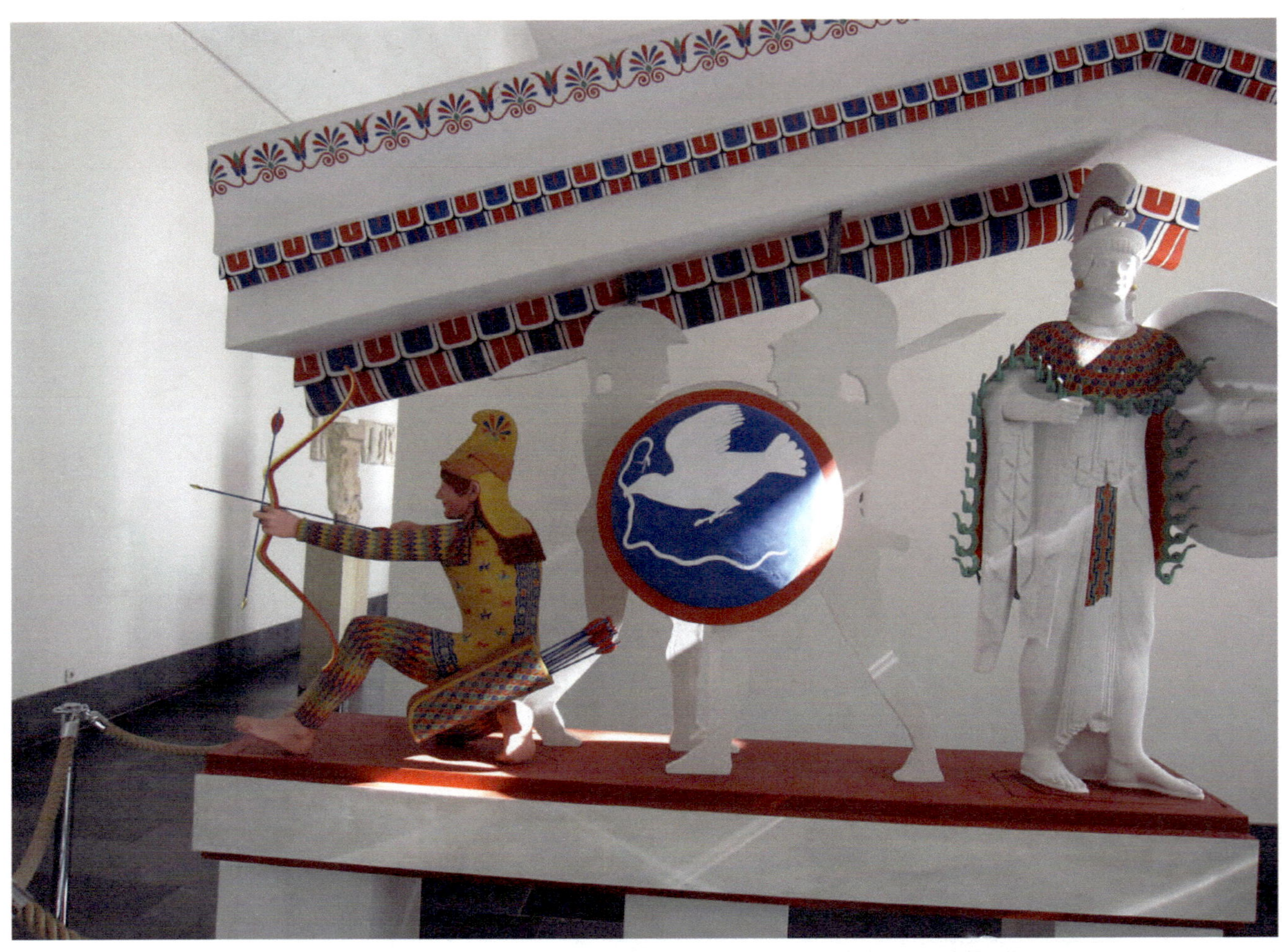

A diorama in a Berlin museum showing how ancient Greek temples and sculptures were originally painted. These bright, vibrant colors are a jarring contrast to our experience of the sculptures and buildings as stark white marble surfaces. Time and the weather have worn away the paint applied to the work when it was created.[1]

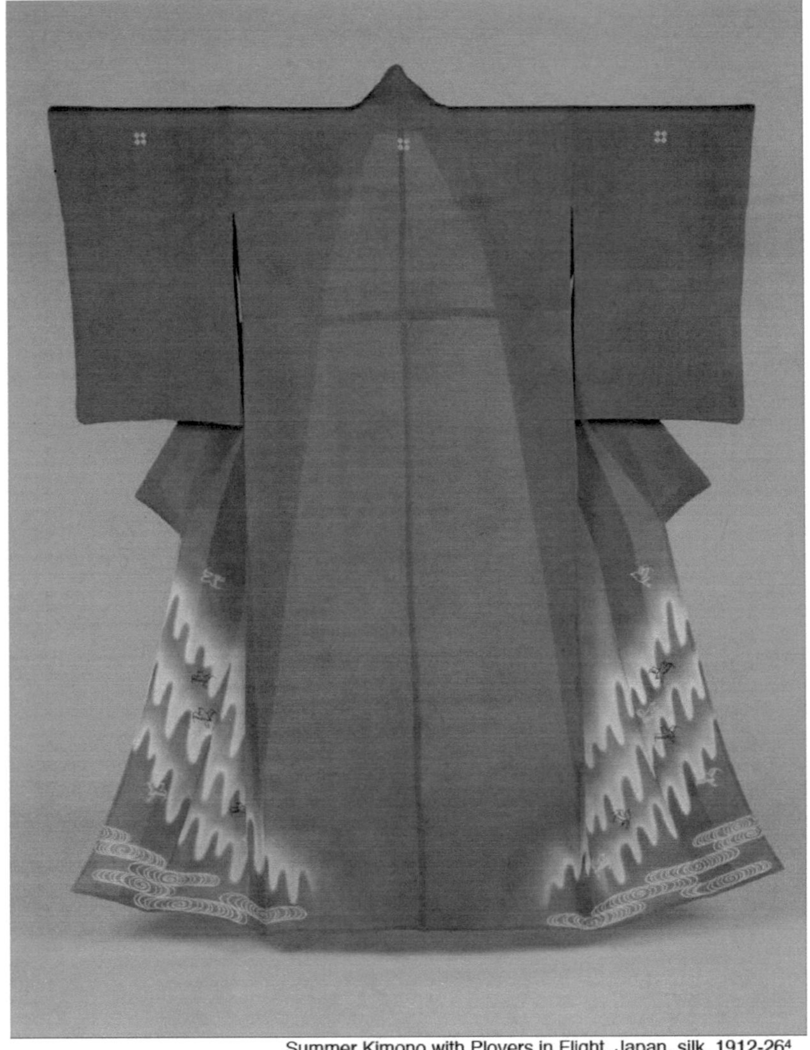

Summer Kimono with Plovers in Flight, Japan, silk, 1912-26[4]

4

ART PRINCIPLES

The principles of art are a way of organizing the art elements in order to make interesting images or objects. When looking at a work, we often generalize about how the principles are used to create a feeling or overall effect. You may also want to think about the elements of art as words and the principles are the sentences that you can create in order to communicate your idea.

As you become a more experienced object maker, the elements and principles of art will become a subconscious part of what you do. You will consider the entire object and make critically informed decisions about what would make it more aesthetically pleasing. Your personal approach to art making will evolve as you find new inspirations and build new technical skills.

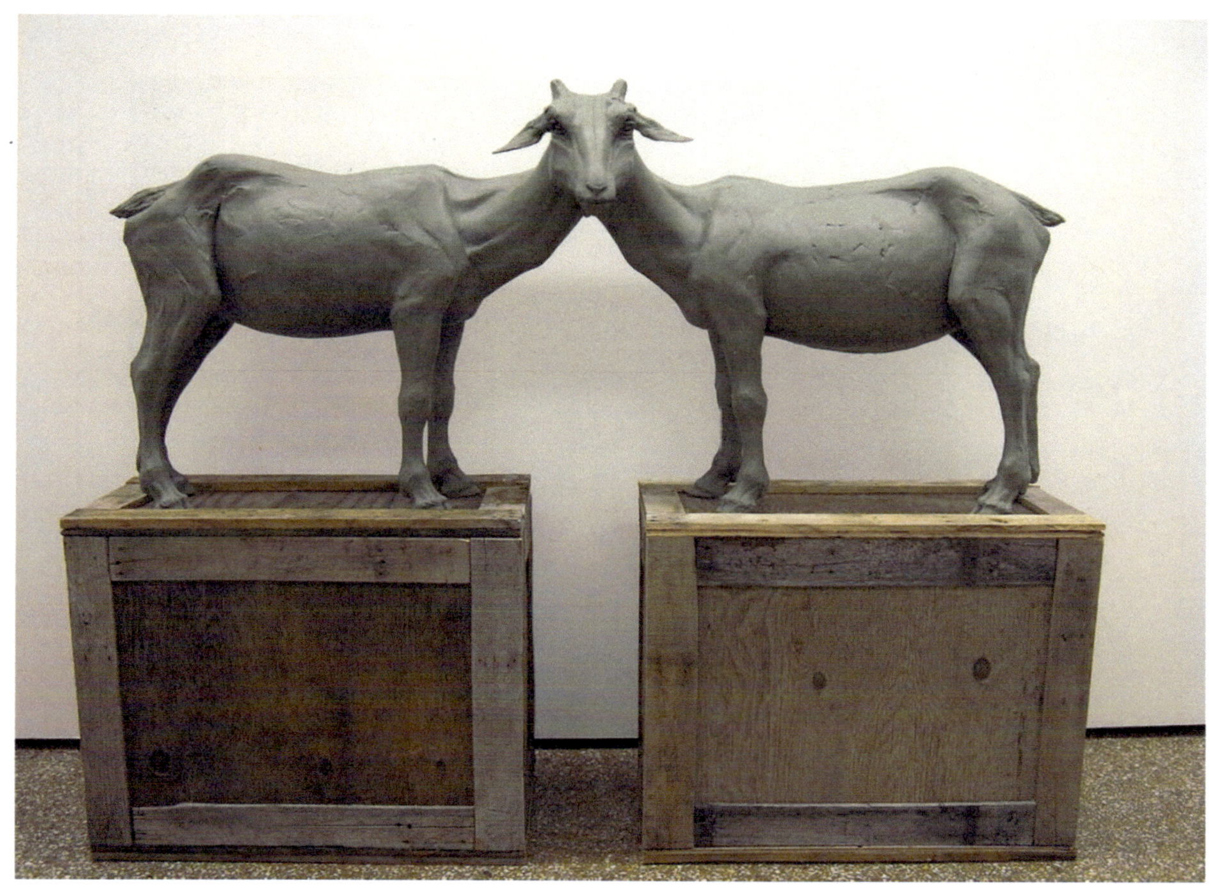

Beth Cavener Stichter, "Inquisitors" showing symmetrical balance.[3]

BALANCE

Balance is the sense of visual equilibrium achieved through implied weight, attention, or attraction within an artwork. In 3d art and design, balance also takes on a physical dimension when dealing with gravity. The work needs to stand on its own or stay attached to something in order to not fall and break. Gravity will always be one of the largest challenges you will face when making 3d objects.

The three types of visual balance most often used are symmetrical, asymmetrical, and radial balance. An object has symmetry when it feels like all parts are a mirror image of the others, for example a round, straight sided cylinder. Asymmetry is when there is an uneven amount of visual weight on one side of the object. The use of asymmetrical balance often creates more visually dynamic objects. Radial balance refers to a circular or wheel-like balance in the shape.

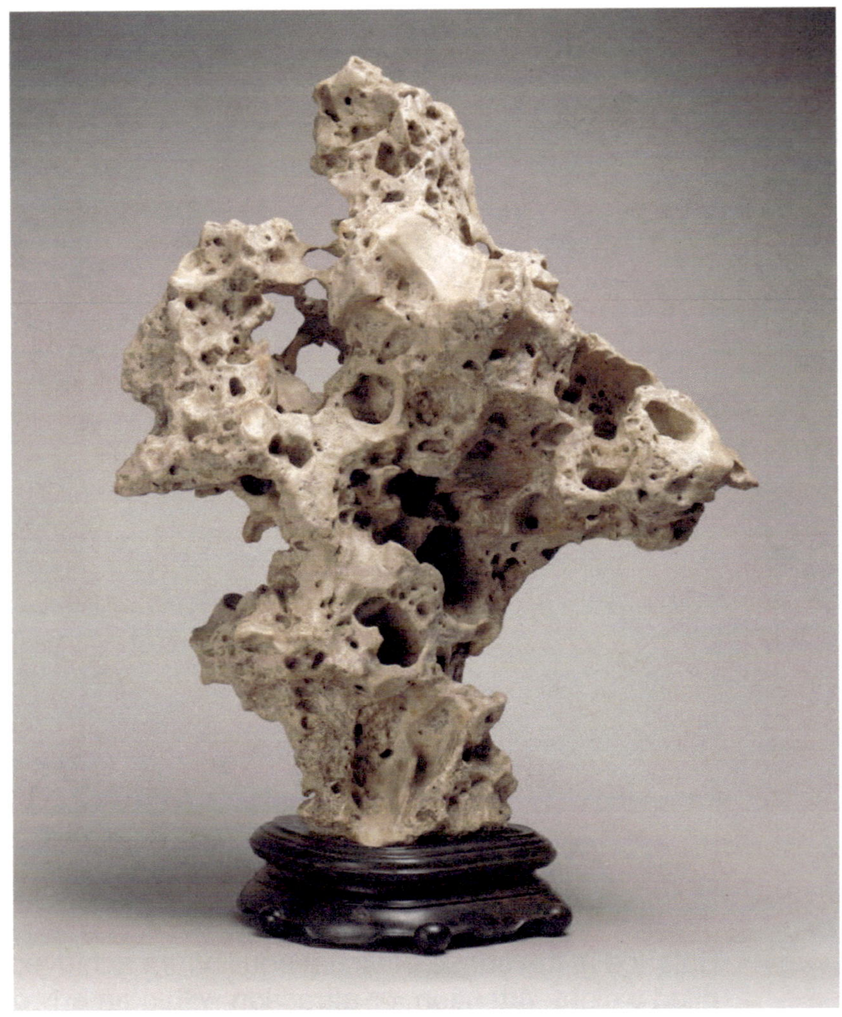

"Scholar Rock", China, natural and altered limestone, 19th century[4]

This found and sculpted piece of limestone is a "Scholar Rock", special pieces of stone that were objects of contemplation for Chinese elites of the time. As an art object, it demonstrates asymmetrical balance with parts projects off into space in unequal ways. Many Scholar Rocks also have specially made custom stands that held the stones. These were often shaped to conform to the asymmetry of the base of the stone.

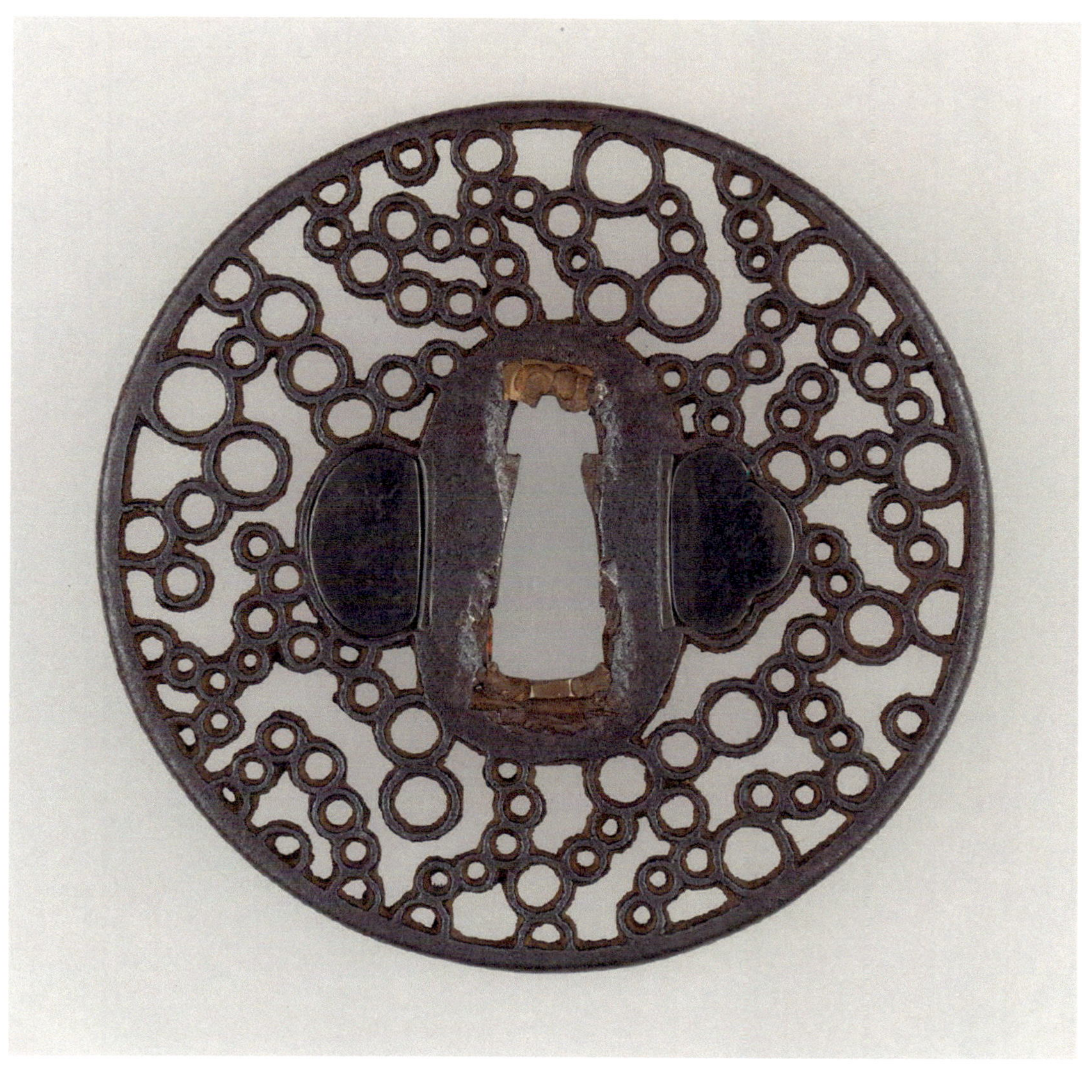

A sword guard (Tsuba) was a circular piece of metal on a Japanese samurai sword that protected the user's hands from getting cut. In this tsuba, the radial balance is obvious as a circular form and the design radiates from the center of the circle.

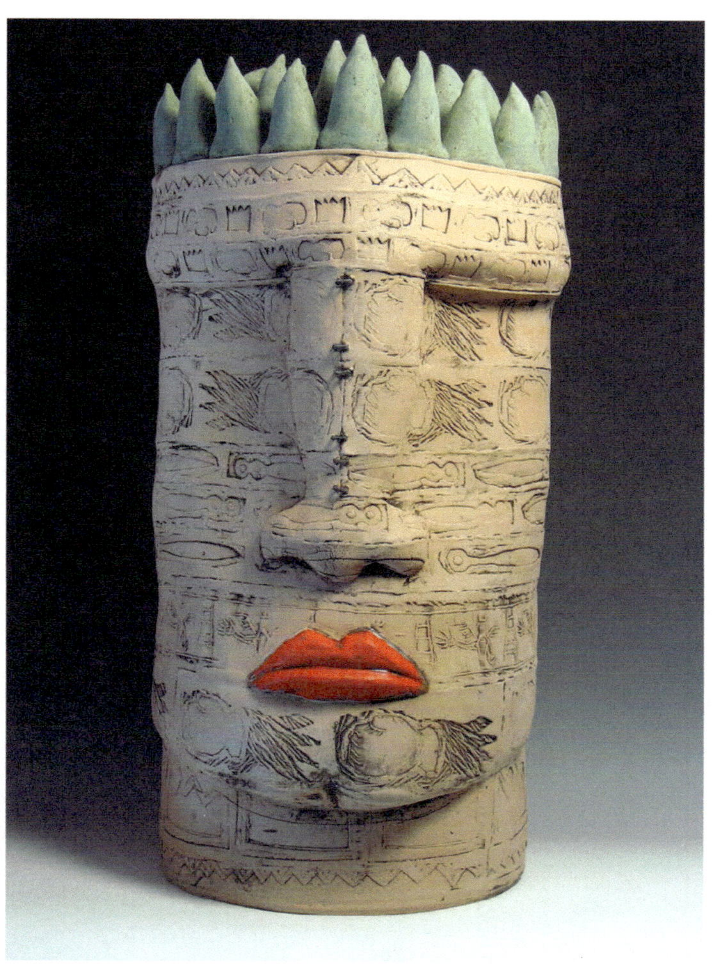

Paul Andrew Wandless, "Prize Fighter"[5]

EMPHASIS

Emphasis (also known as visual dominance) is the creation of visual importance through the use of selective stress. Parts of the object are differentiated from the other parts in order to enhance attraction and interest.

There are many ways to achieve emphasis, including contrasting or exaggerating size, shape, value, color, and texture. Parts of the object can be used to point the viewers attention to the specific element the maker wants to emphasize.

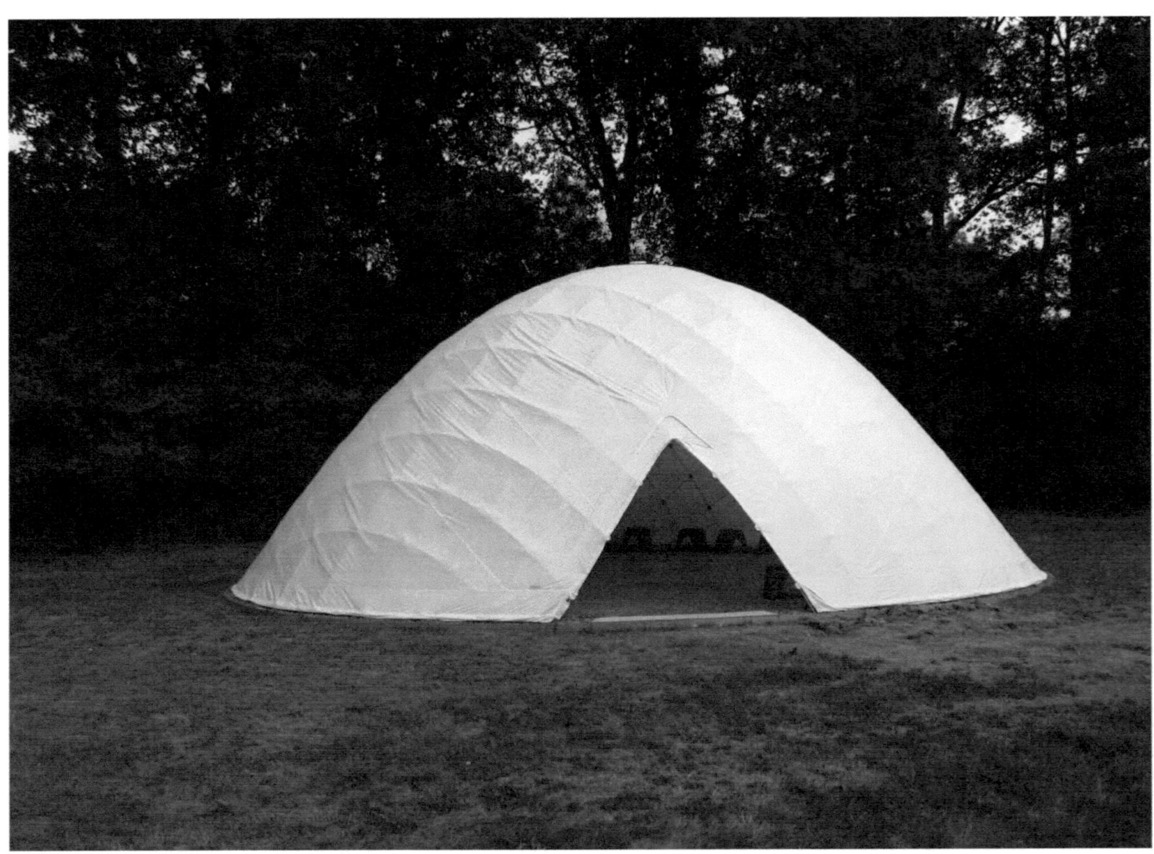

A fabric dome structure at the Domaine de Boisbuchet in France[1]

The darker doorway in this fabric dome draws attention and makes viewers want to enter the structure.

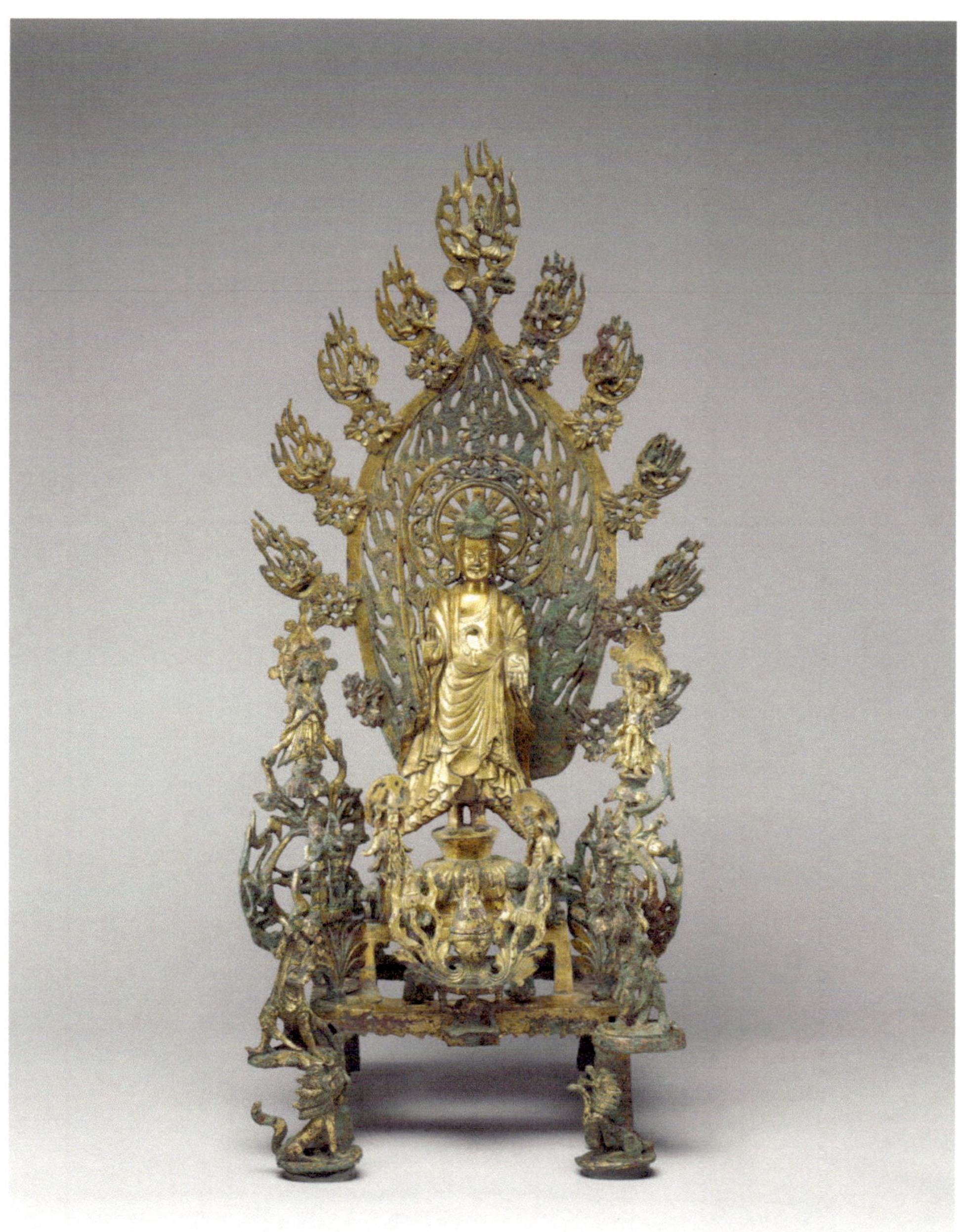

Buddha Maitreya, China, 524 CE, bronze[4]

All the elements of this Buddhist sculpture radiate from and circle the Buddha's head. This creates a point of emphasis that focuses visual attention at the most important point in the composition.

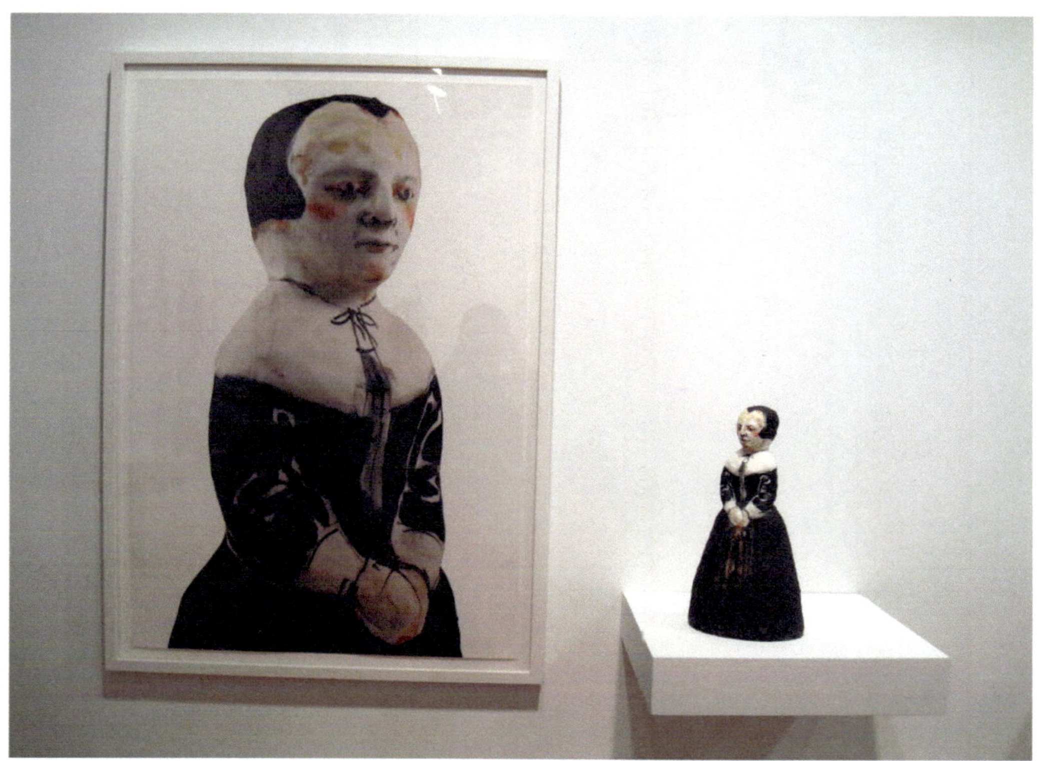

Akio Takamori, "Dutch Grandmother"[2]

PROPORTION AND SCALE

Proportion refers to relative size of an element measured against other elements or against some norm or standard. Proportion often refers to a ratio of the size of parts to the whole. The "Golden Mean" was a proportional system developed by the ancient Greeks that helped create harmony in Western design. It was based on and can be seen in many forms found in nature.

Scale can be another word for size in a work. Scaling can refer to changing the size of an image or object. A comment often heard during critique is that the object would be more interesting if it was a different scale (larger or smaller). As a species, humans relate everything to their own size. Small things like insects are tiny to us but we are the size of buildings to them.

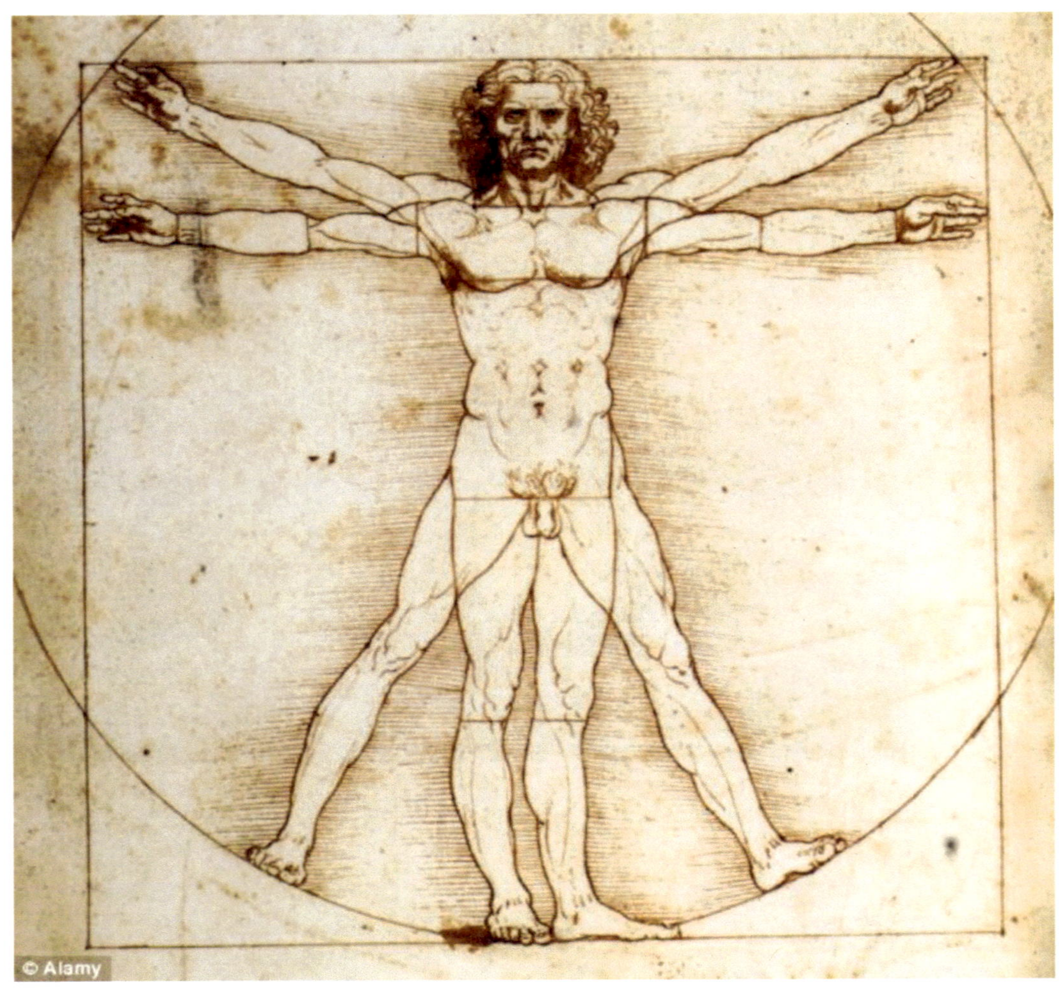

Leonardo Da Vinci"s drawing of "perfect" human proportions[6]

For much of art history, artists were attempting to define the "perfect" human proportion. The problem with that idea is that there is no such thing as perfect. The human body and its parts have varied across time and space and what is seen as "beautiful" or pleasing changes constantly. As a self-absorbed species, the human form has infinite interest to viewer and artists alike.

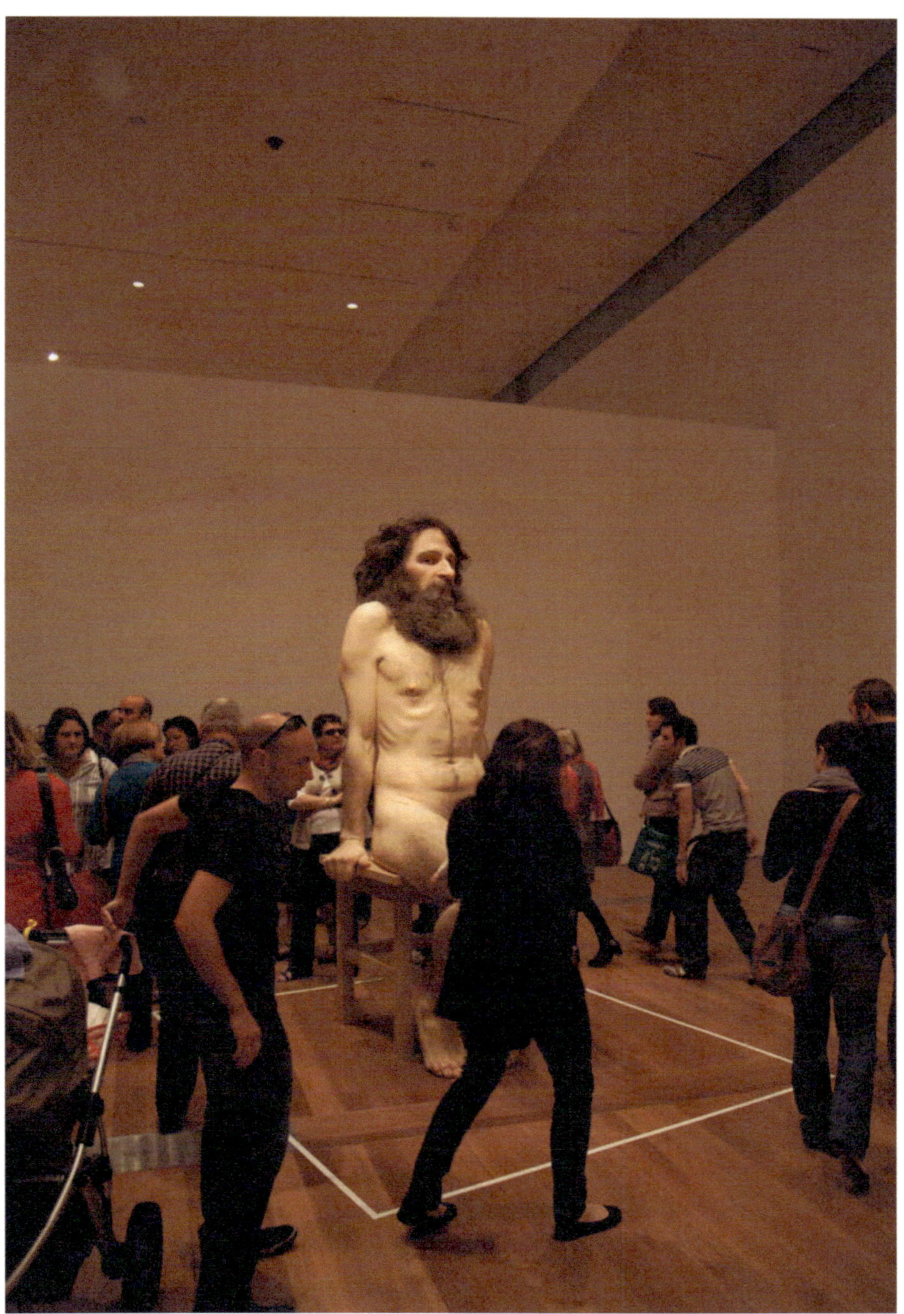

Ron Mueck, "Wild Man"[23]

When an artist like Ron Mueck manipulates our experience of the usual scale of the human body, it becomes unsettling.

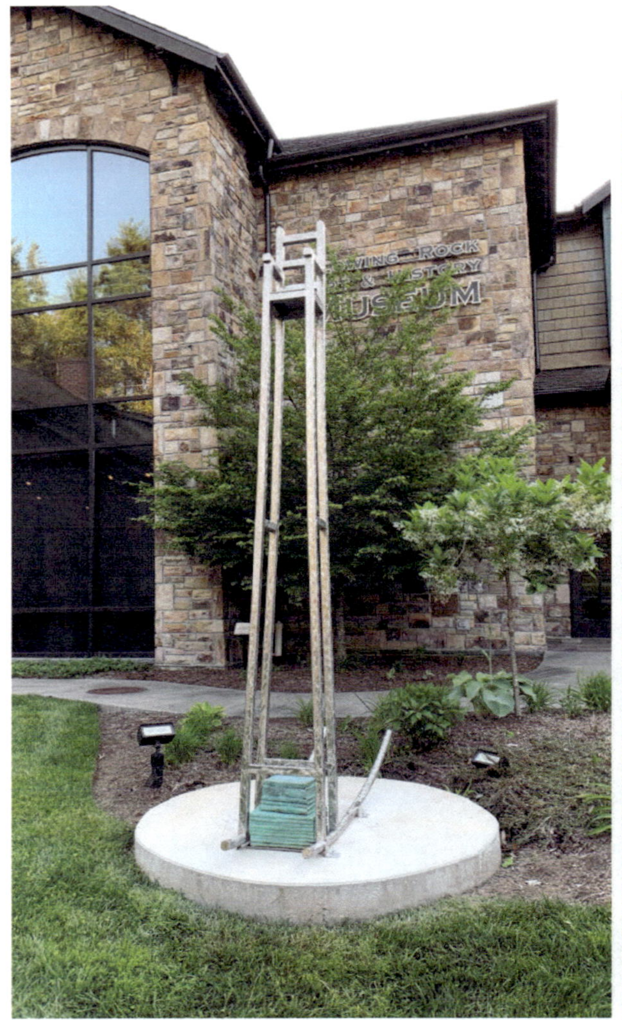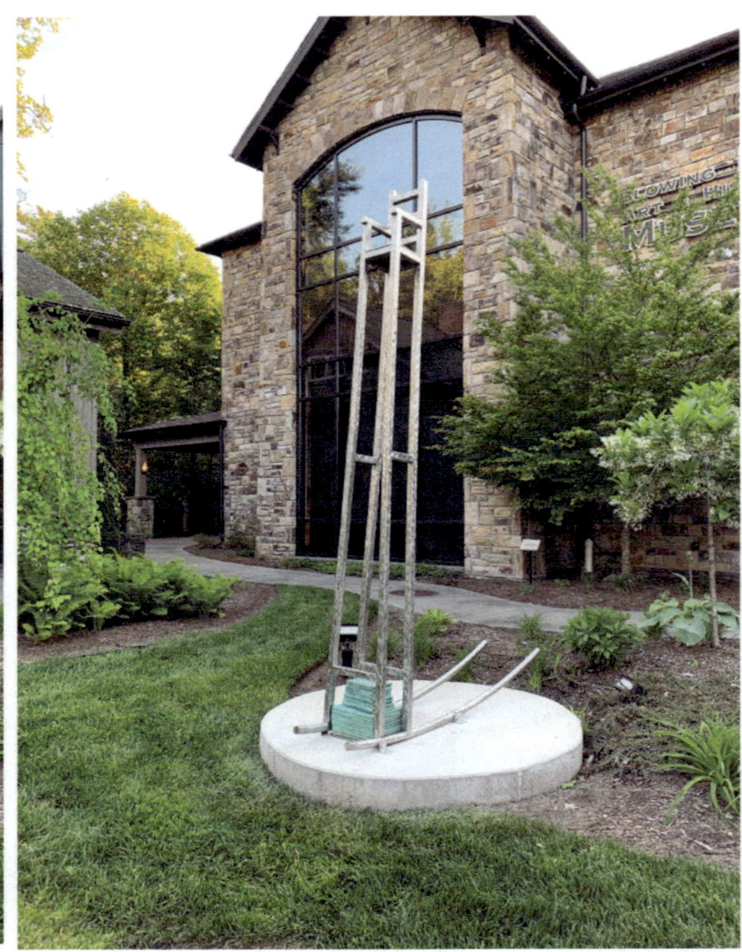

Derek Chalfant[9]

This sculpture by Elmira College Art Professor Derek Chalfant exaggerates the usual scale and proportion of a child's rocking chair. That change makes the work have a greater impact and asks the viewer to consider why this object has moved outside of our normal experience.

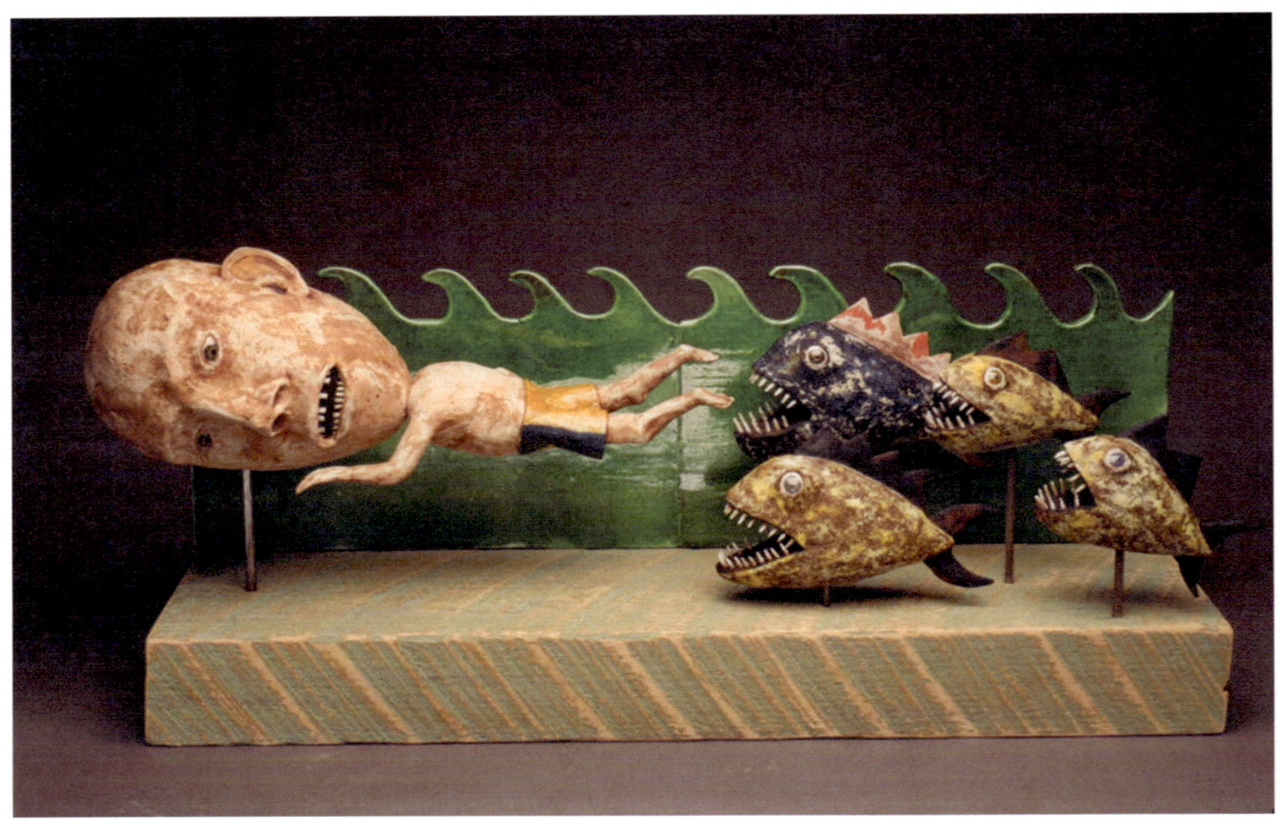
Wesley Anderegg, "Natsoulas 36"[3]

MOVEMENT

Movement (also known as directional force) is the direction and degree of energy implied by the art elements in specific compositional situations and directions. In 3d artworks, the element of actual movement is also possible.

Ways to create movement can include lines, repeated figures, blurred outlines, illusions of growth, and multiple images. An object with implied movement creates the sense that the object has momentarily stopped but will continue. Some three dimensional objects have actual movement (rocking, turning in response to the wind, wheels...) as part of their concept.

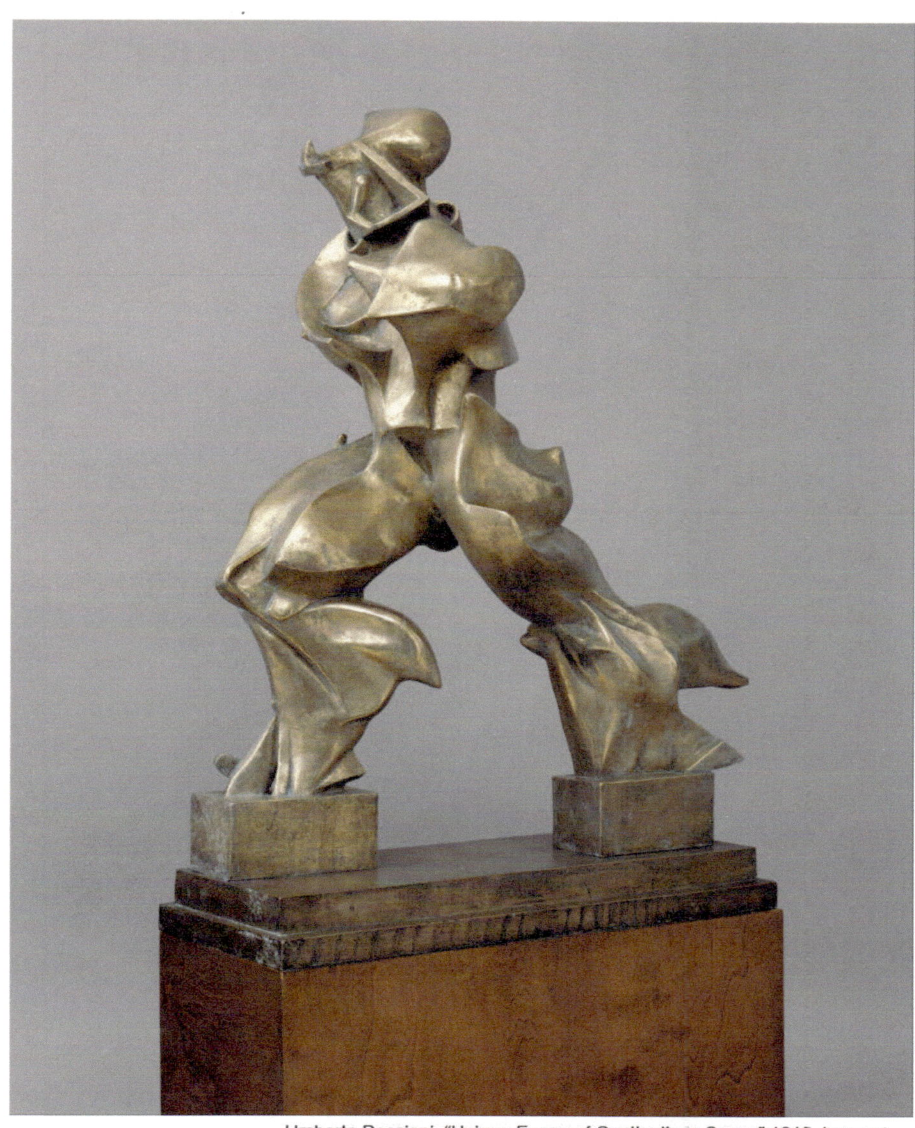

Umberto Boccioni, "Unique Forms of Continuity in Space" 1913, bronze[4]

This famous bronze by Italian Futurist Boiccioni attempts to show a figure in motion. The flowing shapes behind the legs blur the form so it appears to be moving at a high speed. The Futurists were reacting to what they saw was the increased speed of the city and culture at the beginning of the 20th century.

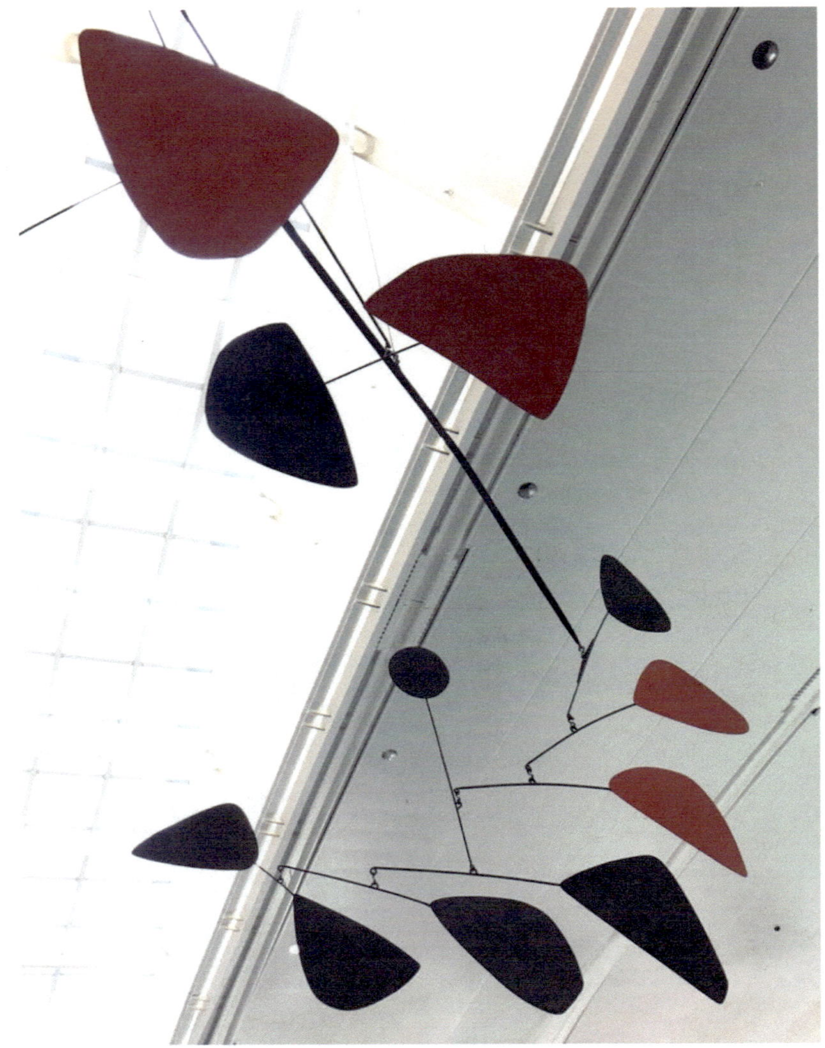

Alexander Calder, "Flight" [24]

Alexander Calder's sculptural mobiles like the work above were highly engi-
neered to move under normal air flow patterns inside buildings. His work was
an important example of early kinetic (resulting from motion) sculpture.

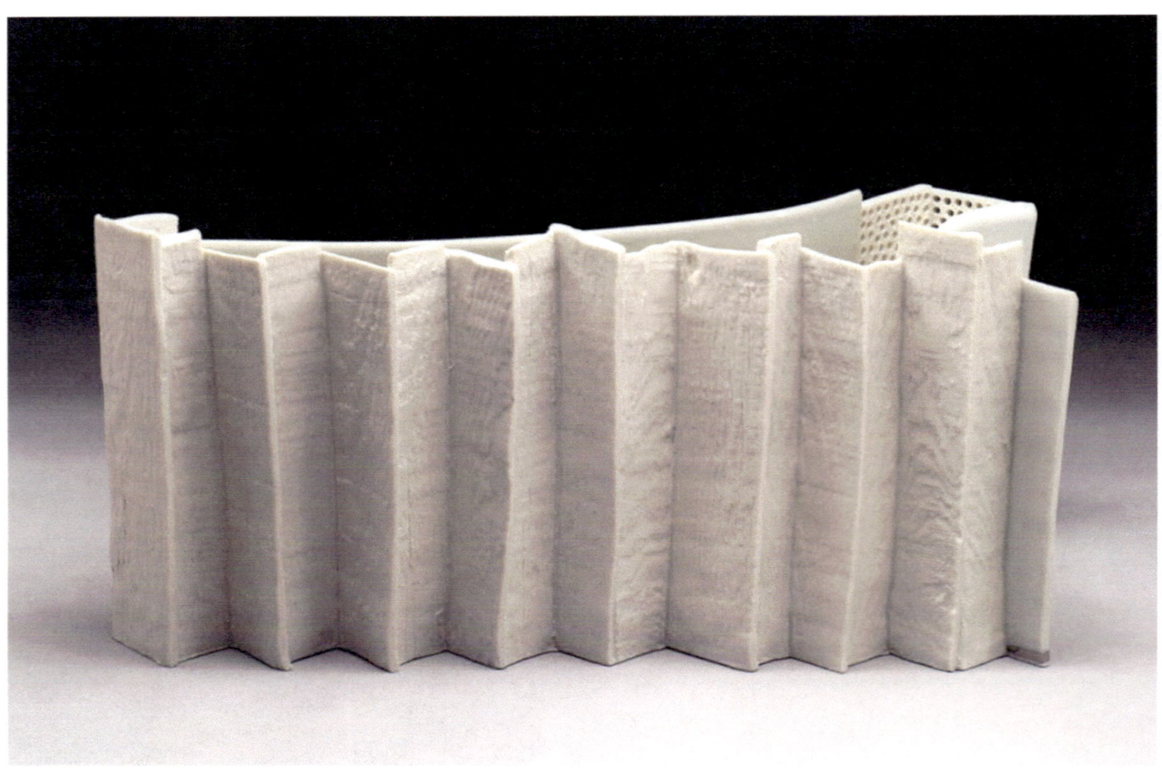

Bryan Hopkins, "Basket"[2]

UNITY

Unity (also known as harmony) is the presentation of an integrated image or object achieved through visual similarity.

A few ways to achieve unity include proximity of parts, coordination of all elements toward one concept, repetition of the same element in decoration, or a rhythm of slightly changing details. Unity can also be achieved by introducing an element of variety in parts that add up to an interesting whole.

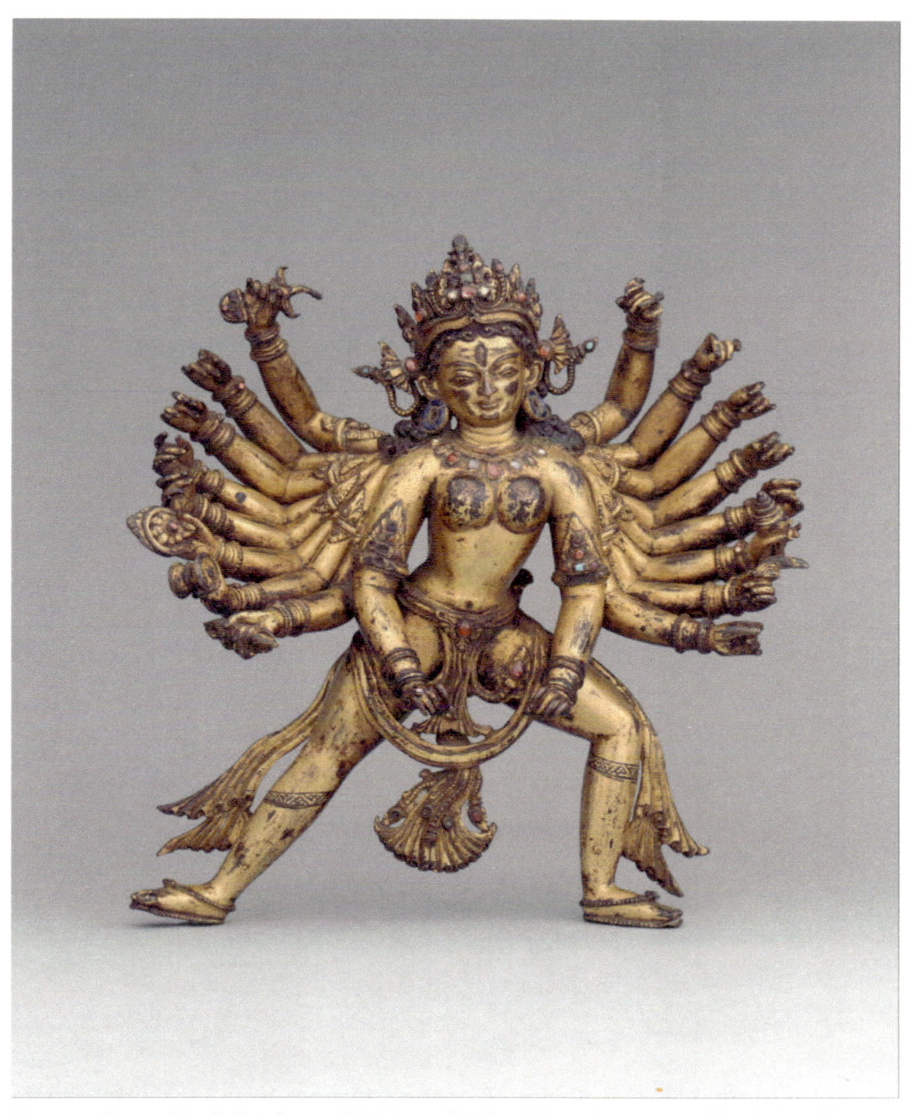

"Durga as Slayer of the Buffalo Demon Mahishasura", 14th - 15th century, copper with set stones"[4]

The sculpture above uses repetition of the figures arms to create a dynamic composition. The Hindu god is depicted having multiple arms which allows the artist to show this dynamic flow in a religious context. The repeated elements in objects do have to be or are not always identical. The variety in parts lends more visual interest.

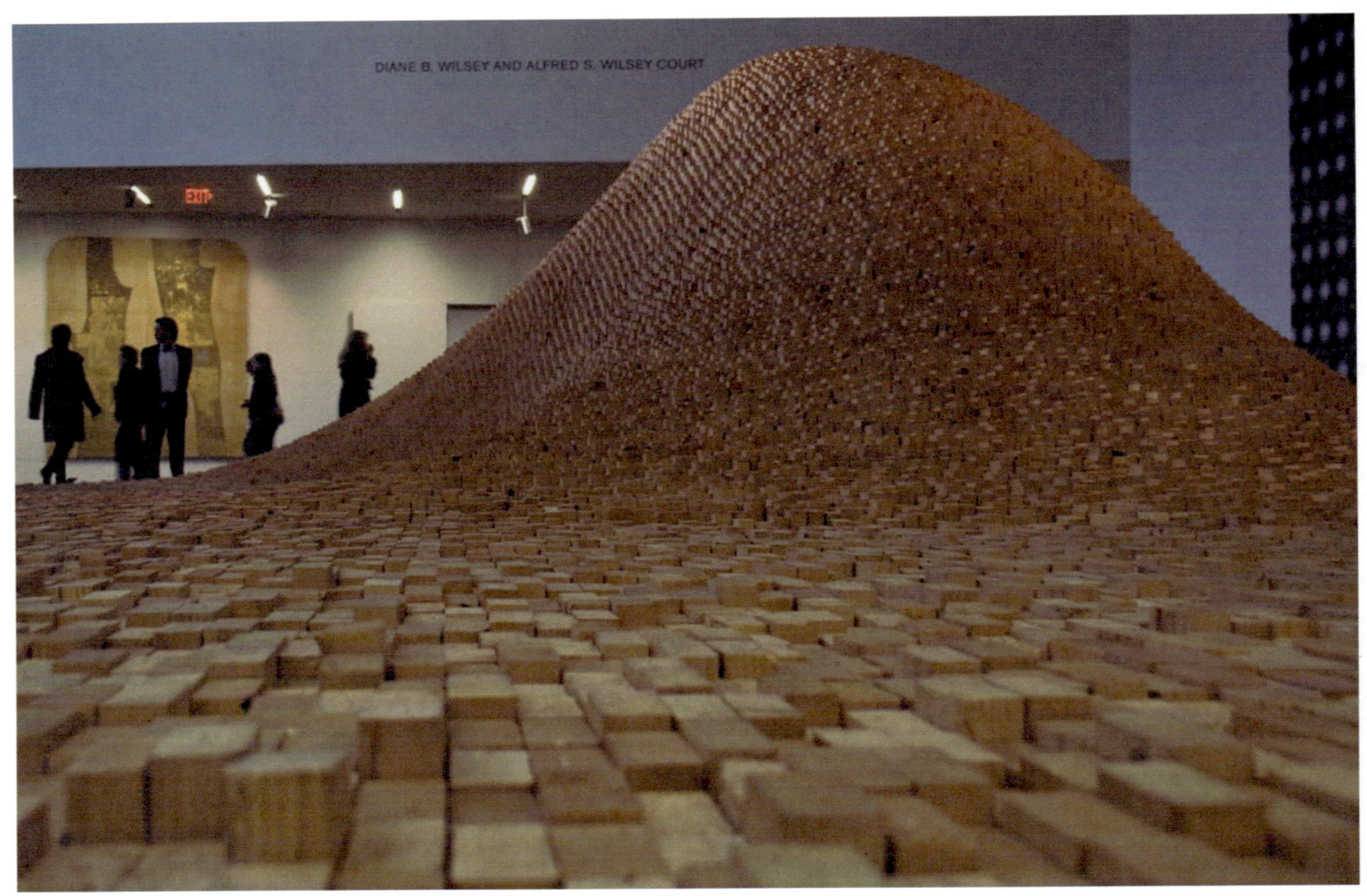

"2x4 Landscape", Maya Lin, 2006, wood[25]

This installation by Maya Lin, the designer of the Vietnam War Memorial in Washington DC, uses the rhythm of repeated wooden pieces to show the a flow of changing landscape. The visual effect of repeated assembled 2x4's of different lengths also creates a surface pattern.

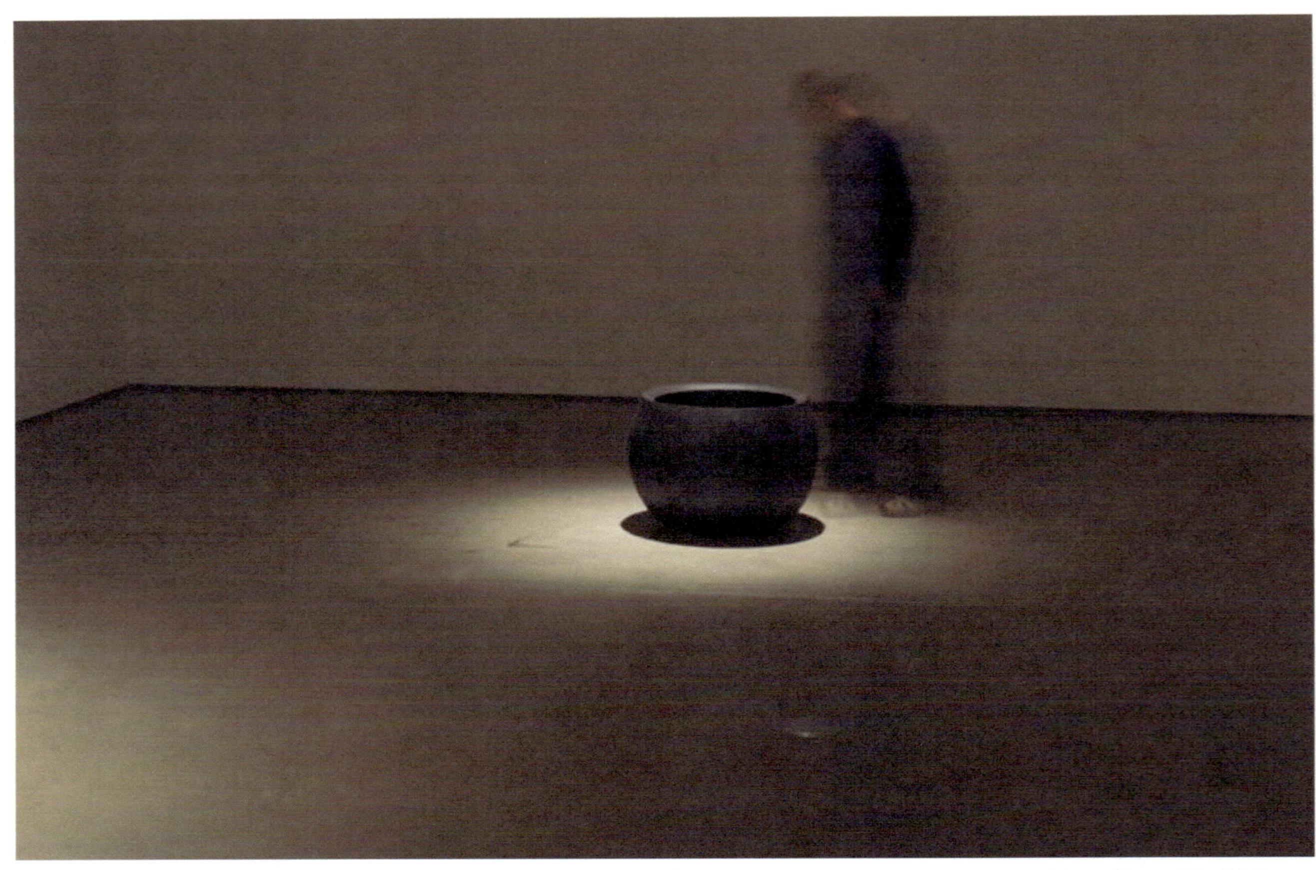

Shawn Murrey, "Crucible"[3]

ECONOMY

Economy is the elimination of elaborate details leaving only the significant essentials of the object or installation. The goal is to pare down without making the work monotonous. Economy is often associated with the term "abstraction" in which unnecessary elements are eliminated in order to show the essence of something.

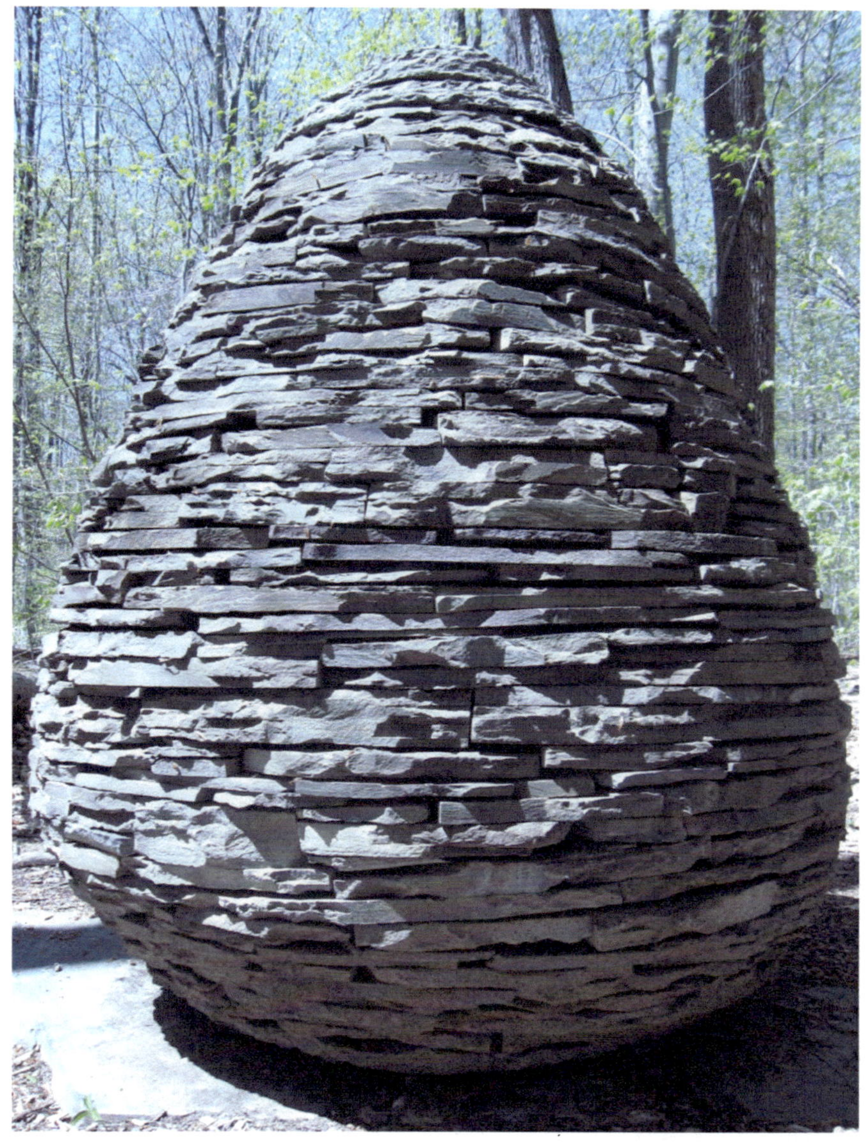

Andy Goldsworthy, "Egg Cairn"[1]

The work above is a stacked stone sculpture by Andy Goldsworthy located at the Ornithology Lab at Cornell University. It uses local stone to build a simple shape into a egg shape about the size of an adult person. The economical shape and surface texture of the stone allows this work to fit into the wooden landscape fo the nature center.

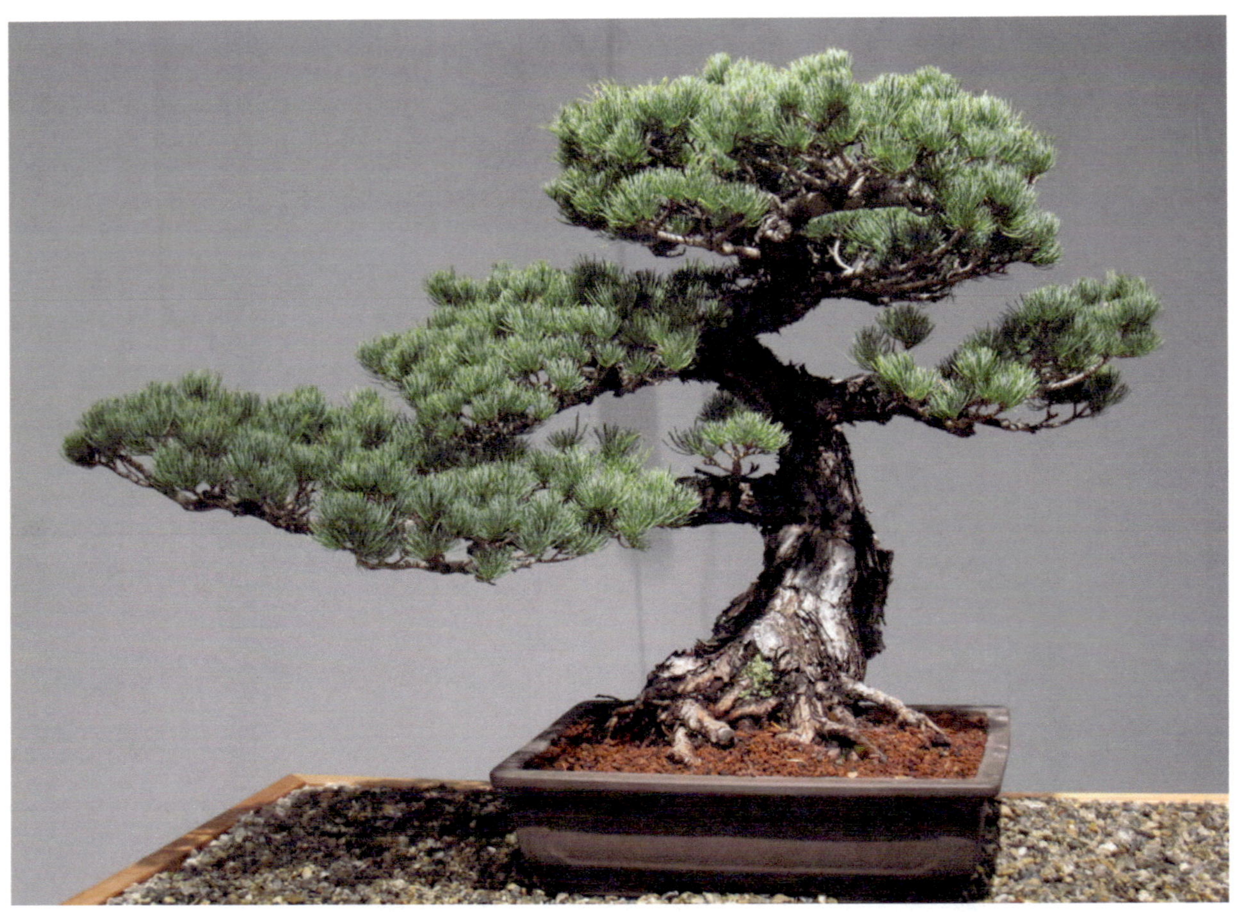

Pine tree at the **Museum** of Fine Arts in Boston [1]

This Japanese bonsai tree is a prime example of taking away all unnecessary detail and getting to the essence of what a weathered pine tree might look like in nature. On some levels, the bonsai artist is working with the living tree to create an abstraction of the perfection in living form.

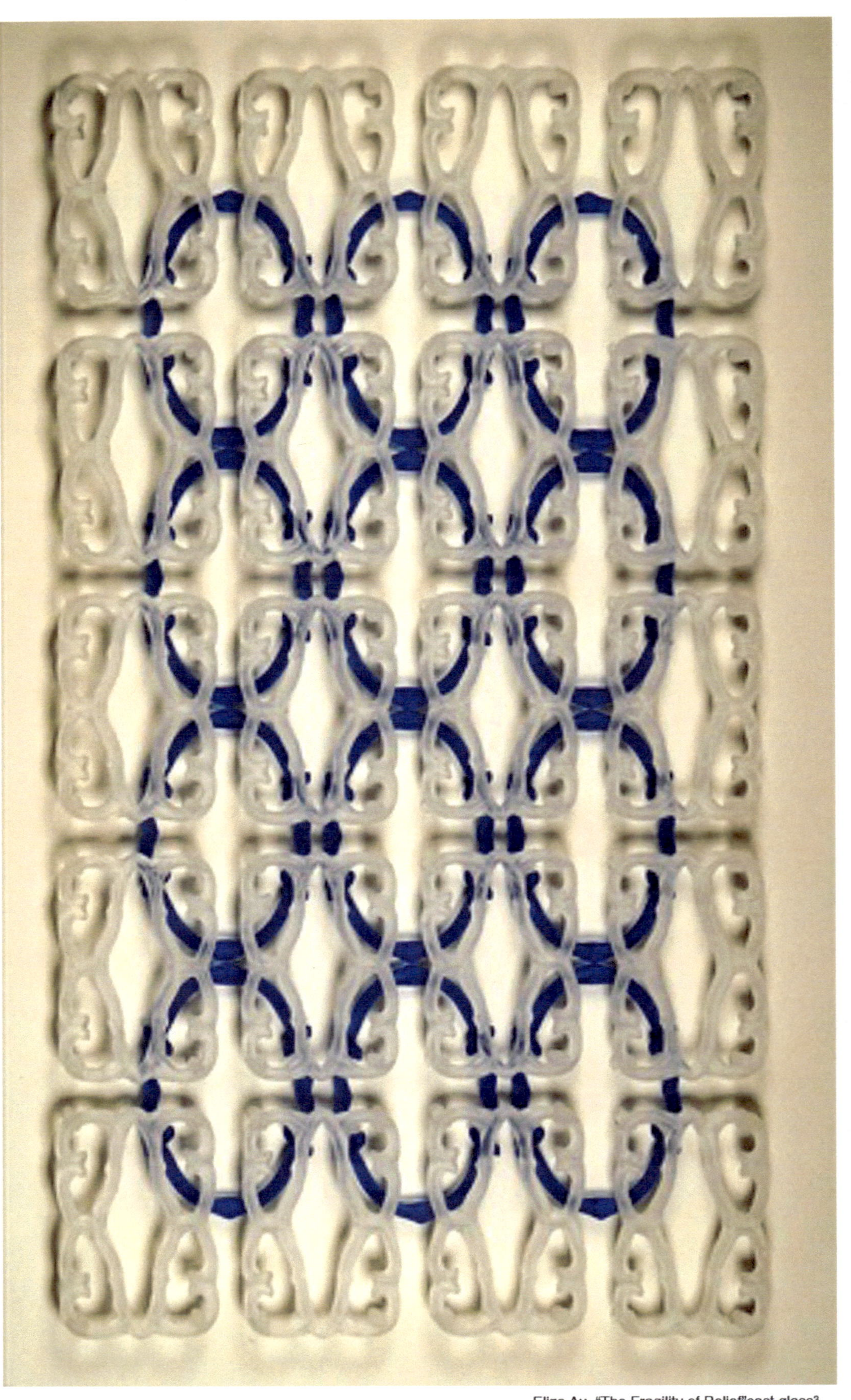

5

GLASS

Eliza Au, "The Fragility of Belief" cast glass[3]

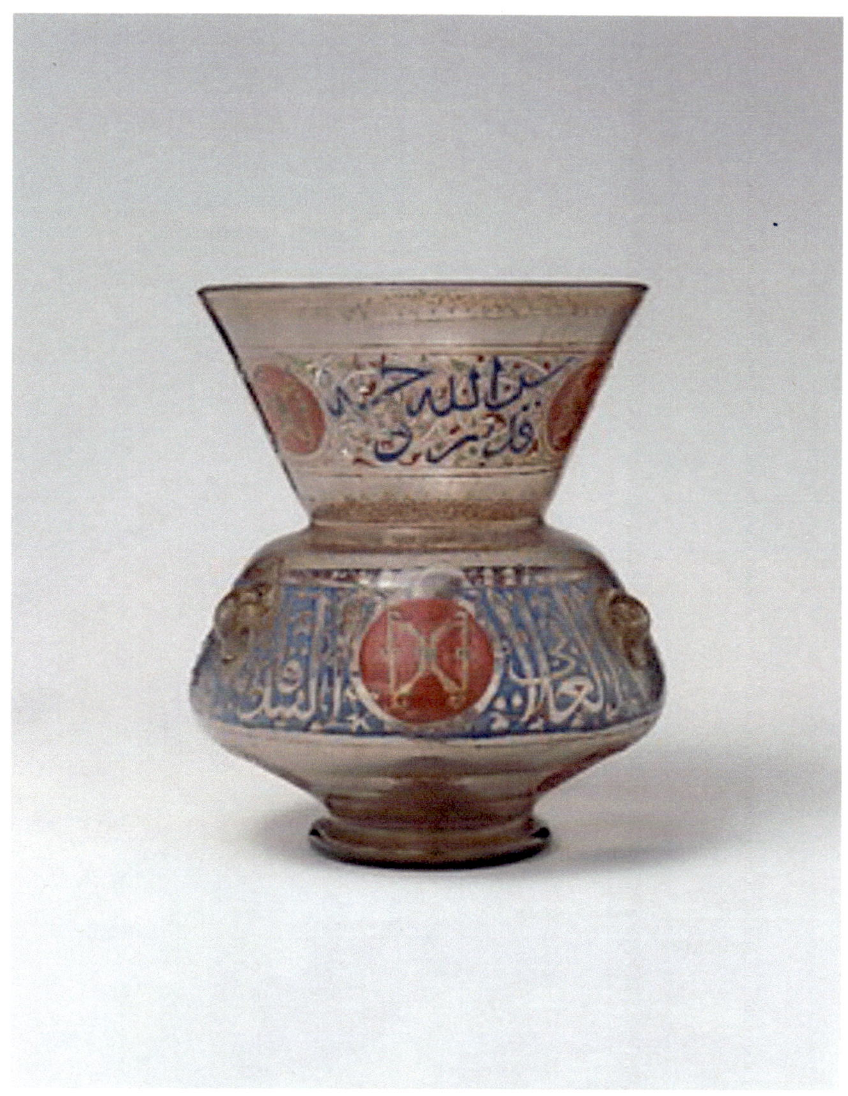

Mosque Lamp for the Mausoleum of Amir Aydakin al-'Ala'i al-Bunduqdar, Egypt, 1285[4]

Glass has a huge part to play in the history of Corning and this region. The design and production of glass objects has been taking place in Corning for over 150 years. The world renowned Corning Museum of Glass is an incredible local resource for seeing glass art that was made thousands of years ago and things being made today. There are a variety of ways glass objects are made and the distinction is often the method used. Cold glass techniques include engraving, cutting, polishing, and laminating forms. Hot glass is using molten from the furnace to blow shapes on a pipe. Kiln working includes fusing glass parts together or casting in molds inside a kiln. Glass is always the raw material and shaping becomes the process that creates the forms.

Glass artists you should know:

Howard Ben Tre, Toots Zynsky, Dale Chihuly, Preston SIngletary, William Morris, Karen LaMonte, Stanislav Libenský and Jaroslava Brychtová, Lino Tagliapietra, Josiah McElheny, Daniel Clayman

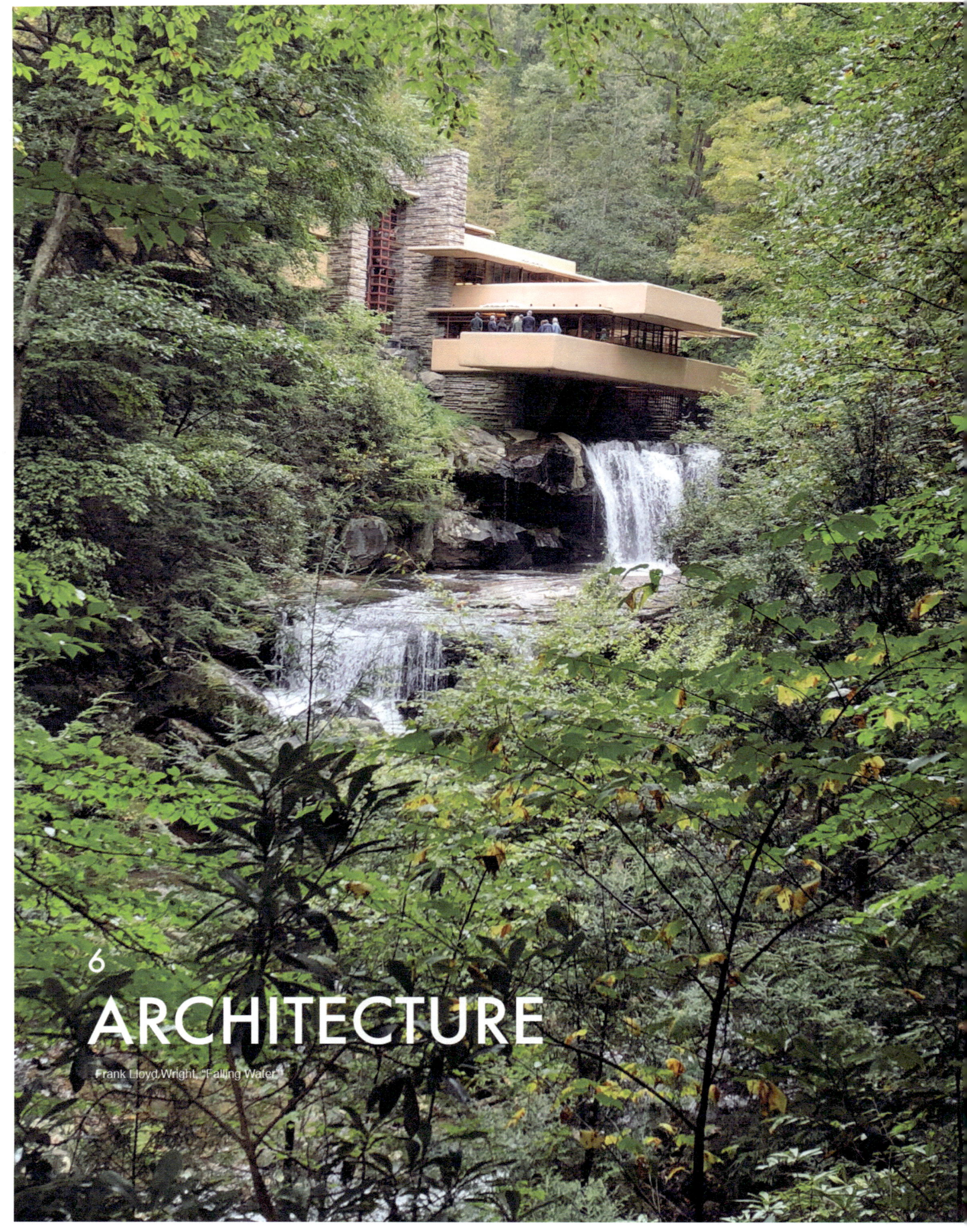

6

ARCHITECTURE

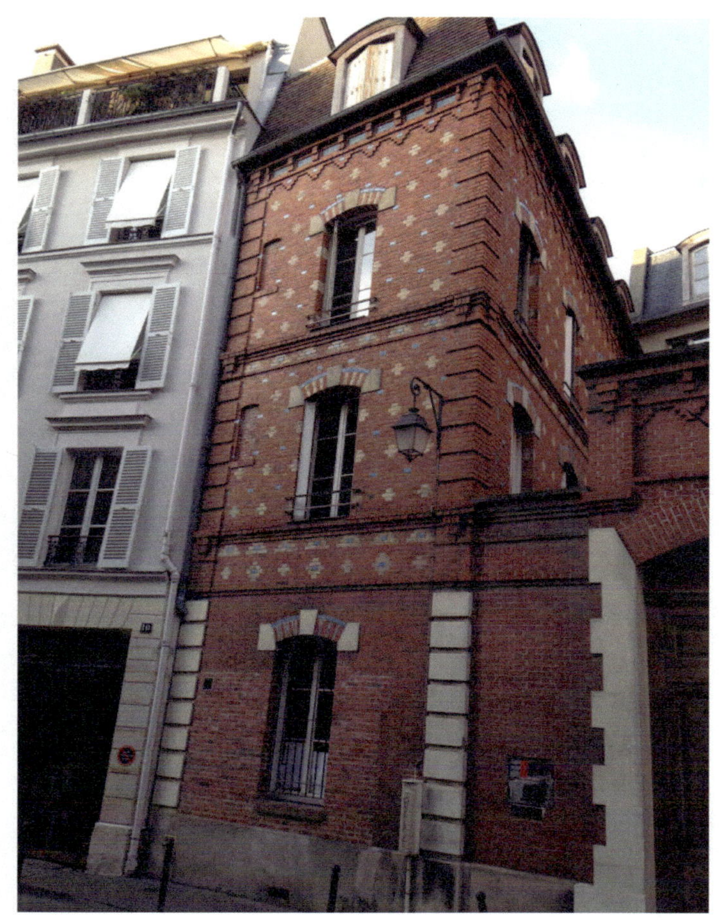
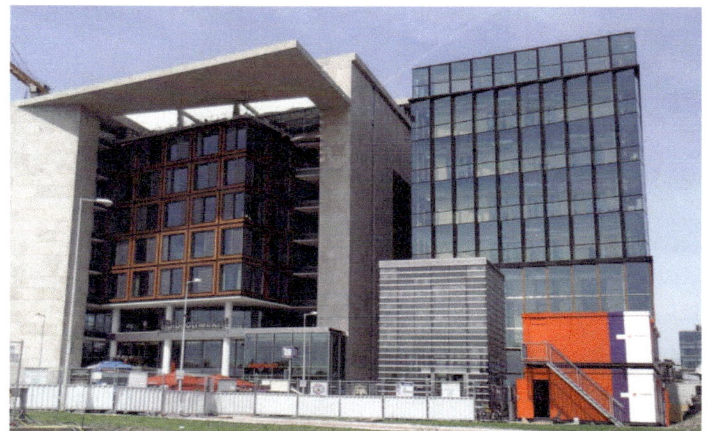
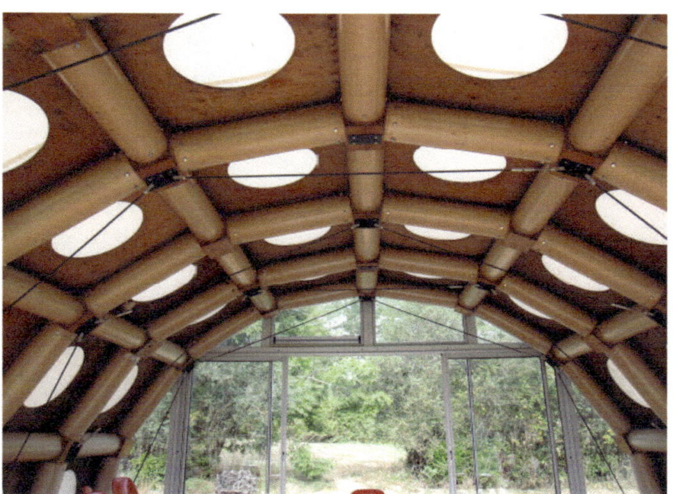

Images this page taken in Paris, Amsterdam, and Domaine de Boisbuchet[1]

The field of architecture deals with designing and constructing our built environment. Every building was designed by someone. That designer considered the shape, function, and location of the structure. When it was being built, a team of workers took over to construct the actual plan to specifications. The building generally becomes the largest 3d designed functional object possible.

Important architects to know:, Zaha Hadid. Maya Lin, I.M. Pei, Le Corbusier, Frank Gehry, Tadao Ando, Robert Venturi, Frank Lloyd Wright

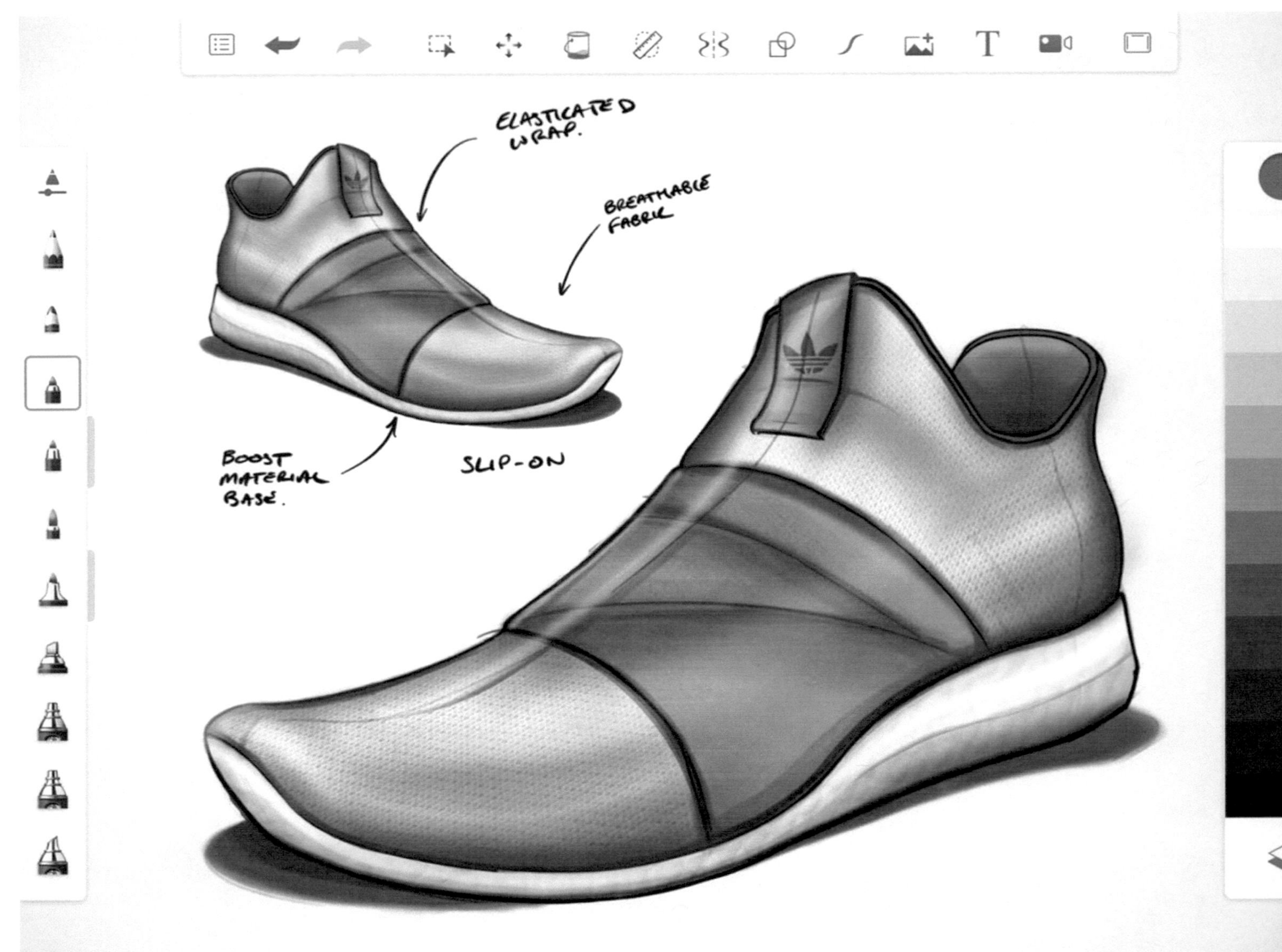

Sketches for new shoe design"[26]

7
PRODUCT DESIGN / INDUSTRIAL DESIGN

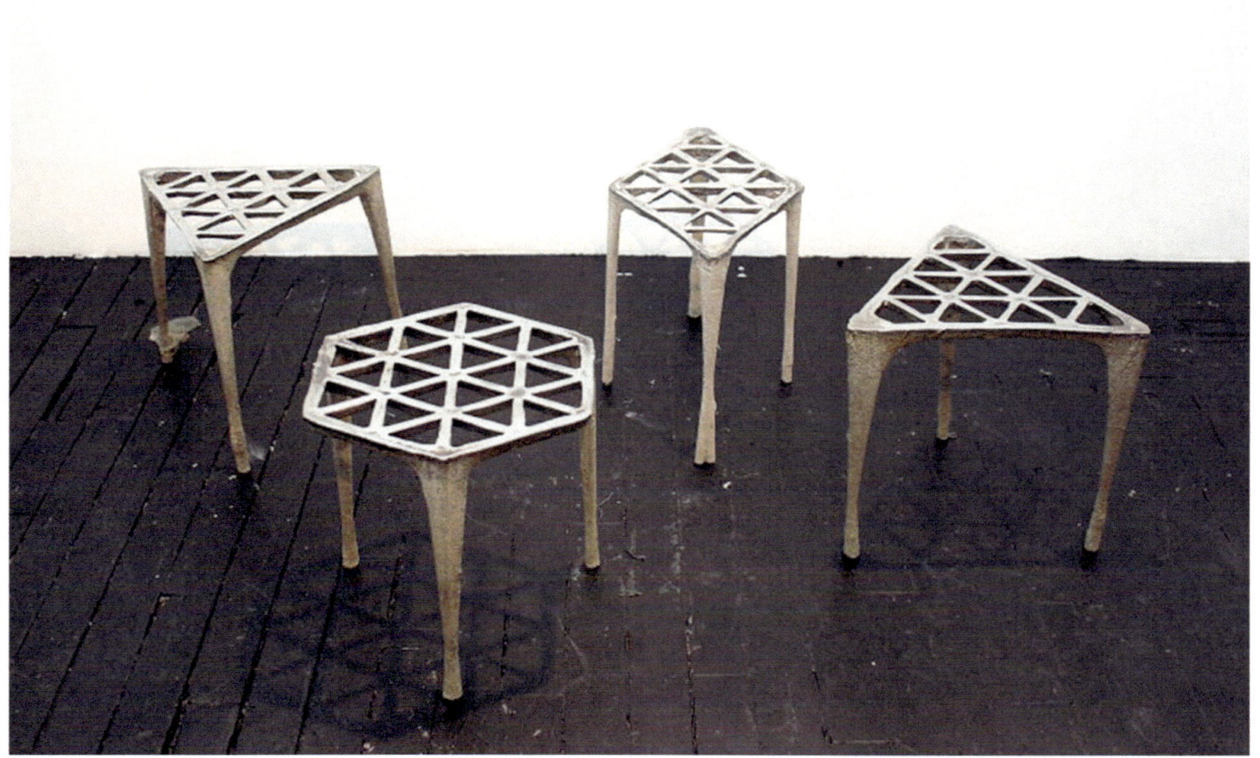

Industrial Design / Product Design / Design is a field devoted to the creation of objects we use everyday. Shoes, furniture, vehicles, computers, cell phones, and almost everything we interact with was designed by someone or a team of people. This area of design uses the same elements and principles of art as every other art form but in this case, function and ergonomics also play a role in the final design.

Important Designers to know:

Jony Ive, Hella Jongerius, Studio Drift, Max Lamb, Karim Rashid, Tom Dixon, James Dyson, Philippe Malouin, Bethann Laura Wood

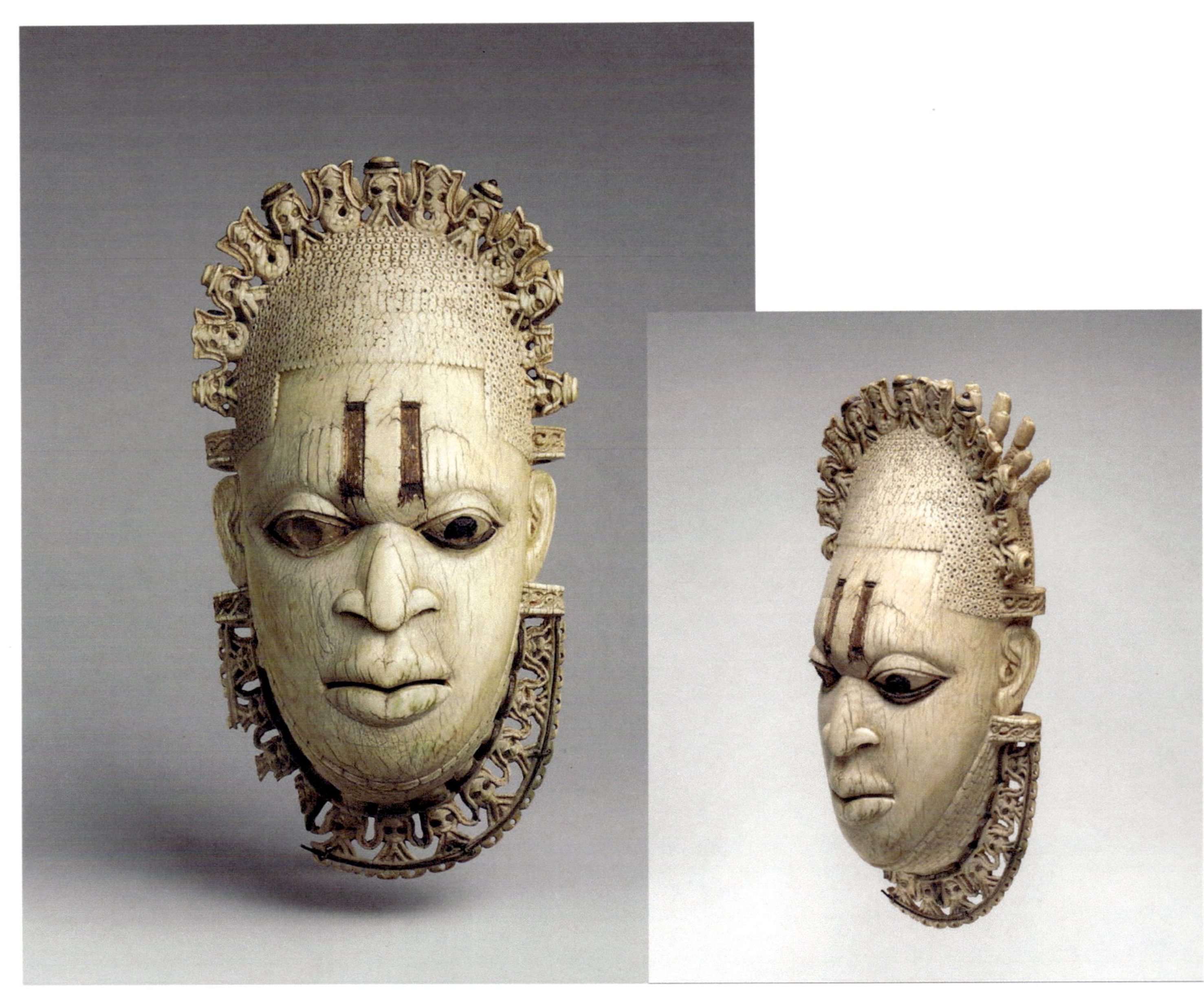

Queen Mother Pendant Mask, Iyoba, Edo peoples, Africa, 16th century CE, ivory, iron, copper[1]

8

SCULPTURE

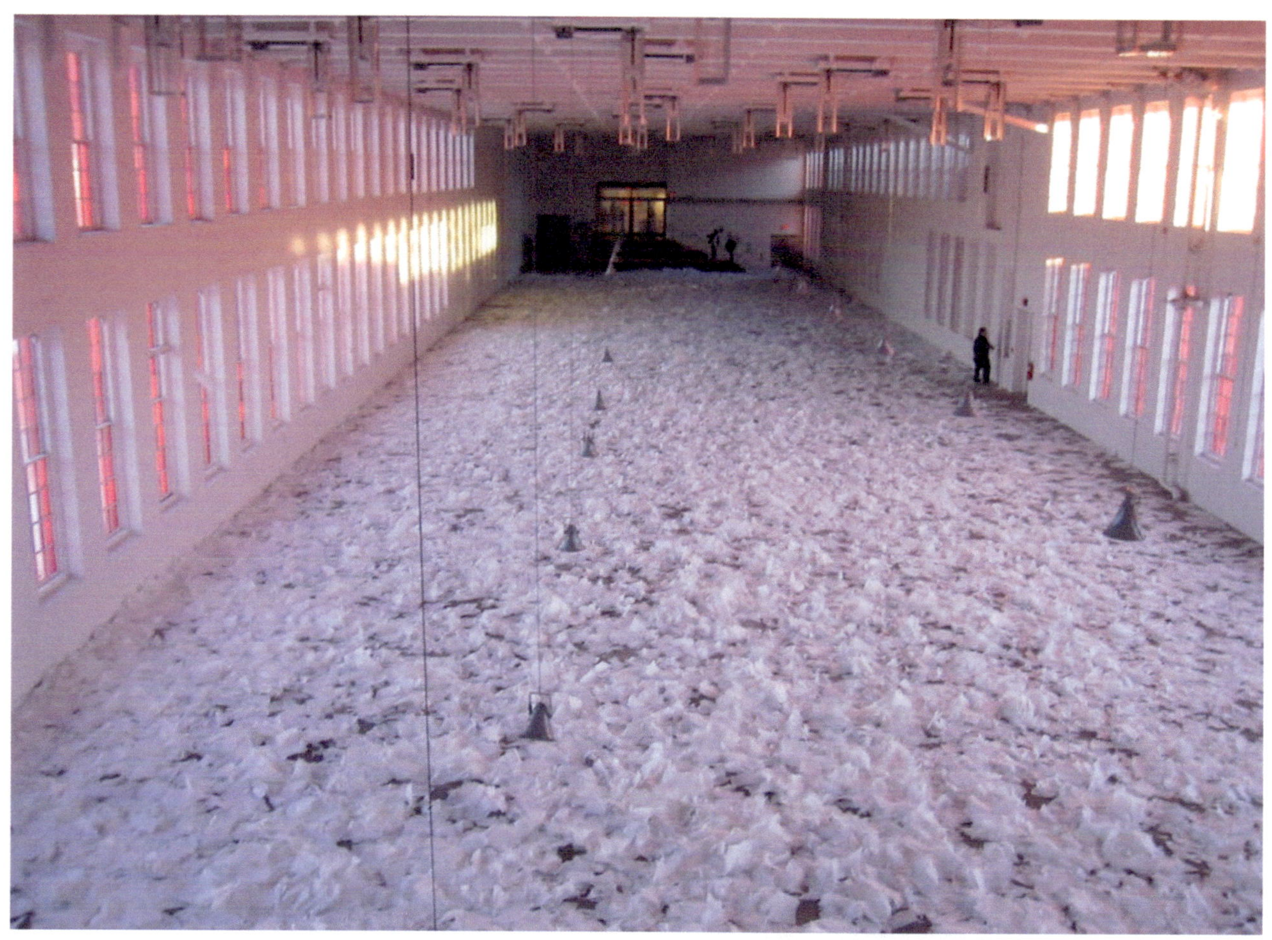

Ann Hamilton, "Corpus", installation at MASS MOCA art center[30]

Sculpture is a field of practice that involves the construction of 3d objects and installations. An installation is a contemporary approach that involves manipulating specific spaces in order to affect the viewers experience of the space. Traditional sculptural techniques include stone and wood carving, metal casting, and assembling mixed material parts into a larger piece.

Artists you should know:

Martin Puryear, Dan Flavin, Joseph Beuys, Anish Kapoor, Do-ho Suh, Ai Wei Wei, Eva Hesse, Rachel Whiteread, Louis Bourgeois, Isamu Noguchi, Virgil Ortiz, Ann Hamilton, Richard Serra

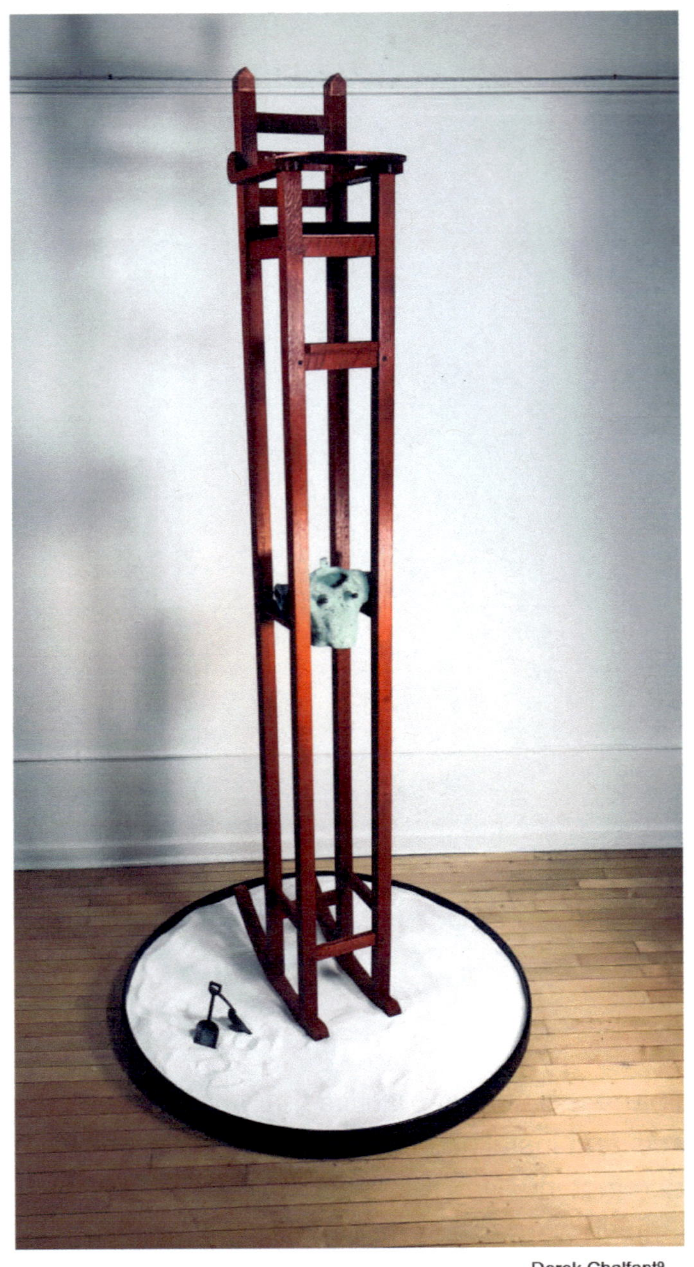

Derek Chalfant[9]

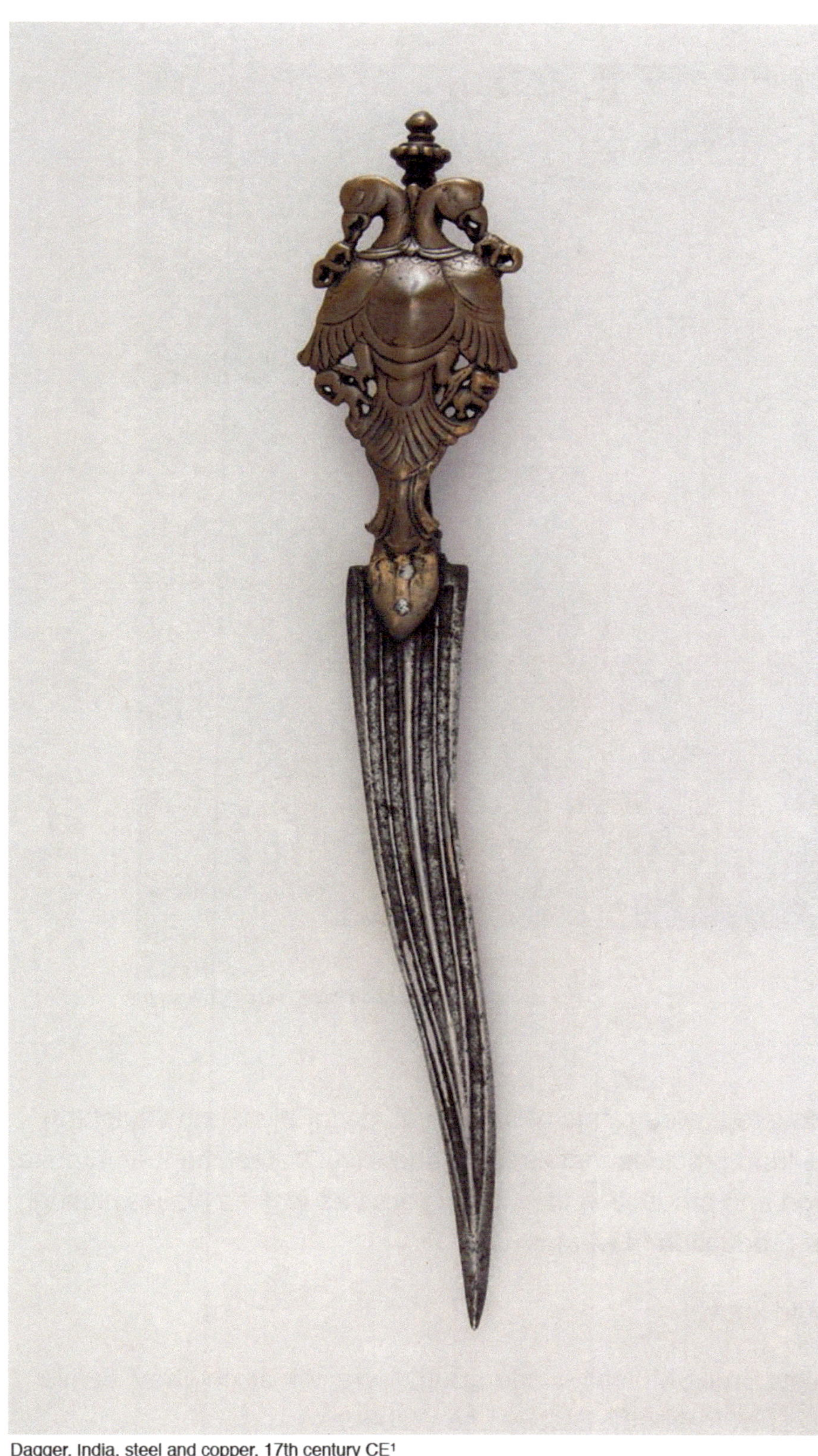

Dagger, India, steel and copper, 17th century CE[1]

9
METALS

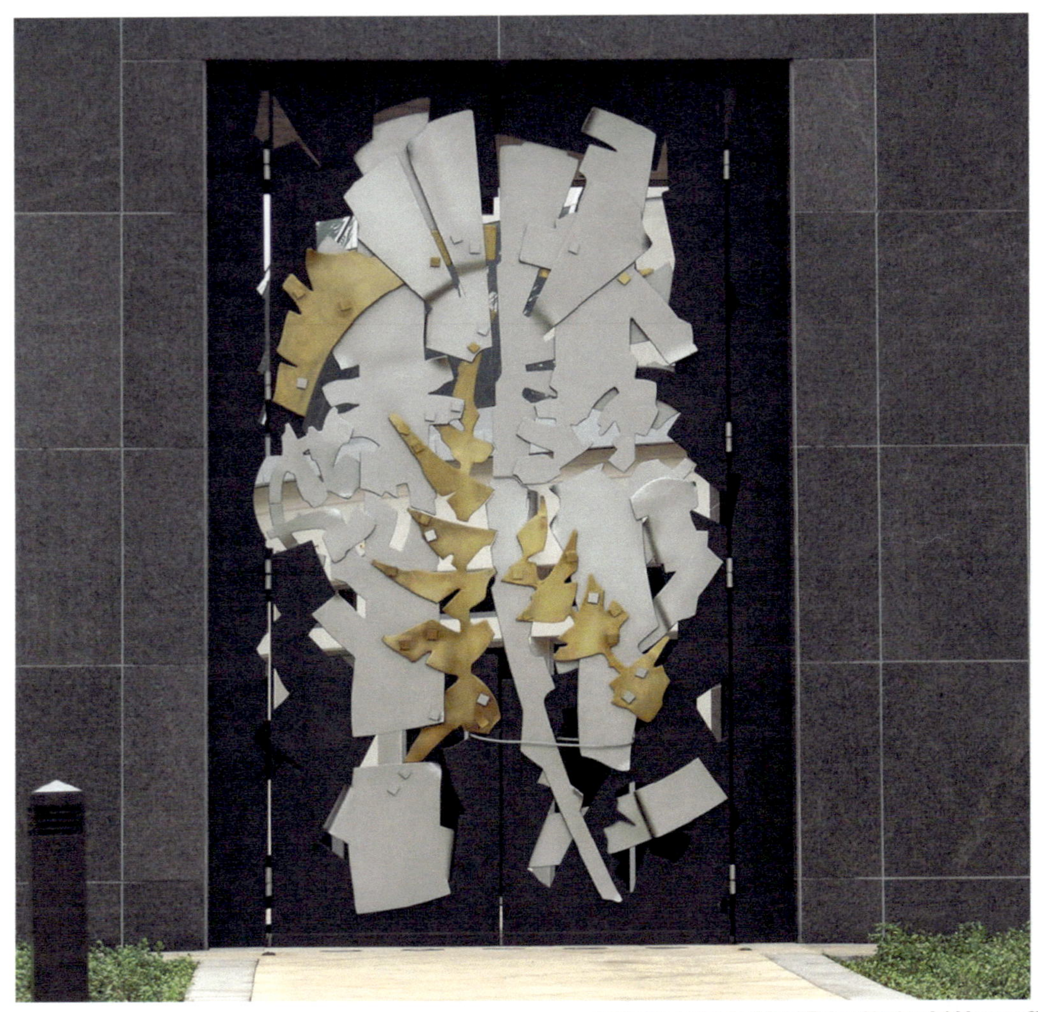

Entrance gates by Albert Paley, Naples Art Museum[29]

The Metals category covers a wide range of functional, decorative, and sculptural objects primarily made from precious metals (gold and silver), steel, copper, bronze, and iron. Jewelry design and production fits into this area as well as blacksmithing, armor making, and the production of weapons.

Metals artists you should know:

Albert Paley, Hoss Haley, Bruce Metcalf, Harlan Butt, Myra Mimlitsch-Gray, Jamie Bennett, Mary Lee Hu, Zack Peabody, Stacey Lee Webber

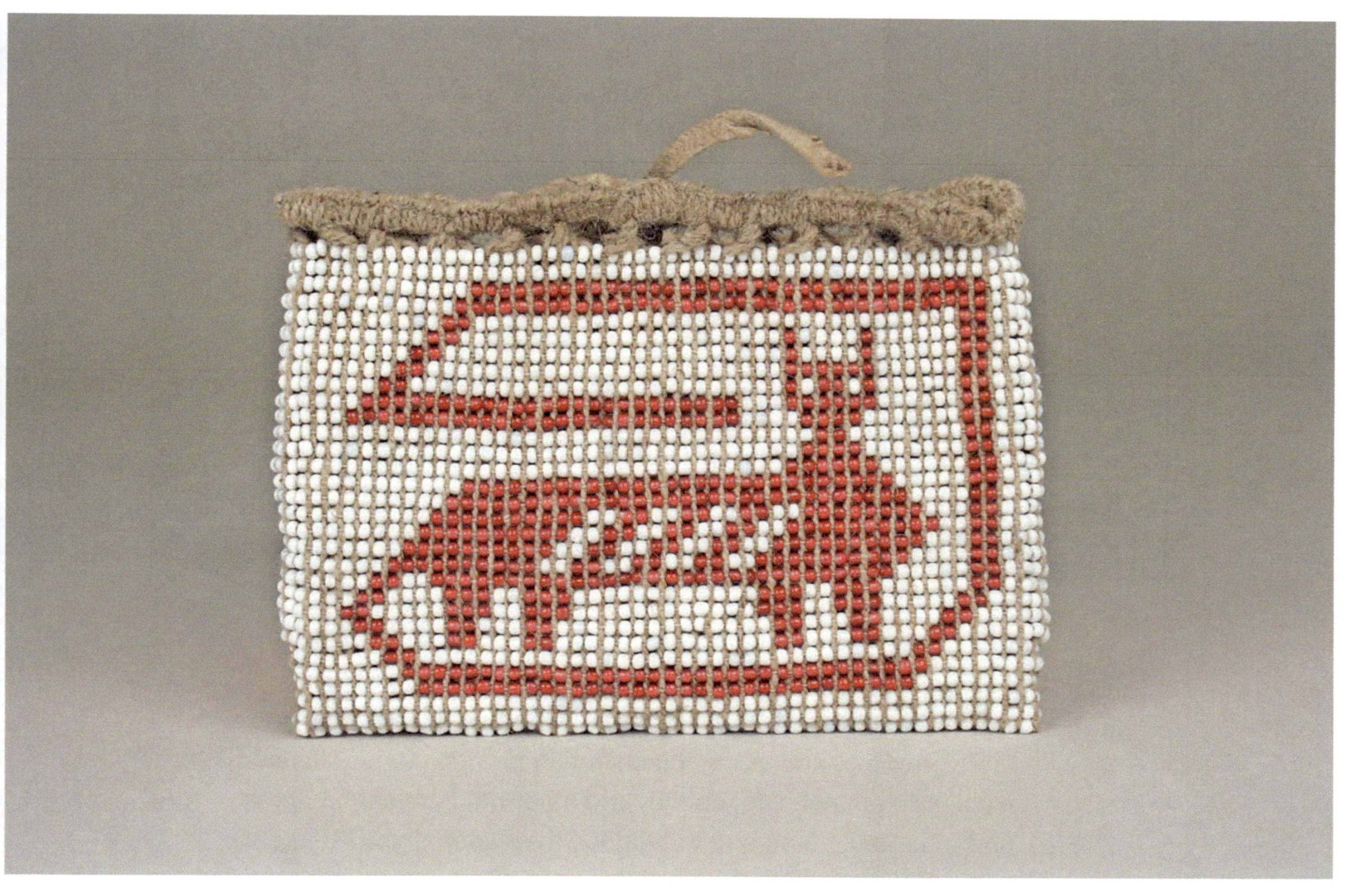

Native American Potawatomi culture, "Business Bundle Bag" 1790-1890, animal hide, wool, glass beads[4]

10

FIBERS

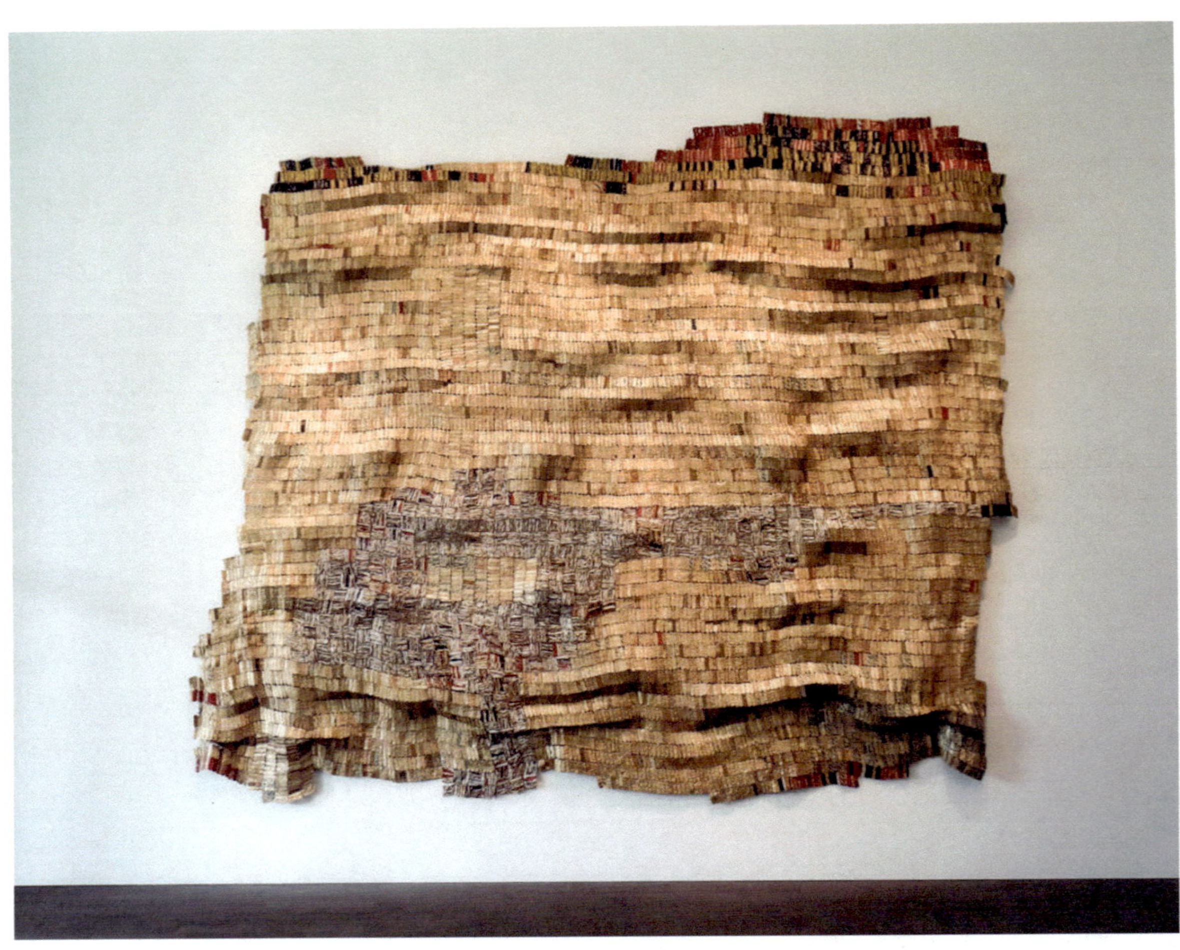

El Anatsui, "Hovor II" 2004, woven aluminum bottle caps and copper wire[33]

Fibers is a category that traditionally dealt with the production of fabric, textiles, and other objects made from materials like spun wool, silk, animal hide, cotton, and other natural fibers. Looms and other tools are used to produce the material used to create traditional works. The focus of this area of art was taking flat thin elements and turning them into a 3d object that could used to cover something including the human body. Contemporary fibers artists have expanded the realm of possibilities and materials into a wide range of functional, decorative, and sculptural objects.

Fibers artists you should know:

Anni Albers, Ruth Asawa, Sheila Hicks, Lenore Tawney, Nick Cave, Magdalena Abakanowicz, El Anatsui

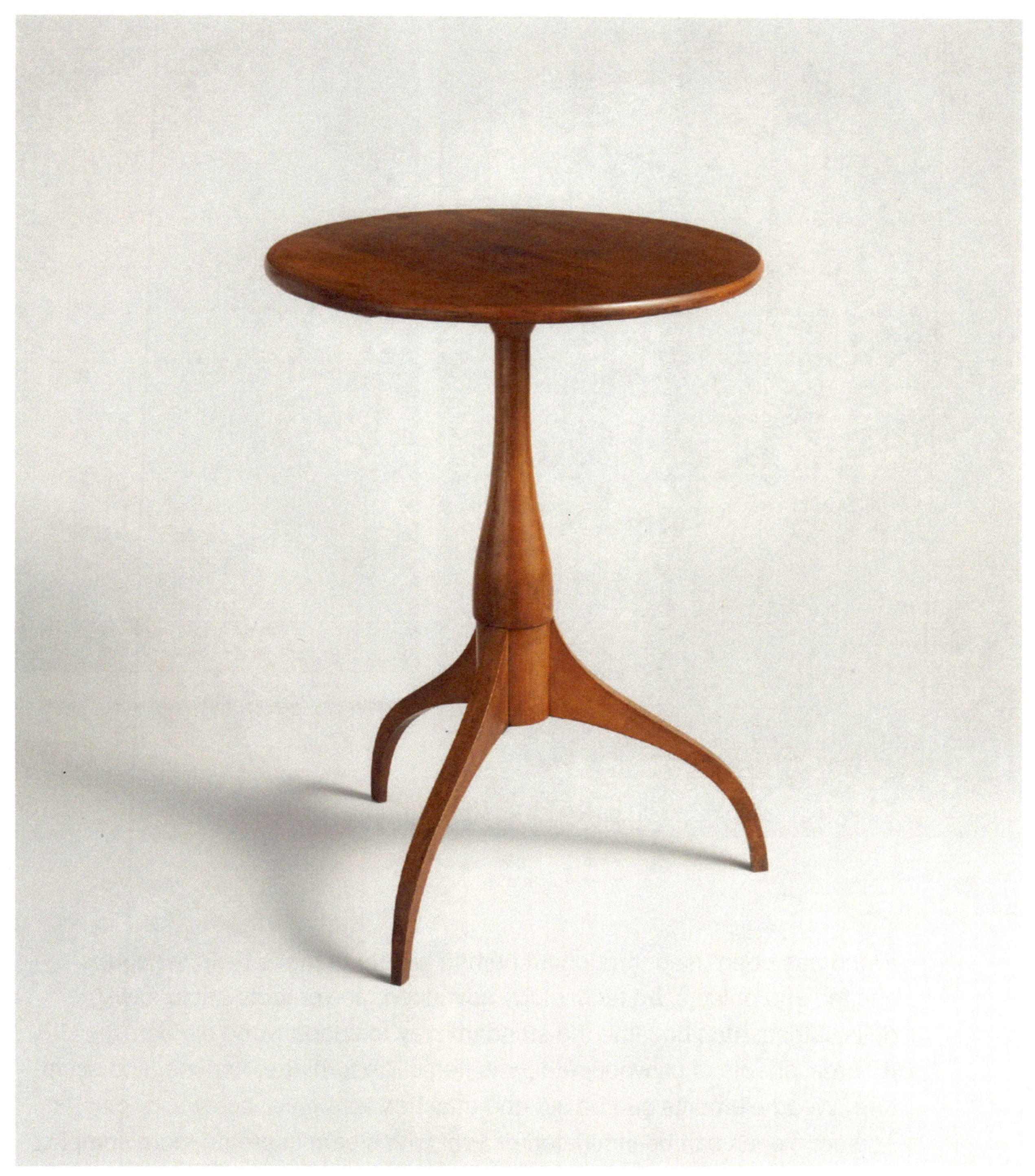

Shaker, "Candle Stand", 1800 - 1840[4]

11

WOOD

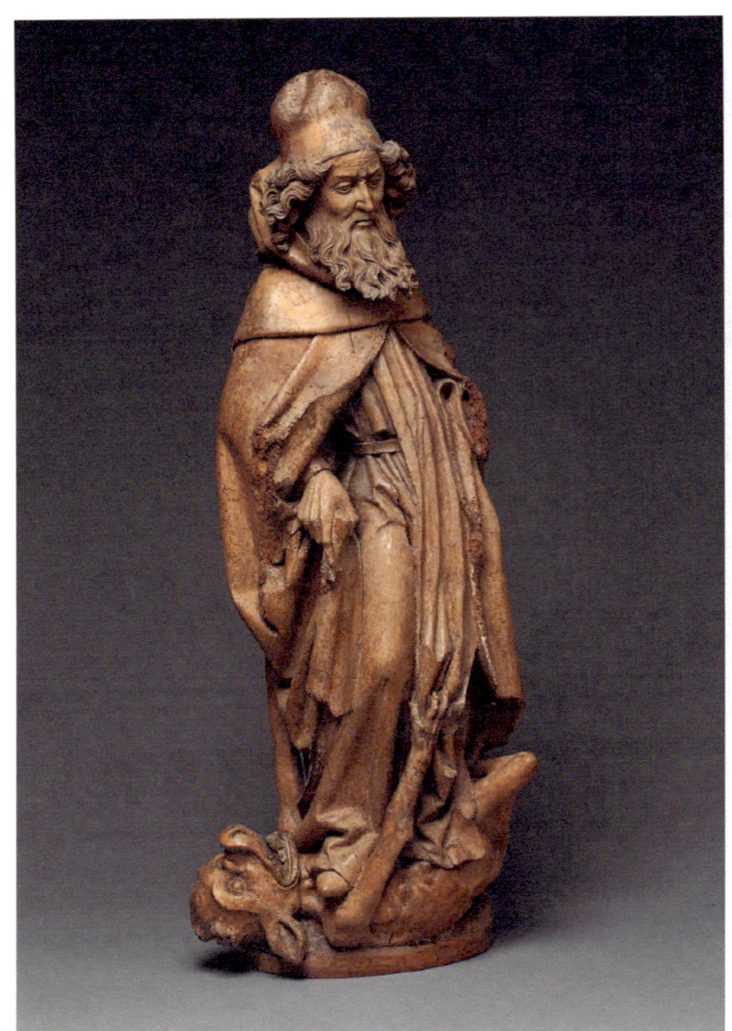

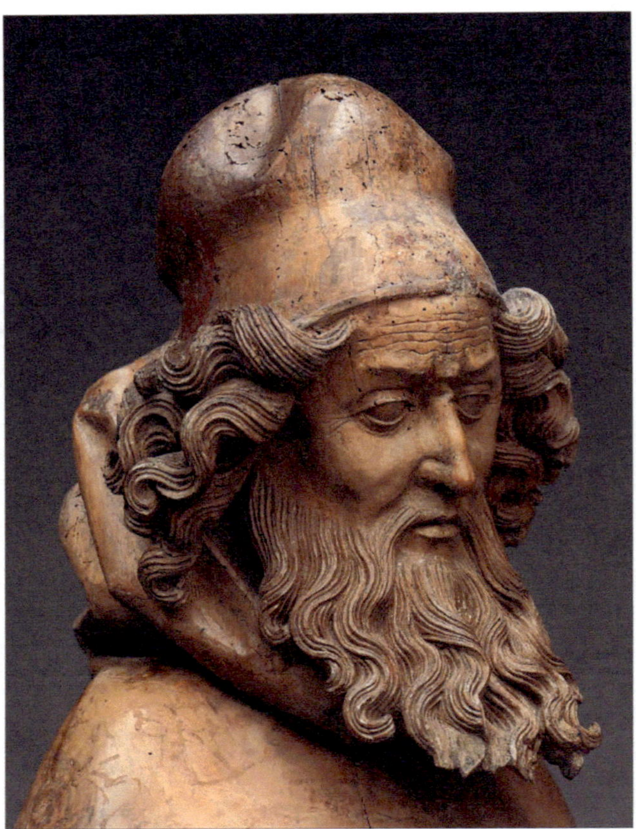

Nikolaus von Hagenau, "Saint Anthony Abbot", wood, 1500[4]

Wood has been used throughout human history to make tools, weapons, shelter, and objects. As technology advanced, power tools (table saws, drills, lathes, etc.) became the standard way to shape wood elements (boards, sheets of plywood, etc.) into items like furniture, houses, and sculpture. Wood elements can be cut and attached with nails, screws, or glue. Thinner pieces can be laminated or bent with steam to create more complex shapes. The natural character of the material can be revealed with stains and polish or painted over.

Artists you should know: George Nakashima, John Reed Fox, Michael Puryear, Sam Maloof, Wendell Castle, Edward Moulthrop

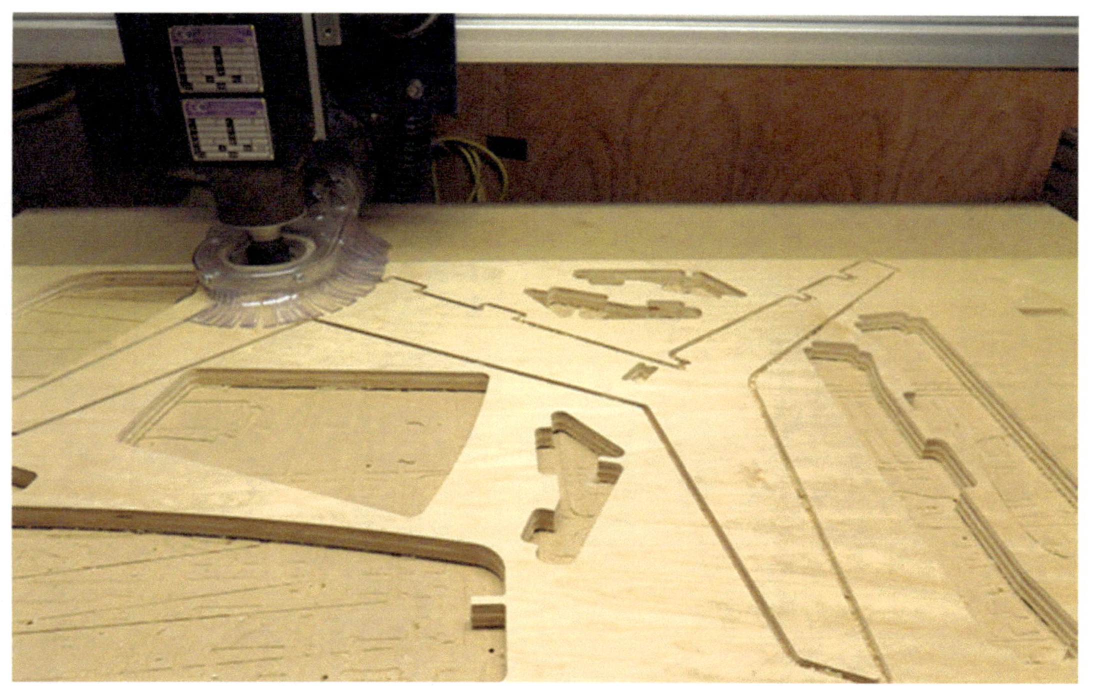

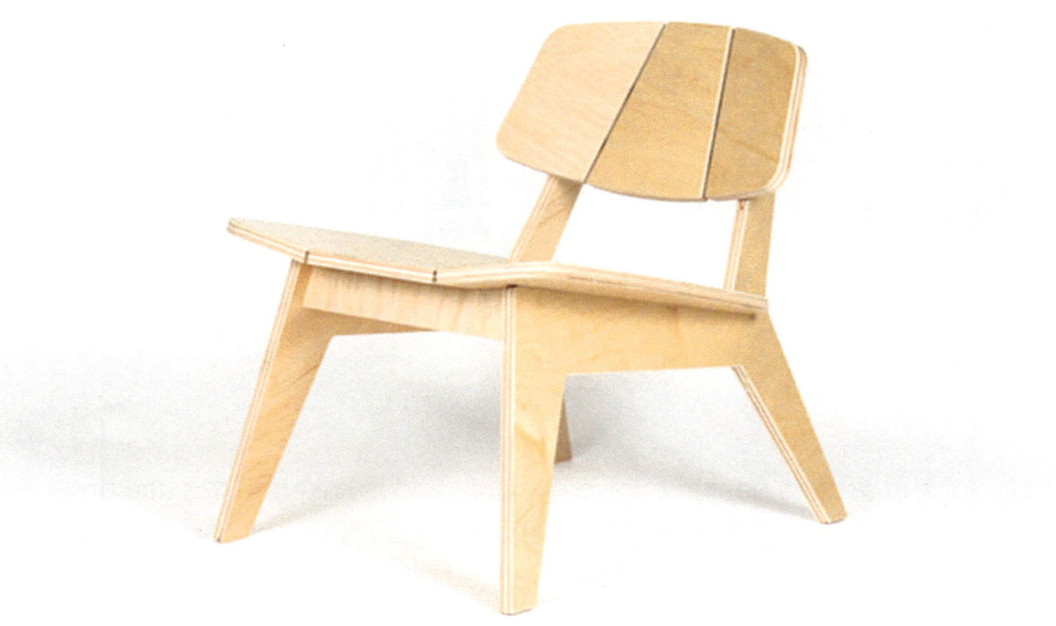

A CNC router cutting shapes from plywood that will be used to assemble this chair design[27]

12

NEW TECHNOLOGIES

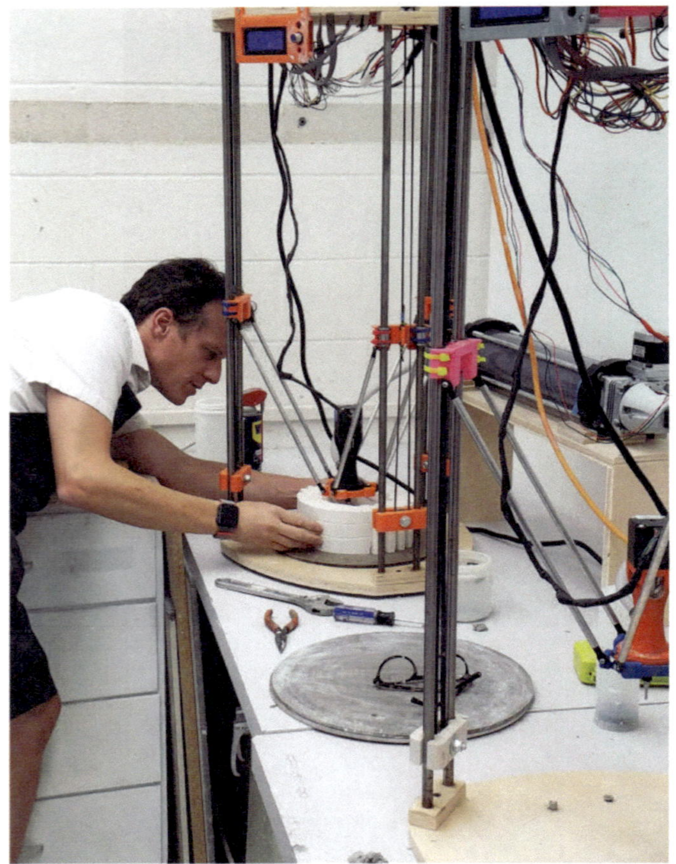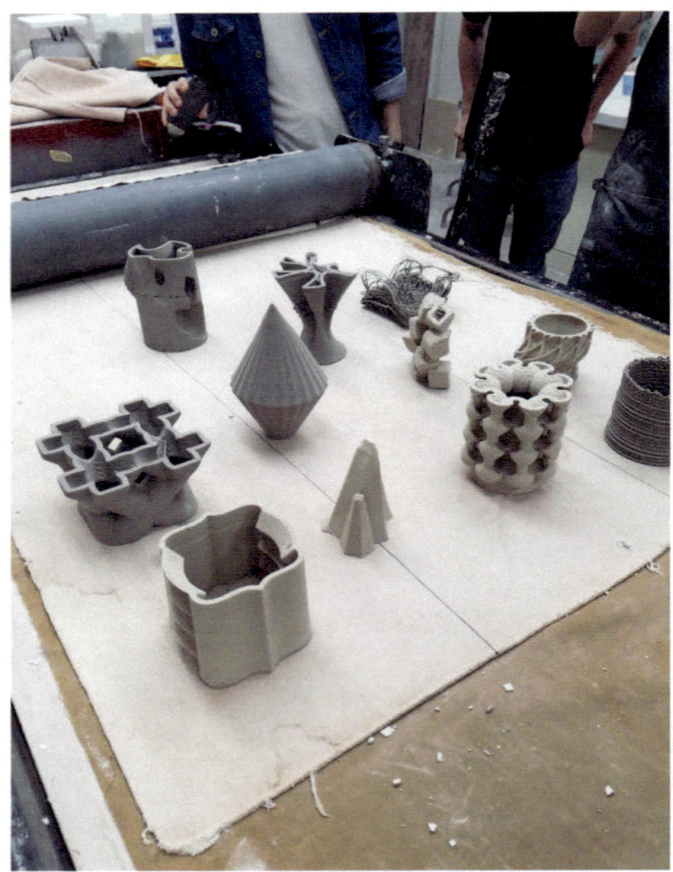

SUNY-New Paltz art professor Bryan Czibesz working with a clay 3d printer and some printed examples.[1]

New technology in art and design evolves quickly and is linked to the use of technology in the larger culture. Artists and designers are often "early adopters" of new tools and help to push them in creative and unexpected directions. In the studio today, they are experimenting with CAD (Computer Aided Design), 3d printing, laser cutting, CNC (Computer Numerically Control) routers and cutters, and computers to control these tools.

Artists you should know: Bryan Czibesz, Jonathan Keep, Studio Unfold, Jenny Sabin, Del Harrow, Andy Brayman, Radical Craft

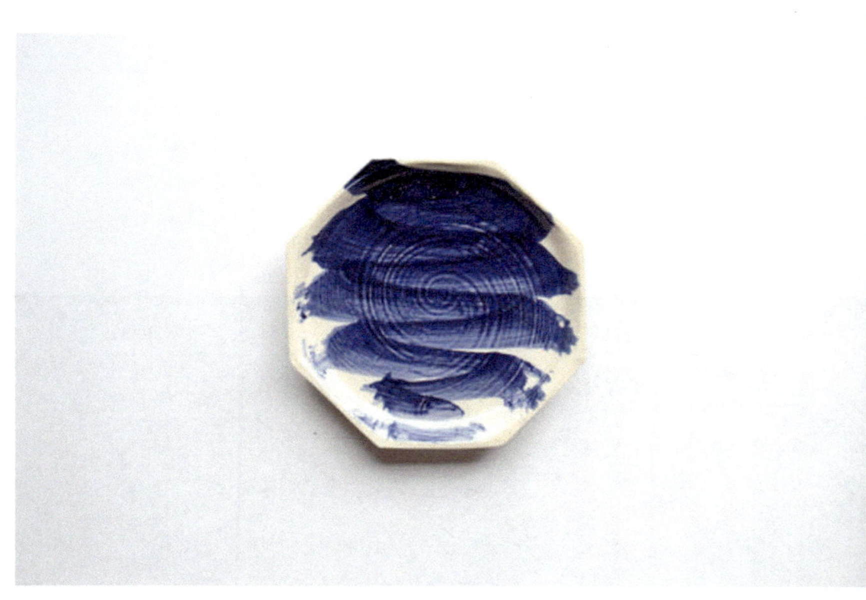

Adam Chau, "Digital Calligraphy" series, CNC decorated porcelain[3]

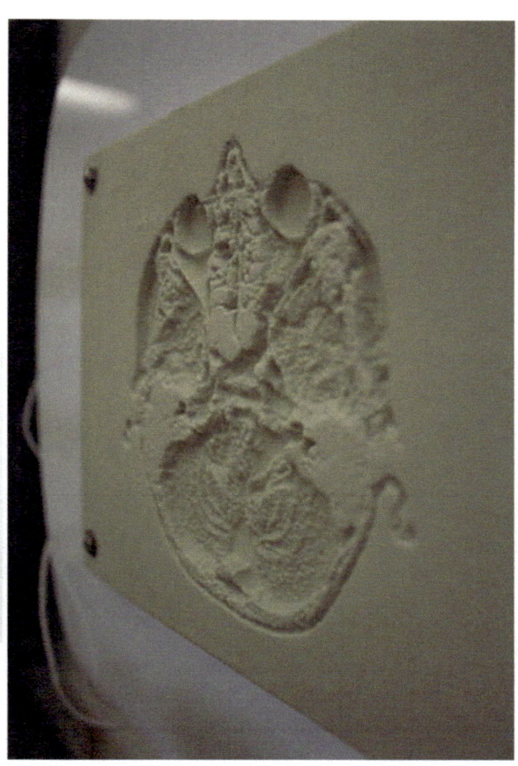

Bryan Czibesz, "Diagnostic: Myopia", CNC milled porcelain[13]

NEW TECHNOLOGY

The ceramics world has always been on the cutting edge of the newest technological and material advances. Ceramics can easily be a blend of some very old methods and the newest cutting edge technologies. One of the avenues that many ceramic artists are exploring today is the use of computer modeling (CAD), 3-d printing, and computer numerically controlled (CNC) tools. Some artists are modeling their pieces on a computer first using CAD software and then using that as a pattern to build the piece. Other artists are utilize the new tools of 3-d printing in order to have the machine build the object they modeled on the computer (or then making a plaster mold of the object) or use milling machines to cut plaster molds. These techniques have great potential to give the artist freedom to invent and construct unique types of ceramics objects.

Resources
Free CAD software: SketchUp: www.sketchup.com
TinkerCAD: www.tinkercad.com

Artists using digital technology to produce their work:
Bryan Czibesz: www.bryanczibesz.com
Del Harrow: www.delharrow.net
Olivier Van Herpt: www.oliviervanherpt.com
Jonathan Keep: www.keep-art.co.uk/index.htm
Adam Chau: www.adamchau.com
Brooks Oliver: www.brooksoliver.com

Data Clay group: www.data-clay.org

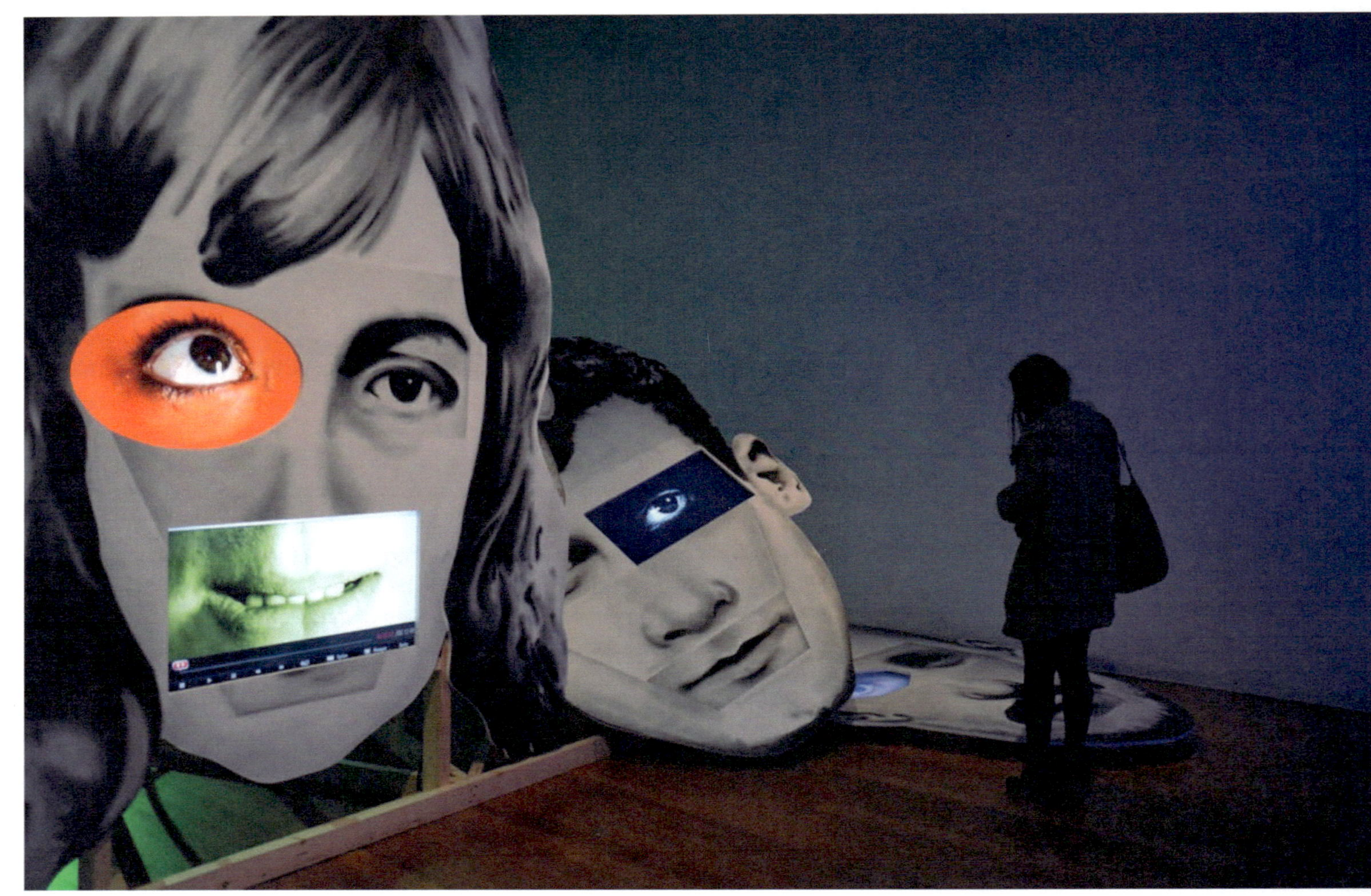

Tony Oursler, "Phantasmagoria" video installation[18]

13

4D ART

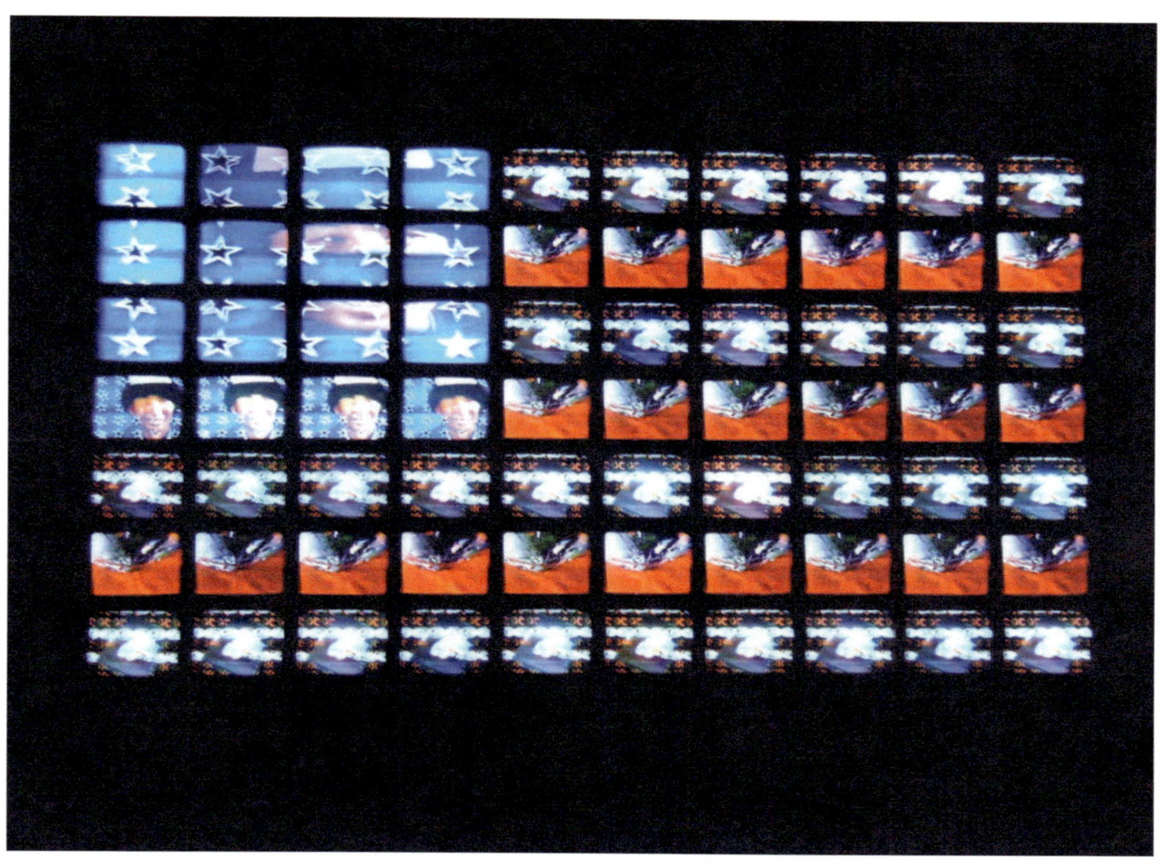

Nam June Paik, "Phantasmagoria" video installation

The ideas of 4d (time is the 4th dimension) art making have evolved as modern technology has developed. Early film, video cameras, and now cell phones have put tools in the artists hand that can record time, motion, and narrative. Sound, video, animation, film projections, computer programming, virtual reality, robotics, and performance art all have also become common art making modes and tools.

Artists you should now:
Edward Muybridge, Tony Oursler, Bill Viola, Nam June Paik, Jenny Holzer, Dan Collins, Arthur Ganson

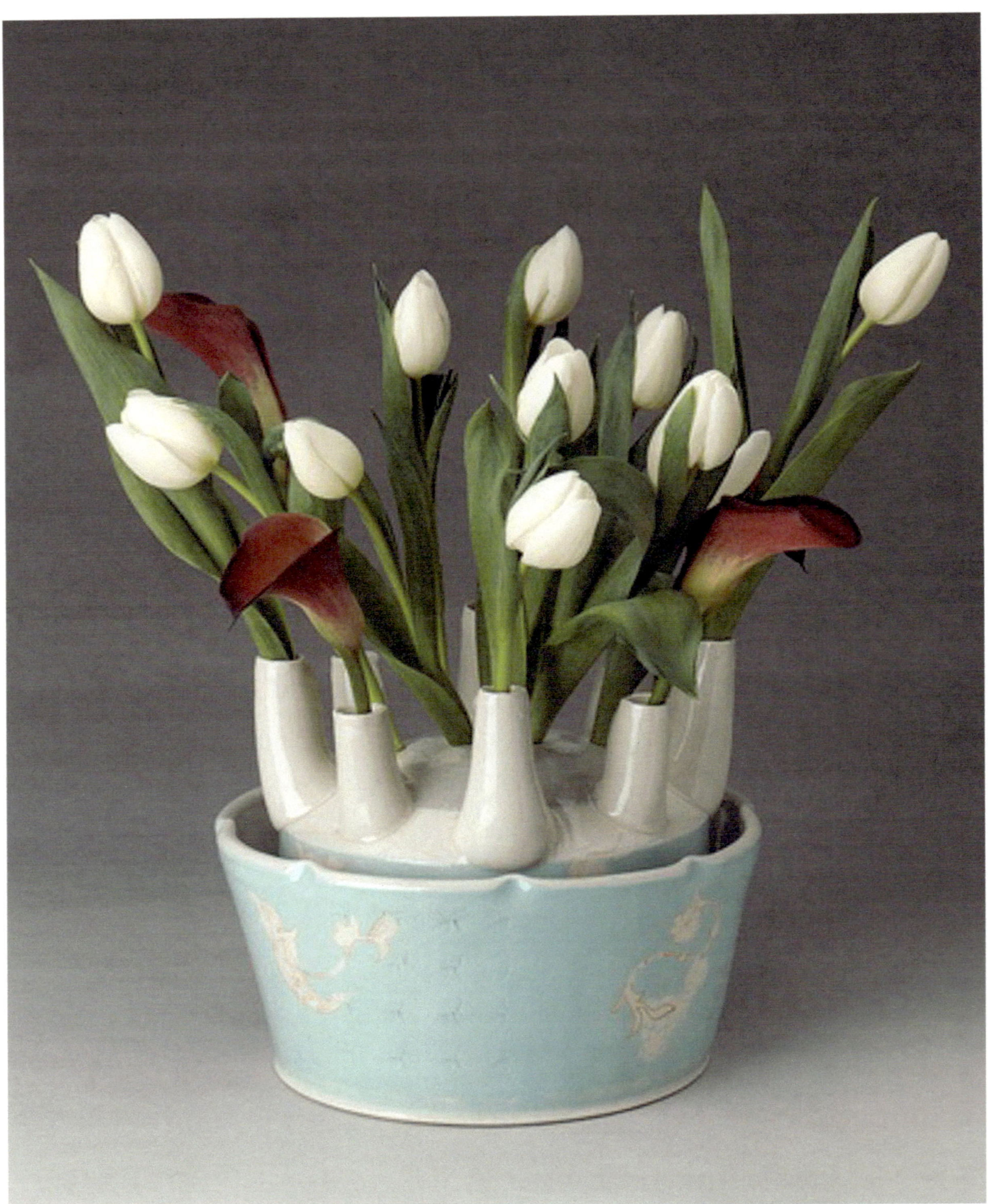

Sanam Emami, "Tulip Vase". porcelain[2]

14

CERAMICS

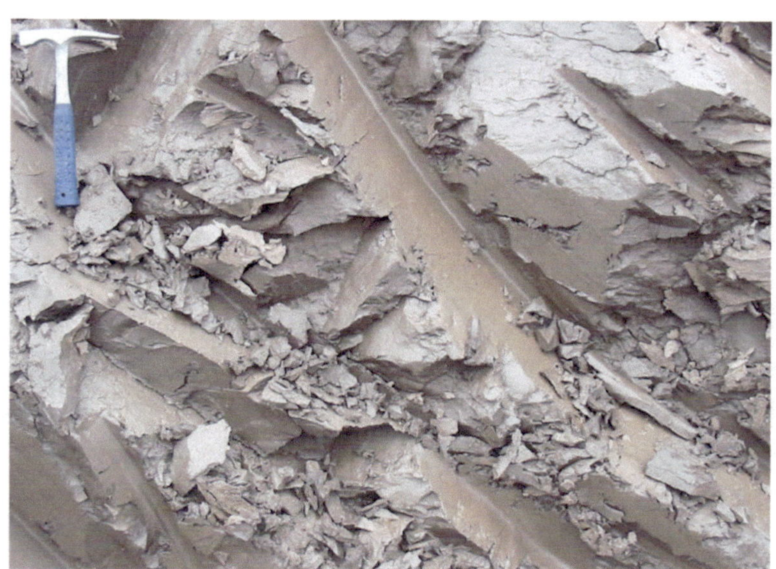

Excavating clay from a natural deposit.[9]

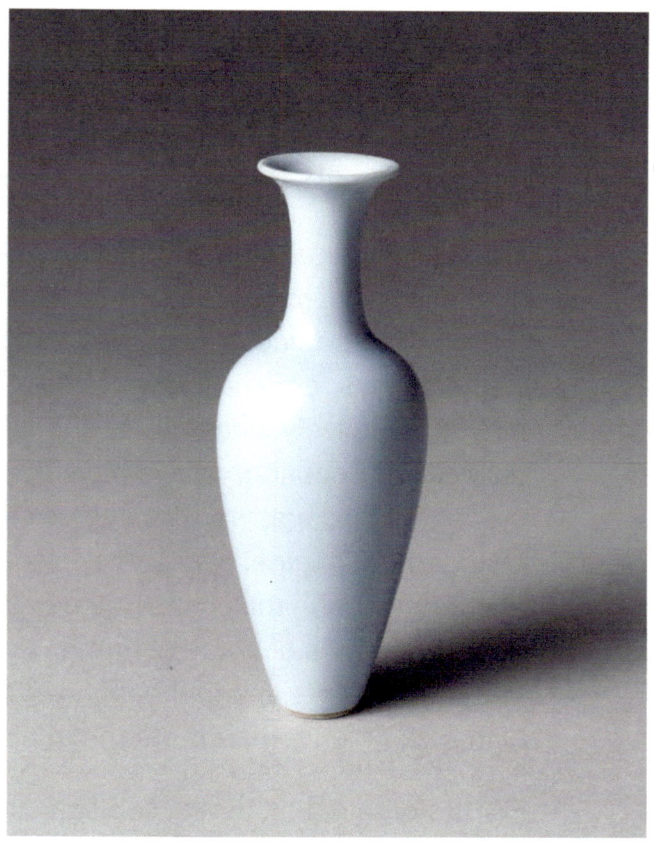

Vase from the Qing Dynasty, China[4]

Clay has been used for thousands of years to make functional objects and sculptural forms. Next to cave paintings in Europe, researchers found bison sculpted in the clay of the cave floor. Fired pottery shapes helped humans store and cook food over a fire making survival easier. Almost all cultures have made objects in fired clay which becomes permanent and provides a lasting record of that culture. In modern ceramics, artists have a variety of tools and materials to work with including potters wheels, extruders, slab rollers, manufactured underglazes and glazes, and other materials from around the world. This section of the 3d handbook contains information also found in the SUNY-CCC Ceramics studio handbook.

Artists you should know: Peter Voulkos, Peter Pincus, Eva Zeisel, George Ohr, Roberto Lugo, Ayumi Horie, Steven Lee, Jun Kaneko, Linda Lopez, Beth Cavener, Peter Beasecker, Kirk Mangus

AL_2O_3 $2SiO_2$ $2H_2O$ --- Chemical symbol for Clay

Clays are naturally occurring alumina-silica materials formed by the weathering of igneous rocks over millions of years. As these rocks were weathered, different types of clay were formed with each having particular characteristics. The two basic forms of clay are primary and secondary. Primary clays remained close to their source feldspathic rock after weathering. This means that they are relatively clean, pure, and often whitish. They are also more heat resistant than secondary clays. Secondary clays have been moved very far from their source. They may have been eroded by glaciers, washed away in rivers, or blown across deserts. The erosion process has changed the original clay particle size and shape and other minerals (most often iron and titanium) have been mixed in. This has created the variety of natural clays found across the planet. Over thousands of years of human history, clay has proven to be one of the most useful and important materials and that continues today. We are in a "ceramics / glass age" using a variety of high tech / high temperature materials in our computers, phones, and vehicles.

For the creation of ceramic objects, there are a number important characteristics possessed by natural clay. These properties include refractoriness (resistance to heat), the ability to become durable and dense after firing, mineral composition (contamination by other minerals), and plasticity (ease of shaping and ability to hold that shape). The plasticity in wet clay (one of its most important characteristics) is caused by a very fine particle size, the thin platelet shape of these particles, and the water moving between the particles (see the image on the previous page). After an object is shaped, it must be dried slowly to prevent cracks from forming and then fired to make it permanent. Once the piece is heated beyond 1,000 F (540 C), it has been turned into ceramic and is no longer a plastic workable clay. Clays found by prospecting in nature should be subjected to a variety of tests such as workability and firing temperature before being dug and used in large amounts.

See David Peters' website www.davidpetersceramics.com/process-gallery-test/ for an example of how clays can be prospected and used by studio artists.

Categories of Naturally Occurring Clays

There are a huge variety of natural clays found across the planet due to the diverse methods, locations, and situations of their formation. Geologists and ceramic engineers break these different clays into broad categories but it should be noted that since these are natural materials, some clays may fit into more than one area. Some brand names of these clays will go extinct or change as mines close or new more profitable sources of materials are found by the mining companies. There are five basic categories of natural clays, they are:

Earthenware (also known as surface clay)

These are the most commonly and easily found secondary clays. Earthenware was the first type of natural clay used by humans and required the simplest kiln technology and lowest firing temperatures. These fine grained clays are often red, orange, brown, gray, blue, black, or yellow in nature. This coloration is due to a high amount of mineral contaminants such as iron, titanium, and manganese mixed in during the long erosion process. Most of the clays found in this area of NY state are fine grained earthenwares. Some commercially available earthenware clays in the US are Red Art, Ranger Red, and Lizella Red.

Ball Clay

These are a large group of high temperature, contaminant free (very little iron) secondary clays. Ball clays are the most plastic of all types and have the smallest particle size which helps to create plasticity. One drawback of a small particle size is a high degree of shrinkage of the wet clay which can cause problems with cracking. Ball clays are often used to increase the workability of a mixture called a clay body (discussed in the next few pages). Some commercially available ball clays are Kentucky OM#4, Tennessee #1, Spinks C & C, and XX Sagger.

Stoneware Clay

These are relatively refractory secondary clays that have a larger particle size than ball clays but are still very plastic. Stoneware clays are often found mixed with small particles of iron and some feldspar due to the erosion process. They usually fire tan, brown, or grayish and are also naturally occurring clay bodies that vitrify (becoming very dense and non-porous) at high temperatures. Some commercially available stonewares include Roseville, Gold Art, and Foundry Hill Creme.

Fireclay

These are highly refractory secondary clays with a very large, heavy, coarse particle size having been deposited early in the erosion process. Fireclays are not very plastic and they do not shrink very much during drying. Kiln bricks may be made from a large percentage of fireclay. Clay bodies formulated for large scale sculpture also have a large amount fireclay since the coarse particle allows thickly made objects to dry out more evenly. Commercially available fireclays include Hawthorn Bond and AP Green.

Kaolin

These are very pure white refractory primary clays. Since they did not move far from their source, few contaminant minerals were mixed in. Kaolins tend to be course grained and non-plastic clays. The name kaolin is derived from the Chinese word for "high ridge". These clays are necessary ingredients for making a porcelain clay body. Some commercially available kaolins include E.P.K., No.6 Tile Clay, and Grolleg (this kaolin is imported from the U.K.).

Clay Bodies

Clay bodies are man-made combinations that blend a variety of clays and other materials. These mixtures are formulated for specific firing temperatures, forming processes, fired colors, textures and other issues. The most workable clay bodies are made from materials that have a wide variety of particle sizes.

There are three main clay bodies used by sculptors, potters, industrial designers, and other 3d artists throughout art history. They are earthenware, stoneware, and porcelain.

Earthenware (also known as Terra Cotta)

This clay body has been used throughout history and by ceramic artists across the world. It is often a reddish orange color (due to its high iron content) and fired to the lowest temperature (around 1,800 F / 980 C) of the three clay bodies. It remains porous after being fired making it very effective for things like flowerpots. However, because of this characteristic, earthenware must be fully glazed if used to functional pottery or the food / drink will be absorbed into the pot surface.

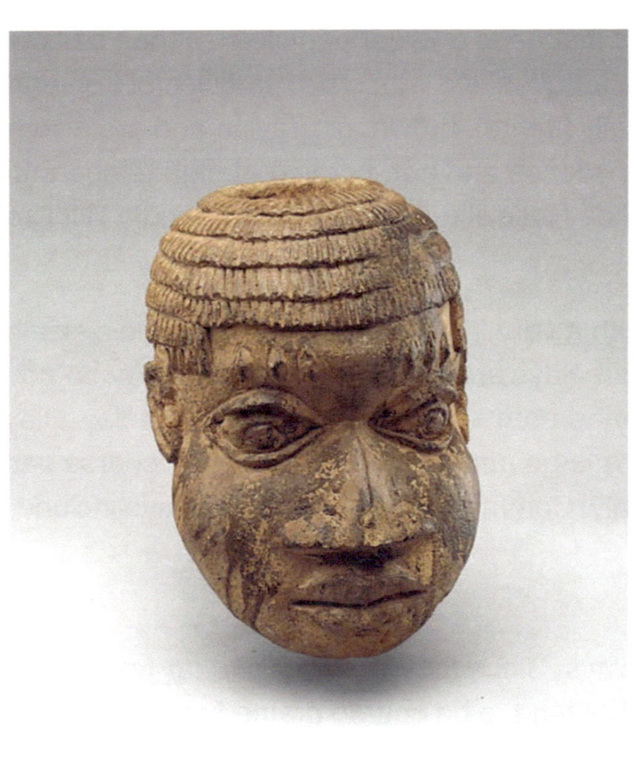

African Benin culture earthenware head[4]

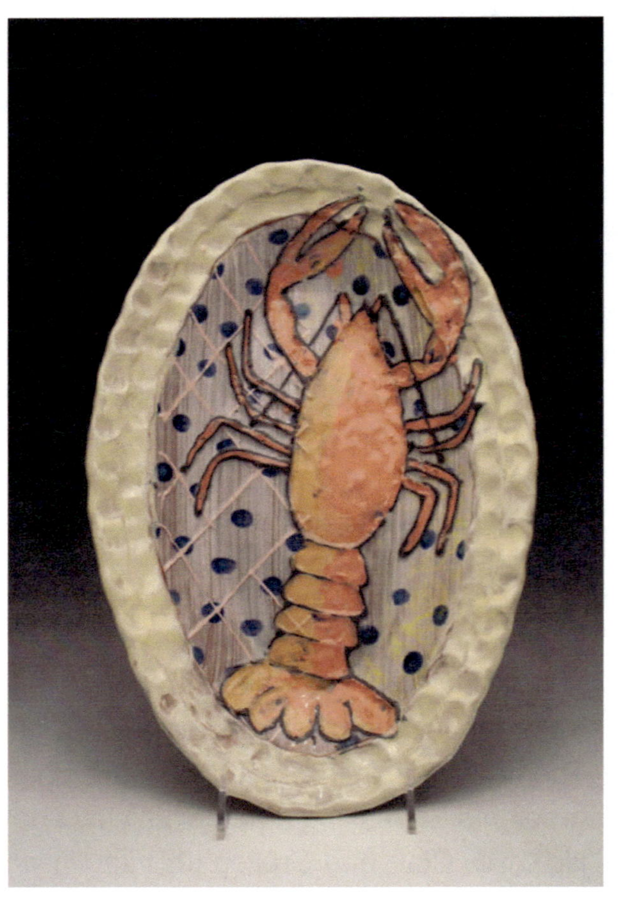

Arthur Halvorsen, "Lobster Platter" glazed earthenware[3]

Stoneware

This clay body needs to be fired to a high temperature (at least 2,150 F / 1,180 C) and often has a tan, brown or gray color. It becomes very dense after firing (vitrified) and has been used extensively for functional pottery. As the need for higher firing temperatures increased in ancient cultures, kiln technology advanced often alongside metal casting. Many of the kiln designs developed hundreds or thousands of years ago are still in use today. The CCC anagama woodfired kiln is based on an ancient Japanese kiln type used to fire stoneware ceramics.

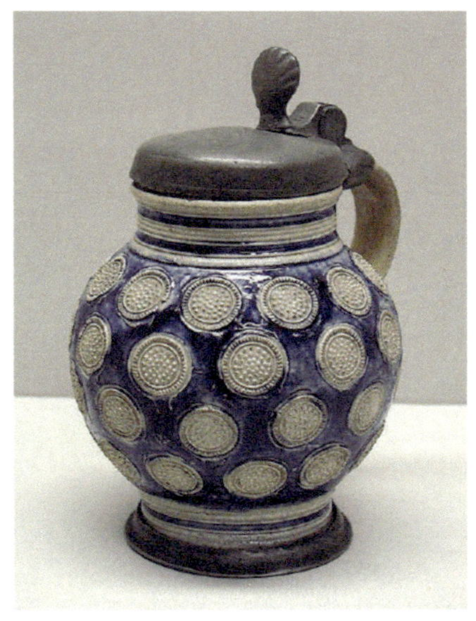

German Westerwald stoneware mug[4]

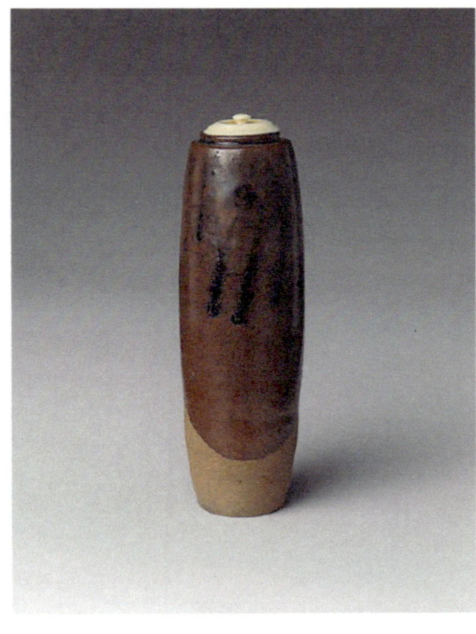

Japanese glazed stoneware tea ceremony jar[4]

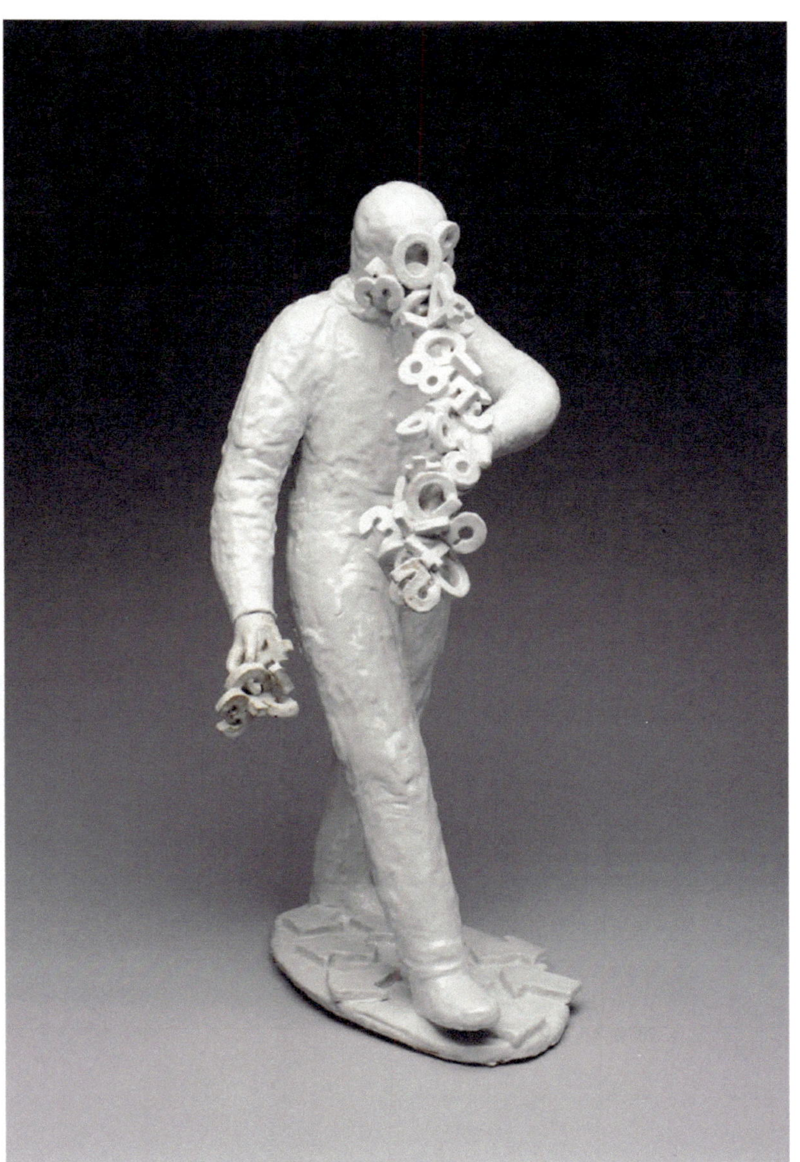

Paolo Porelli, "Excess", stoneware sculpture[5]

Porcelain

Porcelain is sometimes called "China" because of its country of origin. This smooth white clay body is fired to a very high temperature (close to 2,400 F / 1,315 C), after which it becomes very dense, glassy and sometimes translucent. Porcelain can be difficult to work with because of its relatively non-plastic ingredients. The whiteness of porcelain has allowed it to be the perfect surface to paint complex patterns and imagery.

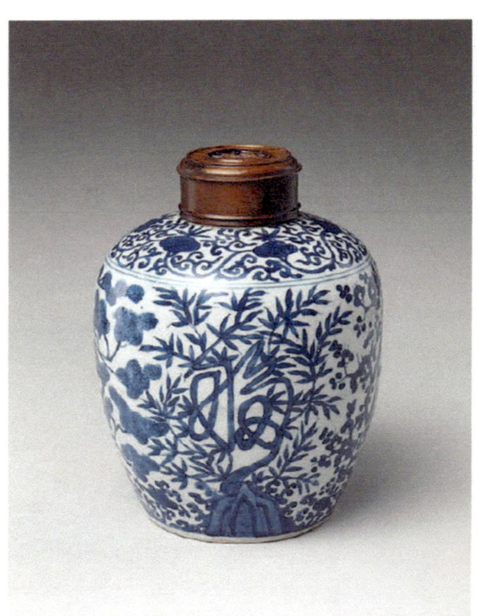

Chinese Ming dynasty porcelain jar[4]

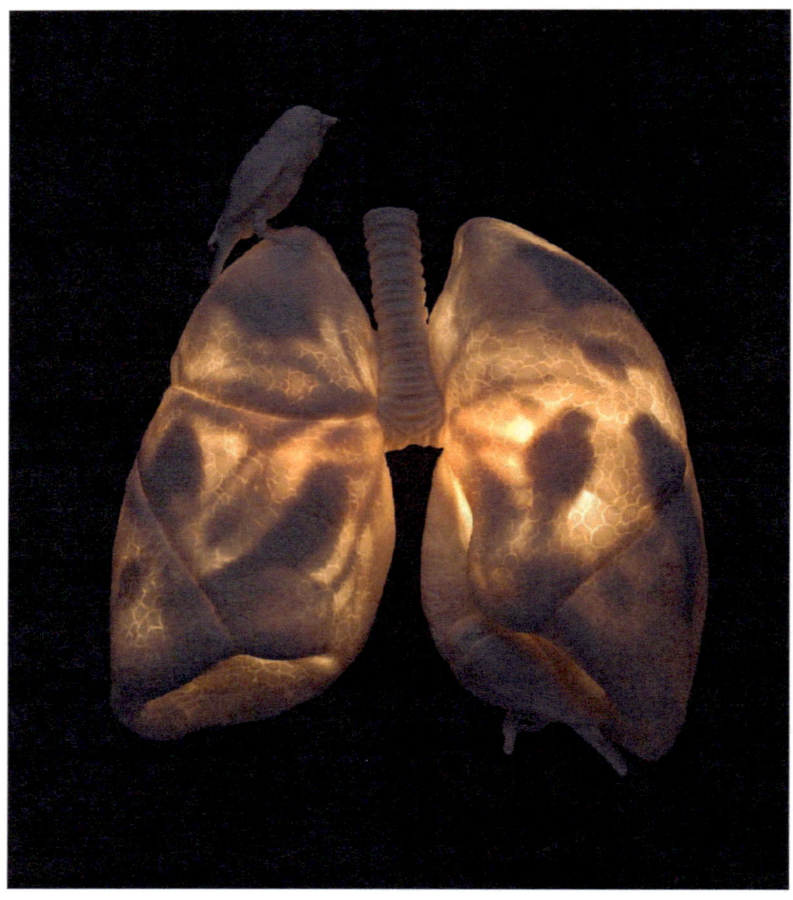

Kate MacDowell, "Canary" porcelain[3]

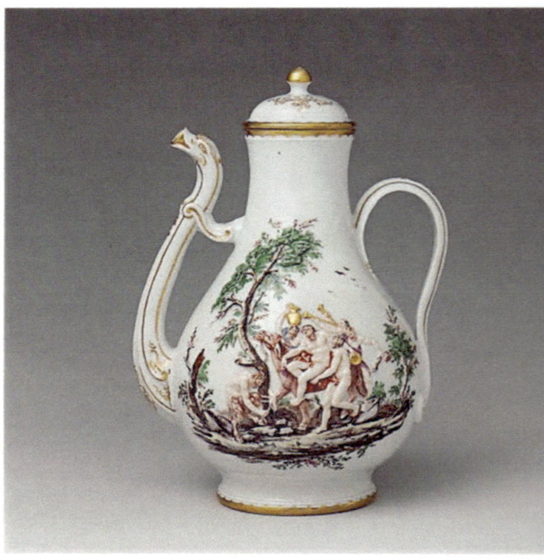

Italian Doccia porcelain coffepot[4]

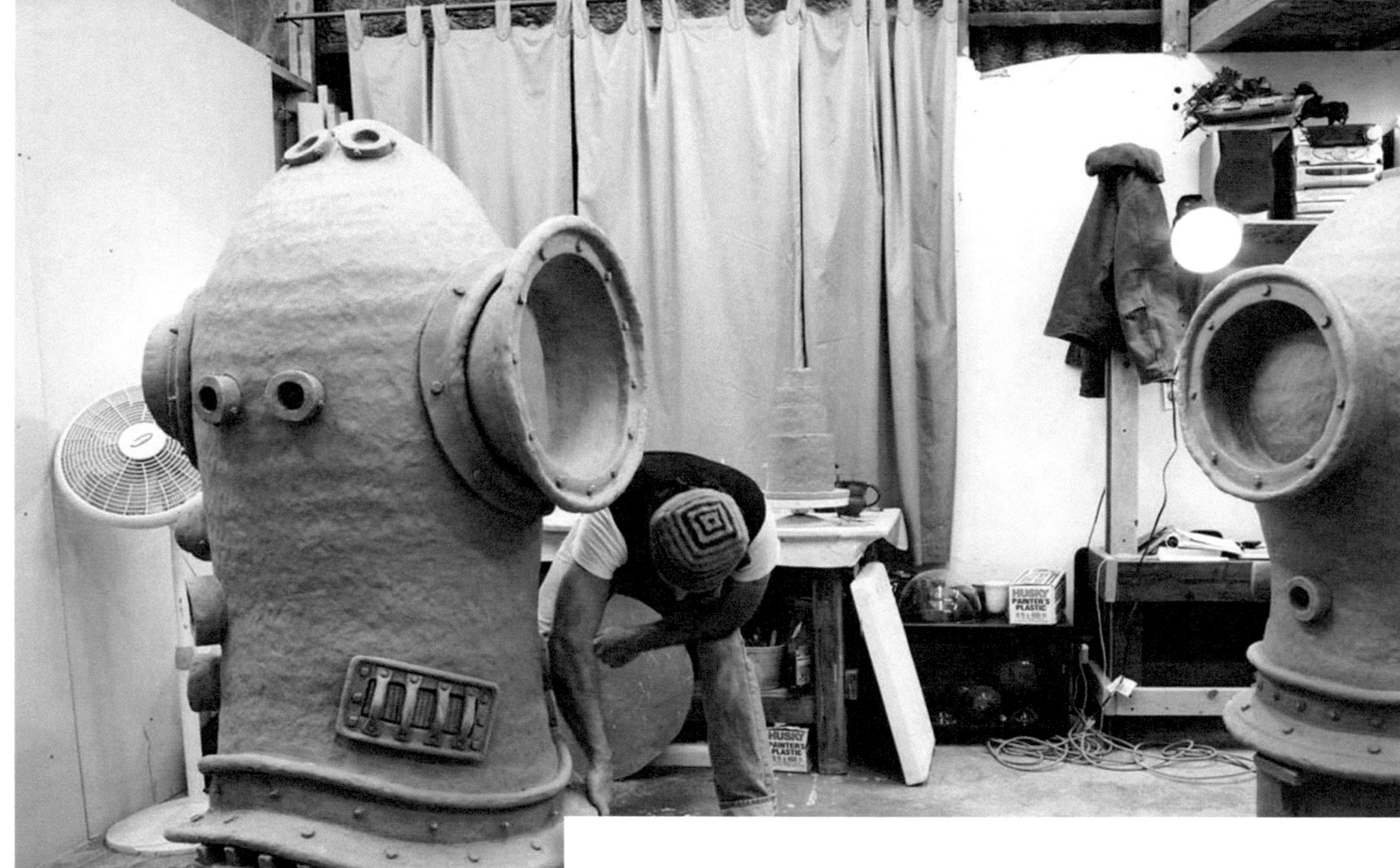

Jacob Foran working in his studio[3]

15

GETTING STARTED

The challenge of working in ceramics comes from the material itself. Clay is easy to shape but as it dries becomes more fragile. Patience and time management skills are developed as each process takes a certain amount of time. Ceramic objects must also be fired in a kiln to become permanent. The firing process has it's own set of challenges including getting the work into the kiln, heating to the correct temperature, and having the final product fit the artist's original design. The fired object can last thousands of years and can serve as future evidence of our culture.

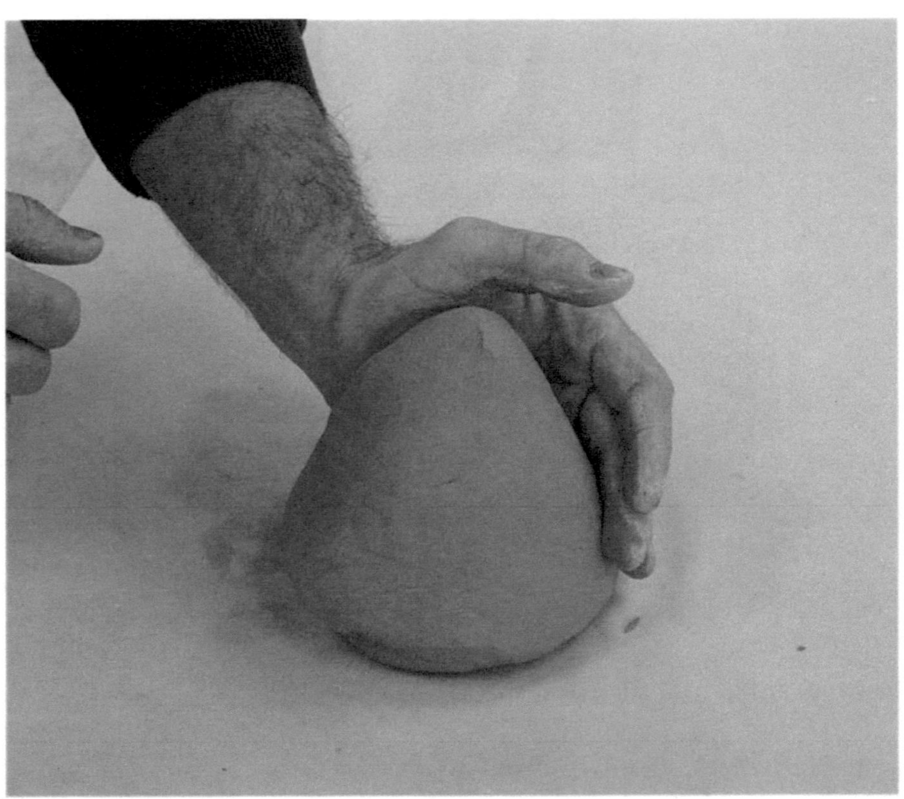

The finished product after wedging[1]

PREPARING TO WORK

One of great appeals of clay is the feeling of direct manipulation of the material. Every touch of hand or tool is recorded on the clay. Clay appeals directly to our tactile sense- one of our most powerful senses. Some of the first objects made by humans were sculpted using clay found in the caves near cave paintings. Finger prints can be found from the makers on pots thousands of years old.

Working with clay is working in three dimensions and fighting against gravity the entire time. A good habit to get into is to step back from your work and to rotate the object to view it from multiple perspectives. Try to be aware of how the weight of the work is affecting the overall shape. If things are getting distorted because the clay is too soft and heavy, look to prop it with paper or clay supports or use a hair dryer to stiffen the form until it will hold up its own weight.

The objects you make in clay are only limited to your imagination, the amount of material you have to work with, and the size of the kiln (and the assignments for class!).

One of the most important steps when you begin any project is to properly prepare your clay. This process begins with **wedging** the clay by taking a lump of clay out of the bin and bringing it to the table. On the canvas surface, you will repeated push the clay down and then rock it back on itself to force out any air pockets and also make the piece a consistent material. If the wedging is done correctly, you will be create a spiral in the clay. If we looked at the clay under a microscope after wedging, we would see the clay particles lining up so they can slide past and over each other. This allows the clay to stretch out and be more easily shaped.

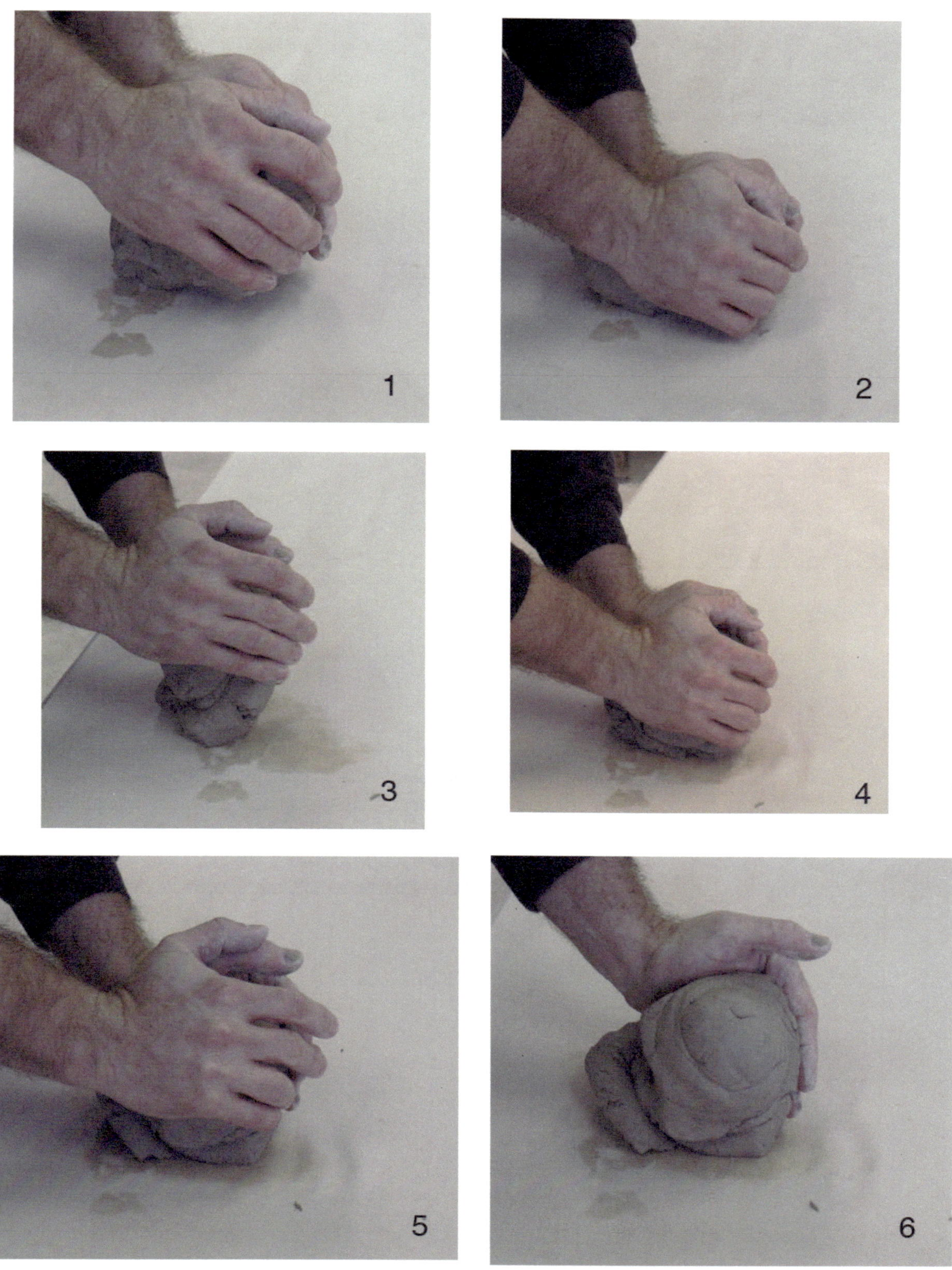

Steps in the wedging process. The rocking motion and a slight angle when pushing down allows the clay mass to move into a spiral. Continue wedging until it feels consistent and dense. You can also check by cutting the mass with a wire and checking for any air pockets or other inconsistencies.

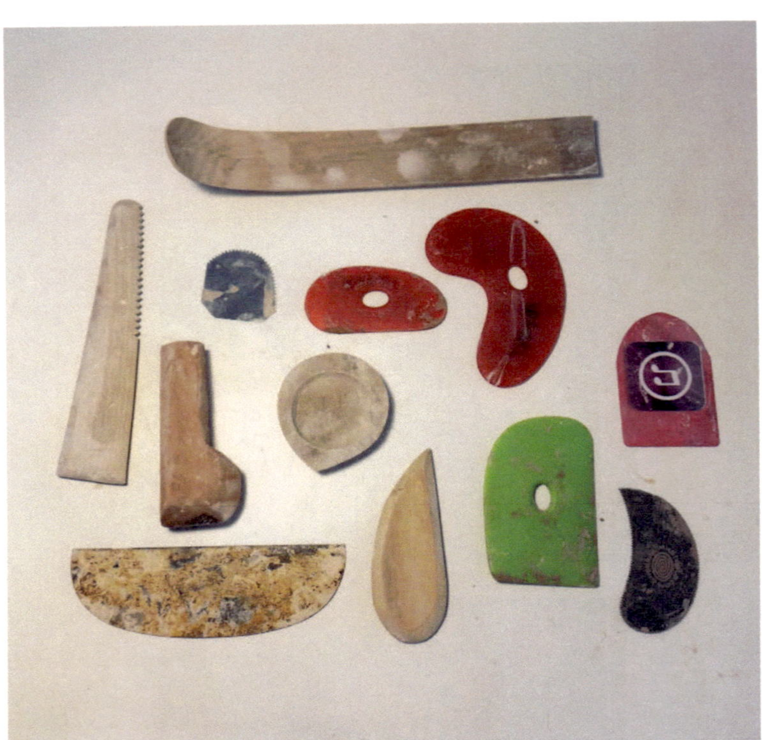

A variety of **ribs** used for shaping and smoothing. Wood, metal, and plastic are common materials. Unique shapes can be easily cut from old gift or credit cards[1]

CLAY TOOLS

Many tools have been invented, altered, and perfected over the thousands of years humans have been making ceramic objects. This process continues today as artists and manufacturers develop new materials and shapes. In addition, tools can be found in other areas (like cooking / baking or woodworking) that can be re-purposed for ceramics. Look at what's around, experiment, and make your own tools in order to create personal effects on your clay work.

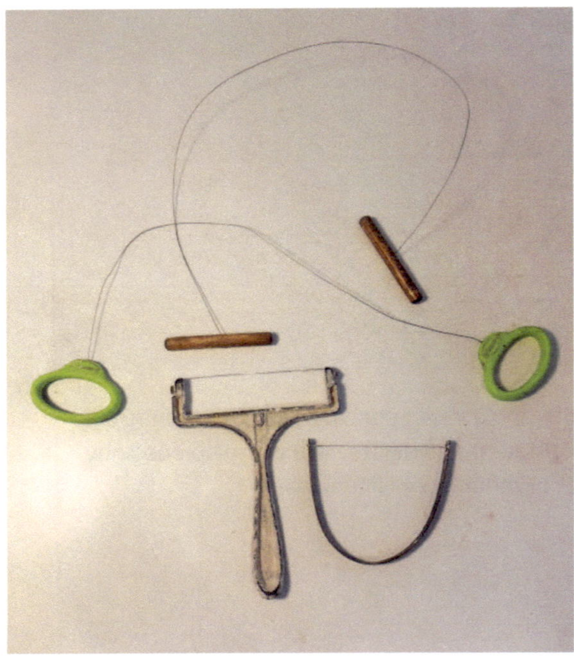

Cut off wires for cutting through blocks of clay. These can be braided metal wire or fishing line. A cheese slicer makes a very effective tool for cutting the top edge of work.[1]

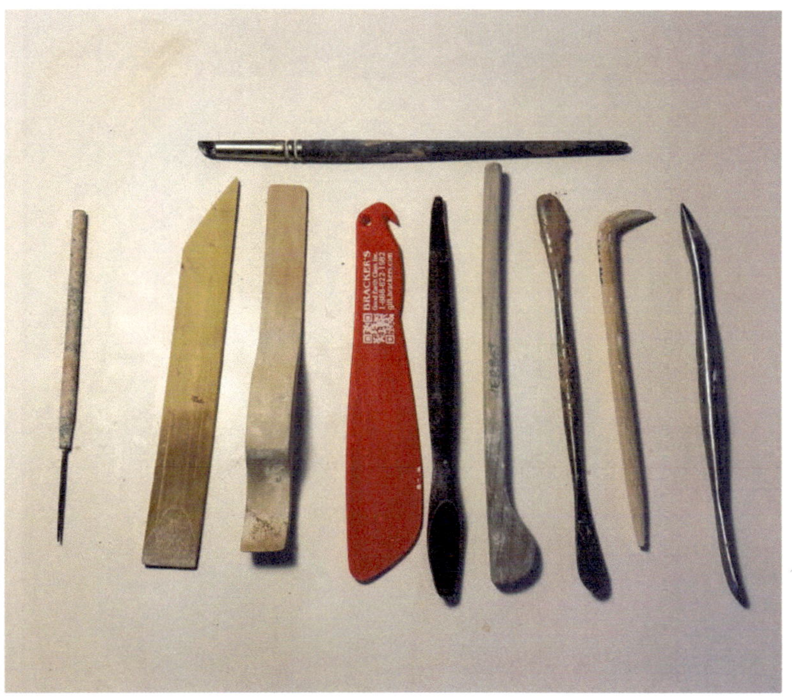

From left side: **Pin tool** (also called **needle tool**) for checking thickness or cutting through edges
Wood knife , next a variety of knife-like or dowel shapes for forming[1]

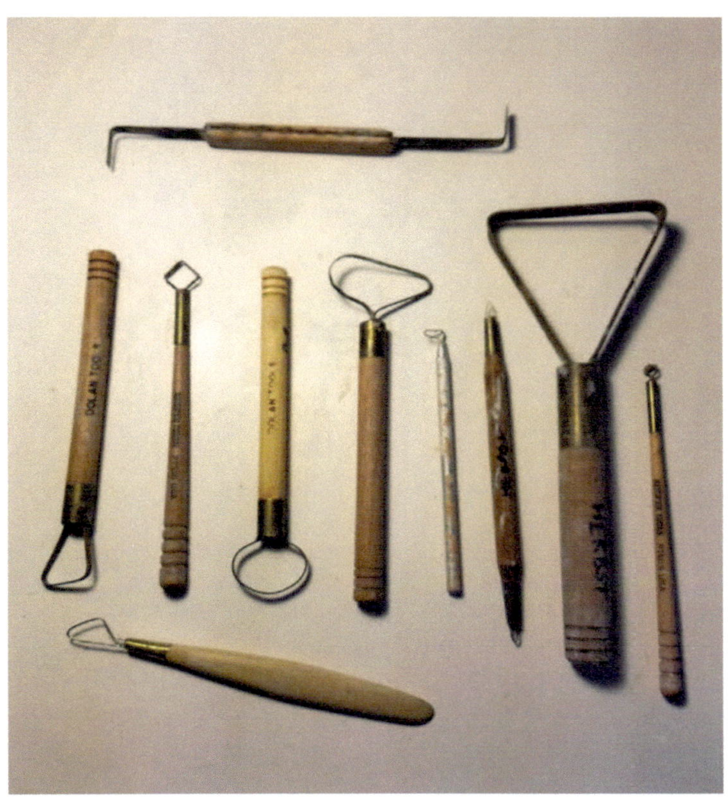

A variety of **loop tools** (also called **trimming tools**) for cutting or carving leather hard clay[1]

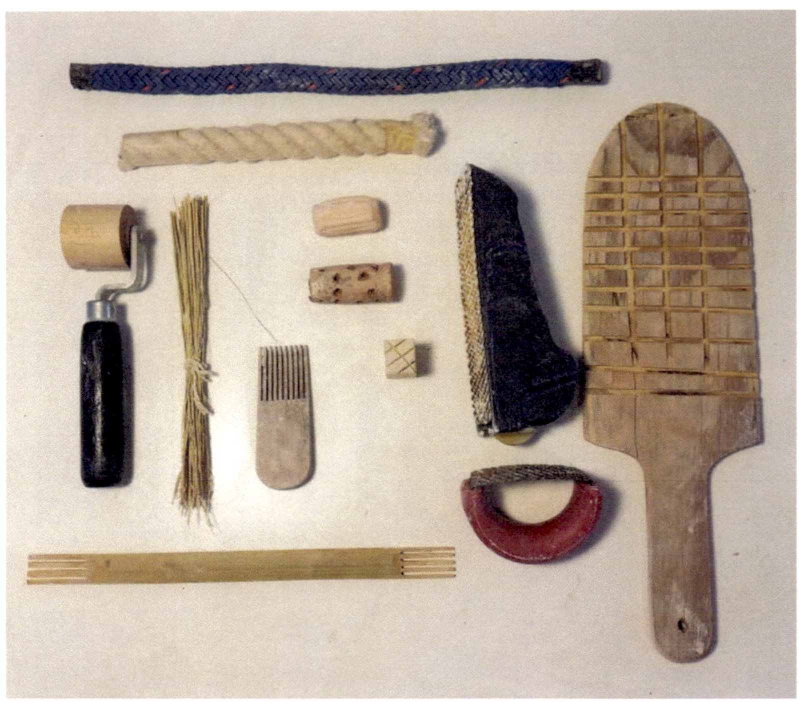

Tools for creating textures: a roller, a brush made from an old broom, bisque fired stamps, carved pieces of wine bottle cork and pieces of rope to roll over soft clay, two **rasp** tools for altering shapes, carved paddle[1]

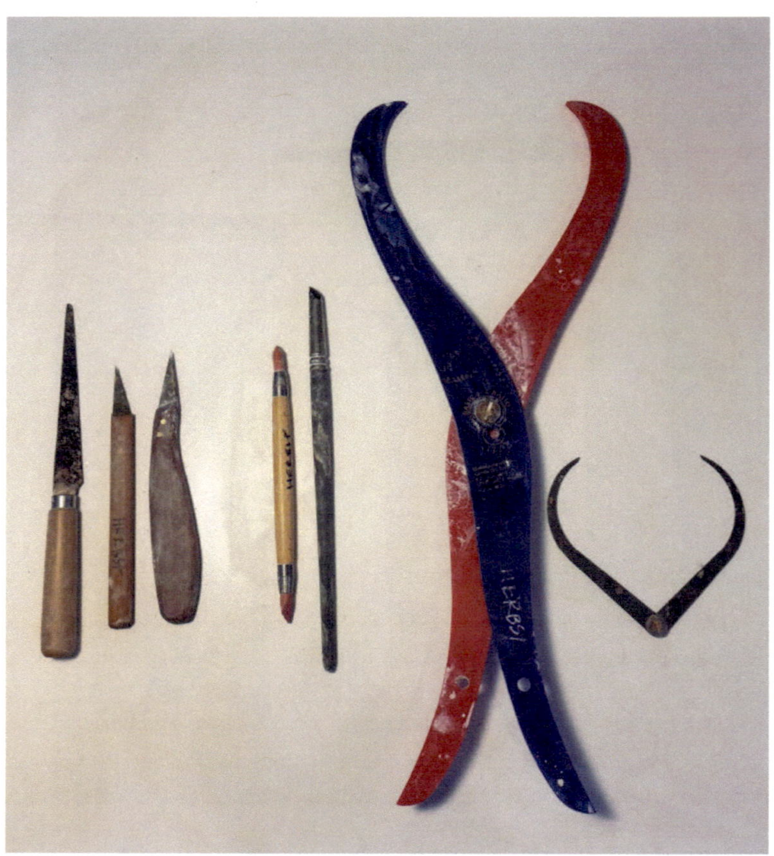

From left: **Fettling knife** and other knives for cutting, two soft tipped tools for shaping, two **calipers** for measuring [1]

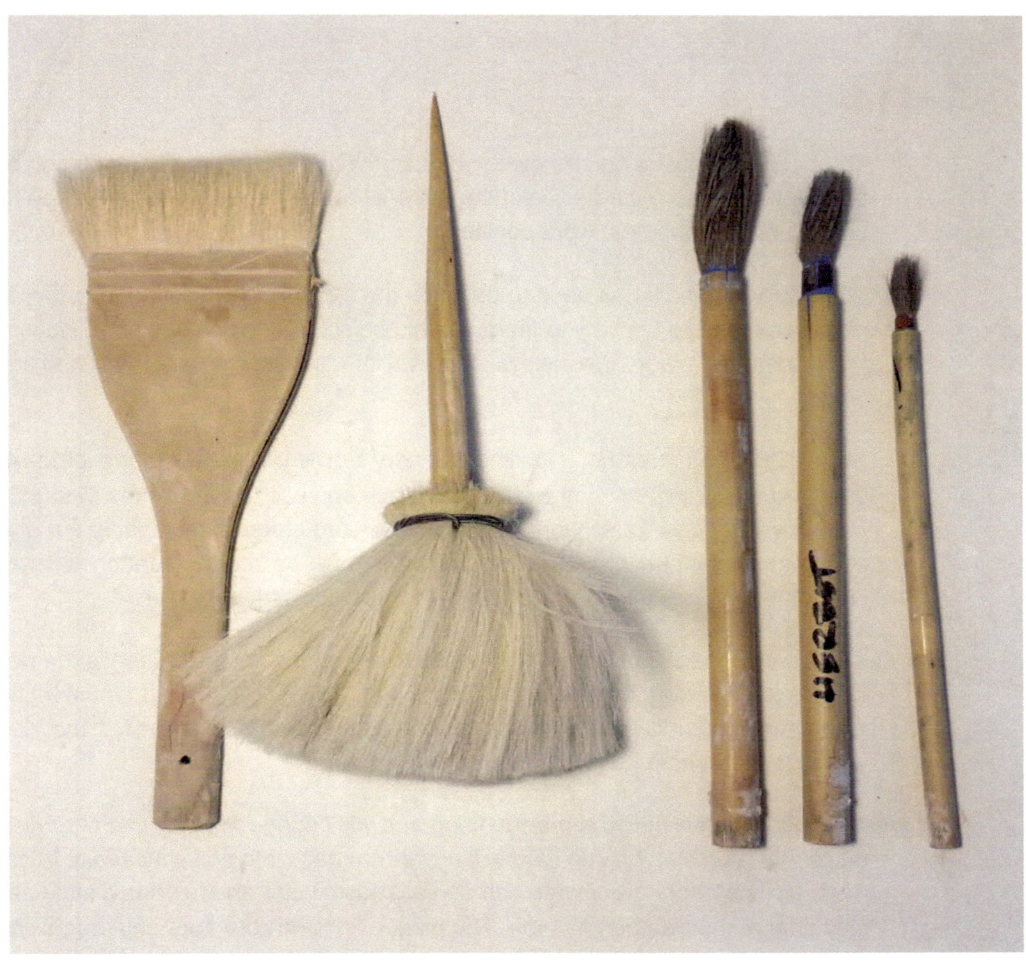

A variety of brushes for painting slips and glazes. The best brushes for ceramics are made from natural hairs and are often used for ink painting. These will hold ceramic materials better than synthetic brushes. Some artists make their own brushes from materials like deer or elk hair glued into a bamboo stem for a handle.[1]

STAGES OF CERAMICS

The field of ceramics has it's own vocabulary just like any area of study and practice. Understanding the basics of the material and its language will help you to succeed in making the best work possible.

There are specific terms used to describe the stages of clay as it goes from a soft workable mass all the way to fired ceramic object. Any piece of unfired clay is in the **greenware** stage. We always start with soft, plastic clay when building the work.

Once the piece is formed, it is allowed to dry slowly until it gets to the **leatherhard** stage. At this point, the clay will not flex much and will support its own weight. Many carving techniques work best at leatherhard stage. Attachments are often done at this point but the surface of the parts must be scored (scratched) and then wet with water or liquid clay slip to help adhere the parts together.

As it continues to dry, the piece changes to a lighter color and reaches the **bone dry** stage. The work is at the most fragile point when bone dry and must be handled carefully or it can easily crack or break apart. Once the piece is fully dried, it will be loaded into a kiln to be fired.

The initial firing is called a **bisque** firing and will change the clay into ceramic. A piece that has been bisque fired will never turn back into soft clay again. In contrast, a piece of dry greenware can be soaked in water and reworked into usable clay after a short amount of time. The bisque firing will burn out any organic material in the clay and also create a stronger, porous material that is easier to glaze.

After the bisque kiln is cooled and unloaded, the pieces will have a liquid **glaze** solution applied. The pieces are loaded into a kiln and fired (usually) to a higher temperature melting the glaze and fusing the ceramic body. When the work is finished it has been glaze fired and ready to be used and displayed.

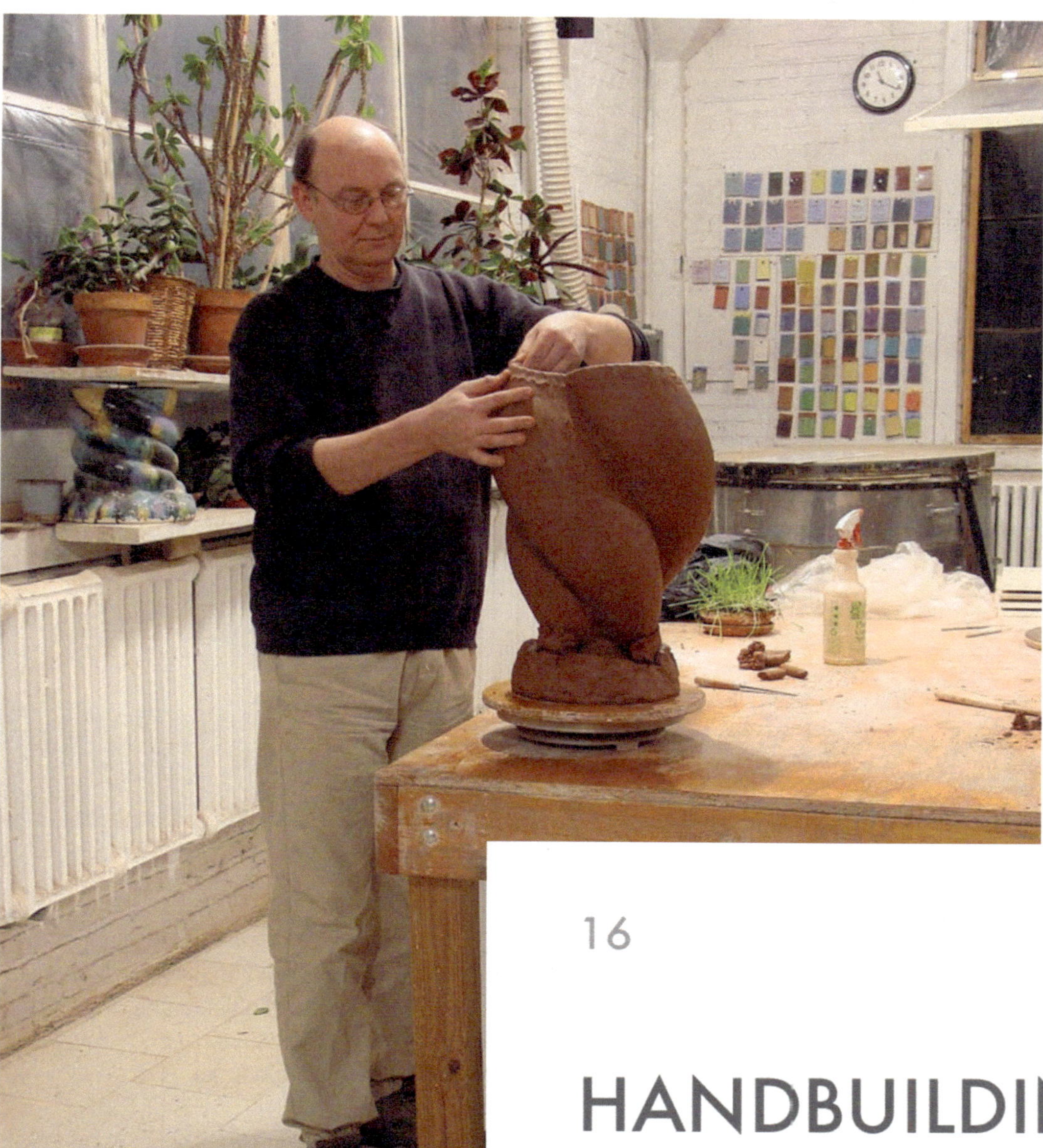

Gary Erickson coil building a sculpture in his studio[2]

16

HANDBUILDING

The processes of handbuilding in ceramics (pinch, coil, and slab) allow for a great deal of freedom and expression. Each method has advantages and disadvantages that the artist must deal with for the execution of their concepts and designs.

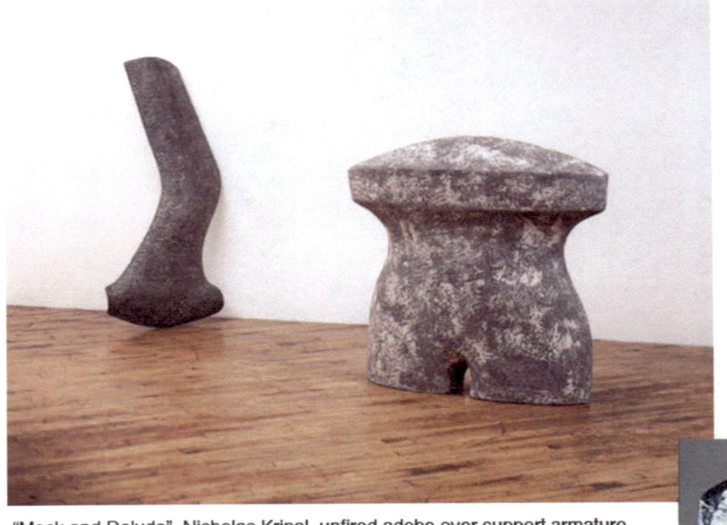

"Mock and Delude", Nicholas Kripal, unfired adobe over support armature, wax, and paint[2]

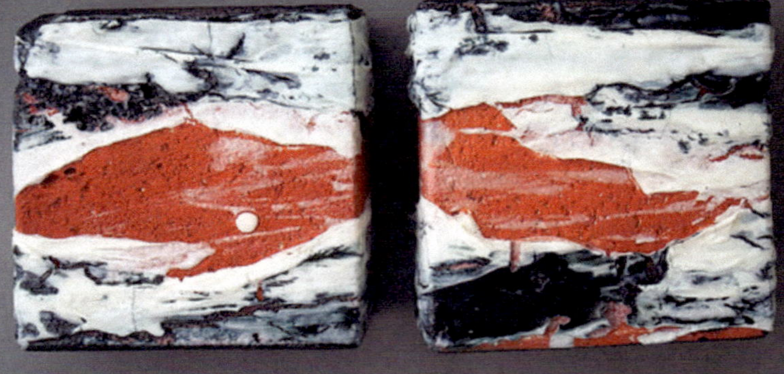

"Landscape Abstraction (red)", Liz Howe, altered kiln brick, slip, and mixed media[3]

breaking some rules

As an art form, ceramics has a long list of traditional "rules" that are taught to help students learn how to succeed with their work. For example, most clay objects are built hollow with an even wall thickness between 1/8" for small objects and up to 1" for large sculptural forms. This approach allows the material to dry out evenly and allows steam to escape safely during the heating process early in a bisque firing.

However in some cases, it is useful to build the object solid. This method is works well when creating small detailed shapes or for complex sculptural shapes that would be difficult to construct hollow. Building solid also allows you to use more force in the shaping process and not worry about the piece collapsing.

The difference is that as the object dries to leatherhard stage, the piece is cut open with a wire tool and hollowed out inside. Try to make your cut at a place that will be easy to repair when the object is reassembled. When hollowing out, it is important to make the wall thickness as even as possible to prevent the form from distorting or cracking during drying. Any areas that are extra thick should be pierced with a pin tool to create channels for steam to get out during firing. After the extra clay is removed, carefully score and apply thick slip to the areas that will be reattached. Press the object back together and reshape the seam to obscure the cut line. Dry and fire large, thick objects slower and for a longer time than usual.

Other rules can be broken or bent in order to create special effects on your pieces. New techniques and discoveries are being made all the time when traditional ideas are challenged. Use your sketchbook as a "research journal" as you work with this material and see what you discover as you develop your own way of working with ceramics.

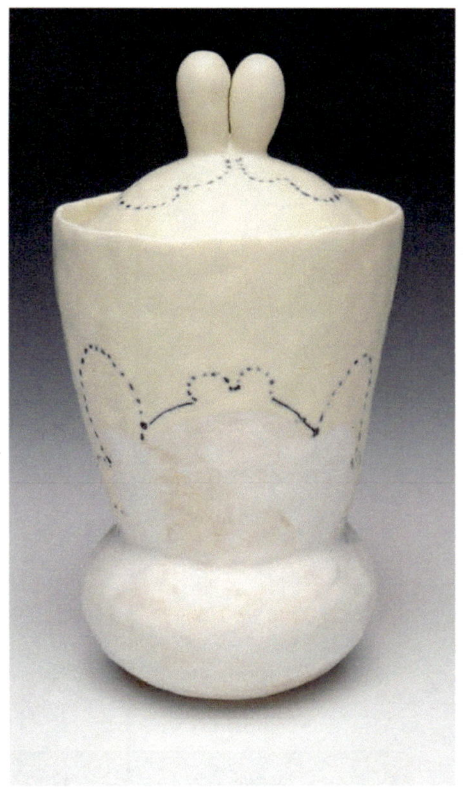

Emily Schroeder Willis, "Jar", pinched porcelain[3]

Julie Tesser, "Seeds", pinched earthenware[3]

PINCH

Pinch construction is one of the most direct and useful building methods. Starting with a solid mass of clay, you will slowing open and squeeze the walls between your fingers and thumb to create the shape desired and thin out the walls. The standard wall thickness for most clay work is between an 1/8" for small forms to a 1/2" for larger forms. You can also easily increase the size of your object by adding strips of clay to the top edge or by joining two separately pinched shapes.

The pinch technique will help to build your sensitivity to how clay reacts to your touch. Some artists prefer to leave the marks of their fingers on the work, others will spend a large amount of time smoothing or refining the clay wall to disguise the forming method.

To create any object using the pinch technique, start with a solid piece of clay (1). Push your thumb into this mass of clay (2) and begin to squeeze the clay between your thumb on the inside and your fingers on the outside (3). Slowly spin the clay and continue to squeeze / pinch the form as you thin out the walls (4) Depending on the shape intended, leave some areas thicker so that the clay can be carved away or manipulated later (5). Continue to work the form until the desired thickness, shape, and surface texture are achieved (6).

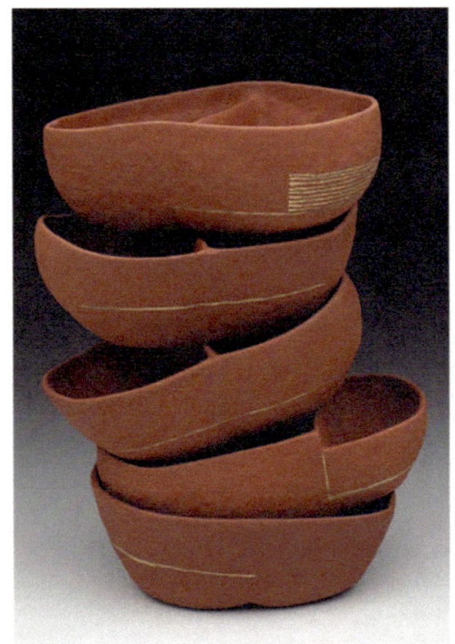

Lilly Zuckerman, "Untitled", pinched earthenware[3]

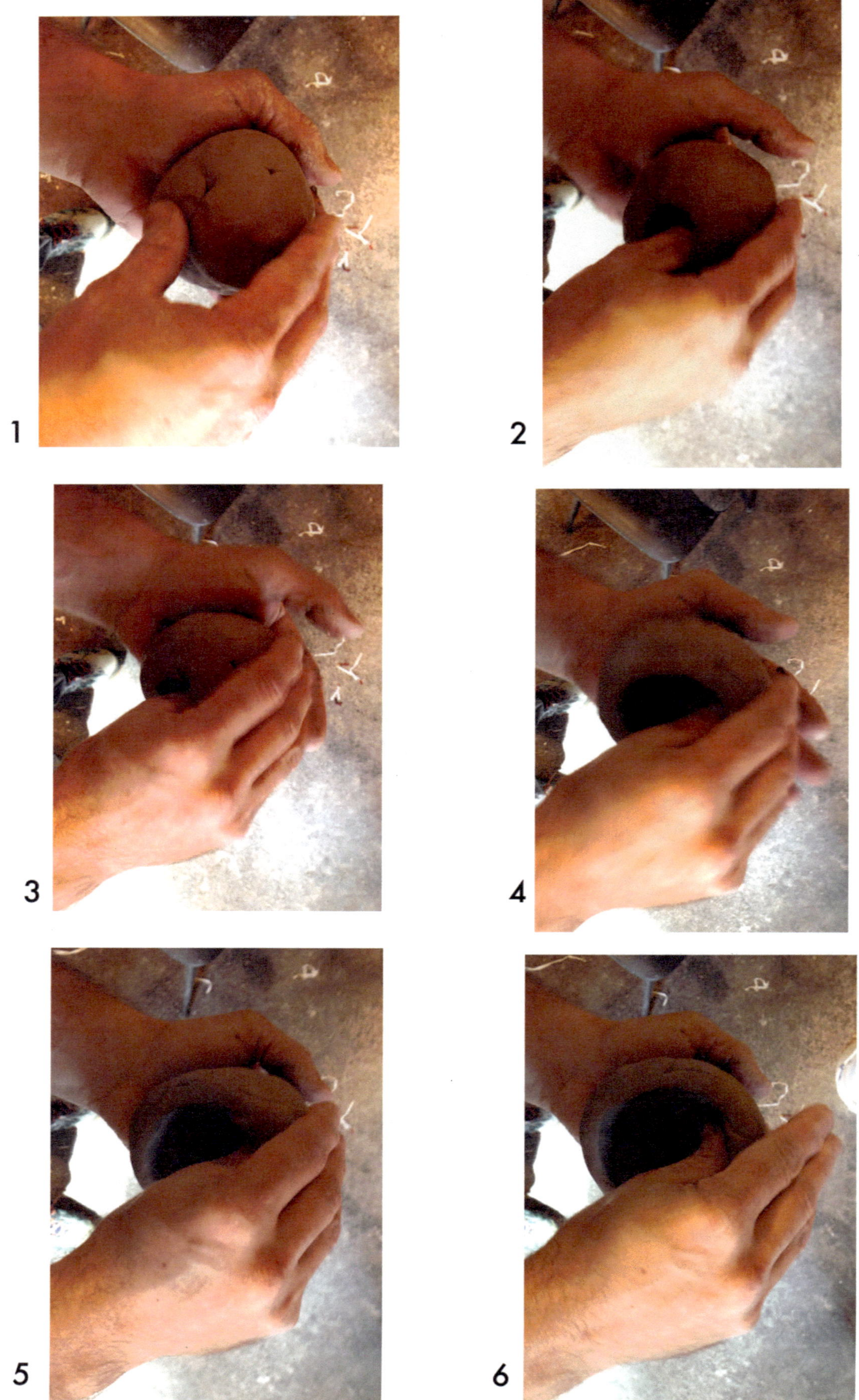

1
2
3
4
5
6

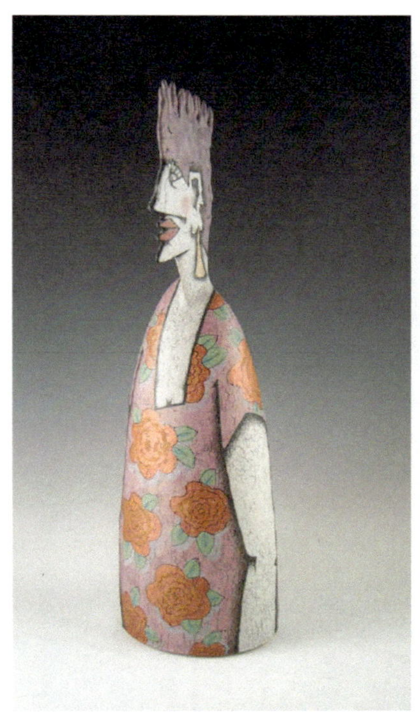

Rimas VisGirda, "BJT", coiled stoneware[3]

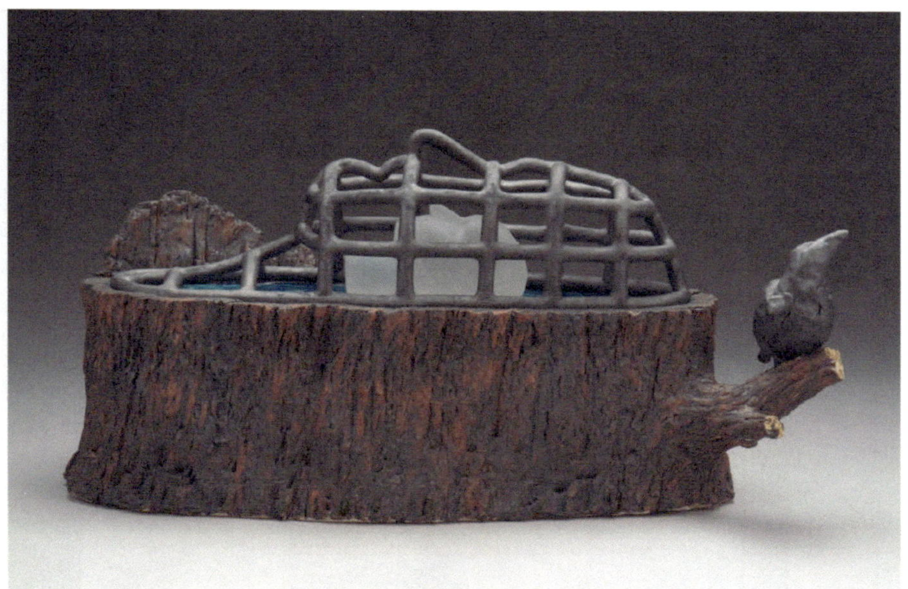

Ted Vogel, "Head Cage", coiled stoneware and glass[2]

COIL

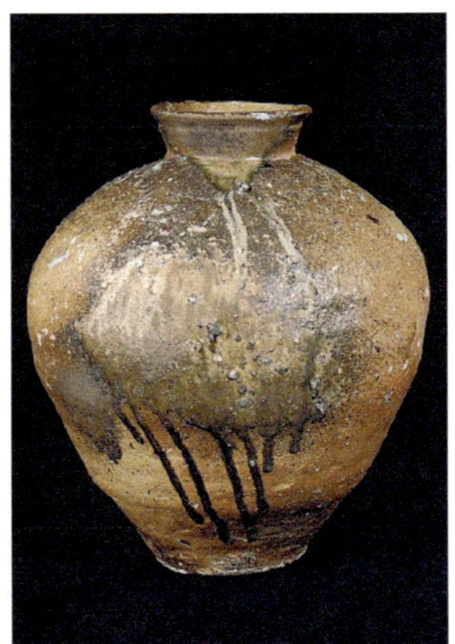

Japanese Shigaraki coiled stoneware jar[4]

Coil building can be a very useful technique for creating shapes at a larger scale. The method involves stacking and blending together layers of coils (both on the inside and outside) to build the form. Coils are made by rolling clay on the table or using the extruder to make multiple coils at one time.

This building method will take longer and each object will take multiple working sessions to complete. To prevent the piece from collapsing under its own weight, you must pause to allow the lower levels to dry just enough to help support the new clay. The drying process can be accelerated by using a hair dryer or fan, or putting the object in the sun.

When new coils are added to existing firmed up wall, the top edge must be scored (scratched) heavily and wet clay slip painted on. The new clay can then be blended on and smoothed. If sections aren't scored and slipped well enough, cracks will form or the piece may come apart.

Large forms may need to have some variation in wall thickness. Slightly thicker coils at the bottom of the piece will help support more weight above. Switch to thinner coils when nearing the top or completing the piece to reduce the overall weight of the object.

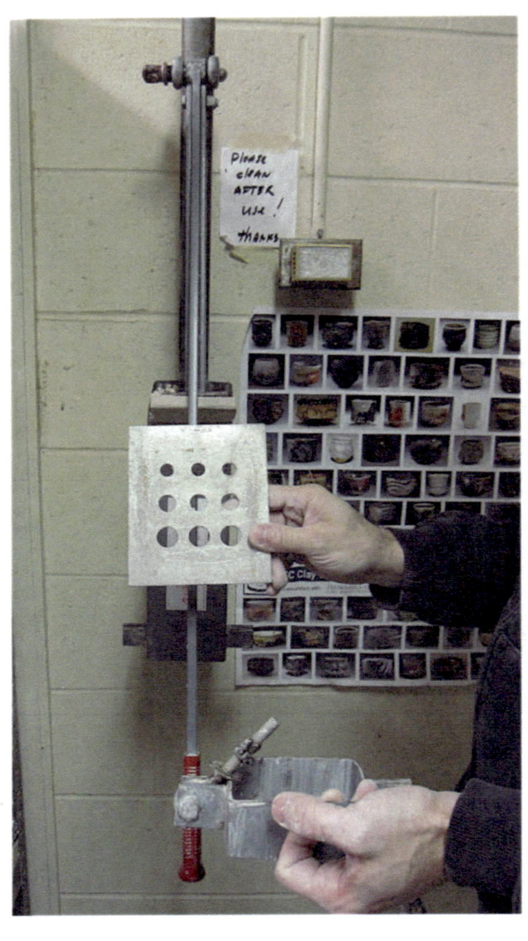

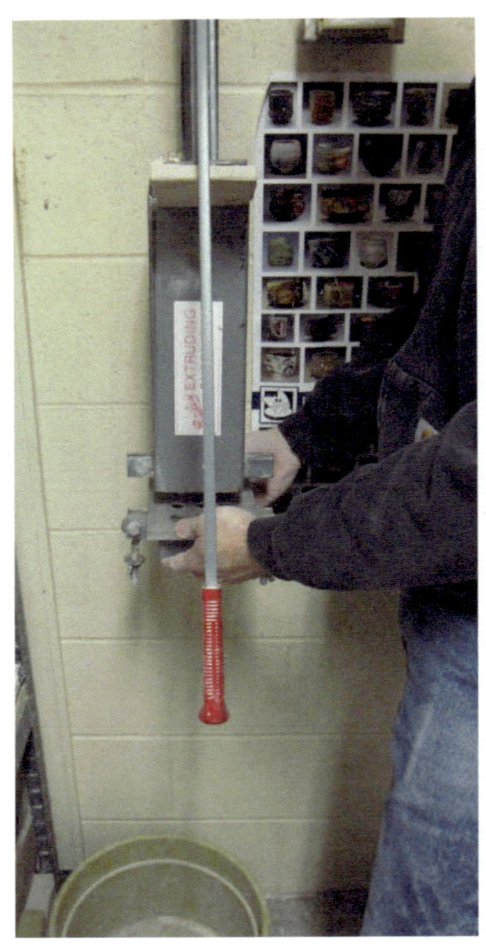

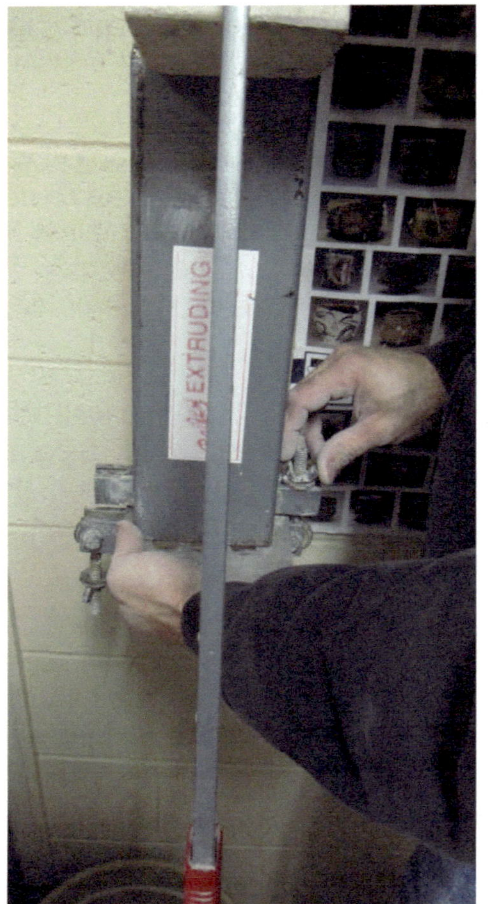

One way of speeding up the coil building process is to use the extruder. The extruder is a great tool for making a variety of shapes including solid coils, hollow tubes, and other geometric extrusions.

For coil building, the extruder allows you to make a number of coils at the same time. First select the coil die and attach it to the bottom of the tube. This is done by place the support ring under the die and tightening the wing nuts over the side tabs. Try to get the die to seal tight to the bottom of the tube.

On the next page, you will see that you then fill the tube with clay. Try to wedge and then block up the clay so it fits into the tube easily. Next, fit the plunging plate into the tube and use the bar to press it down. Continue to press down as the clay gets extruded out the bottom through the die. Tear off the coils and bring to the table before they break o and fall on the floor!

After you are done using the extruder during a class or wo session, take the die off the bottom and clean it off. Also use a stick or tool to scrape out all the clay inside the tube.

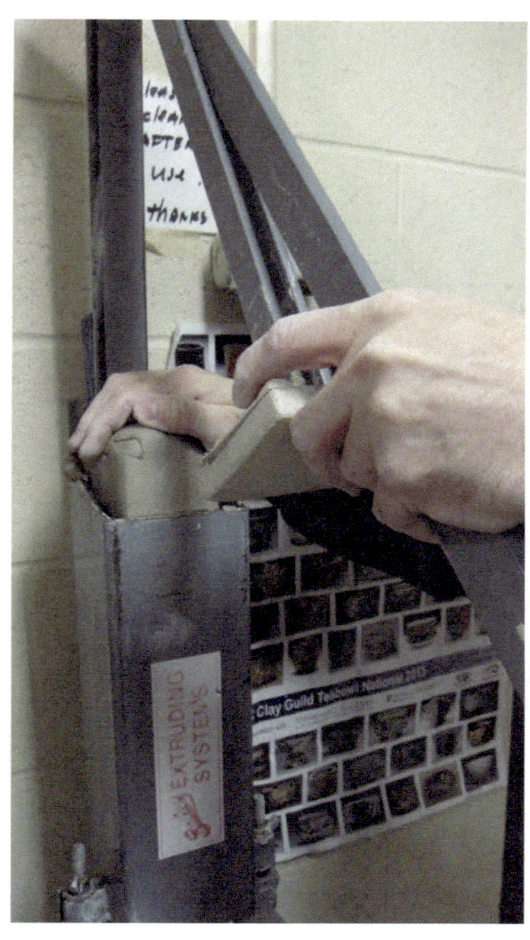

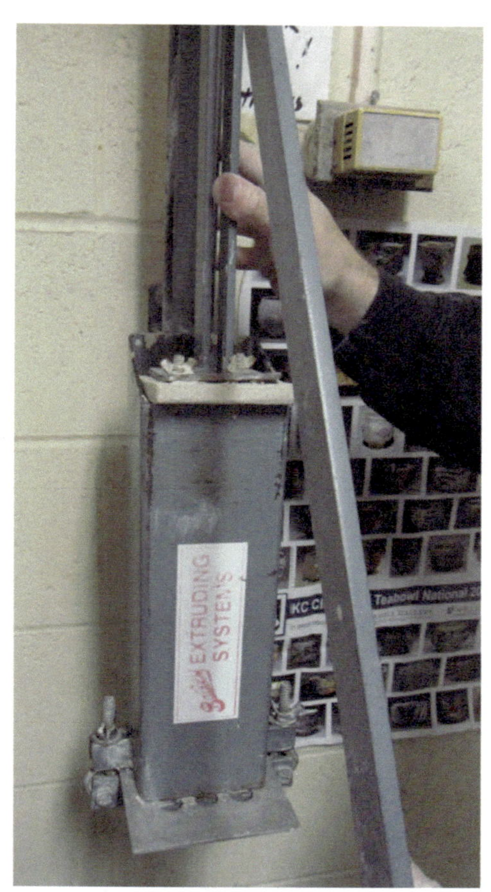

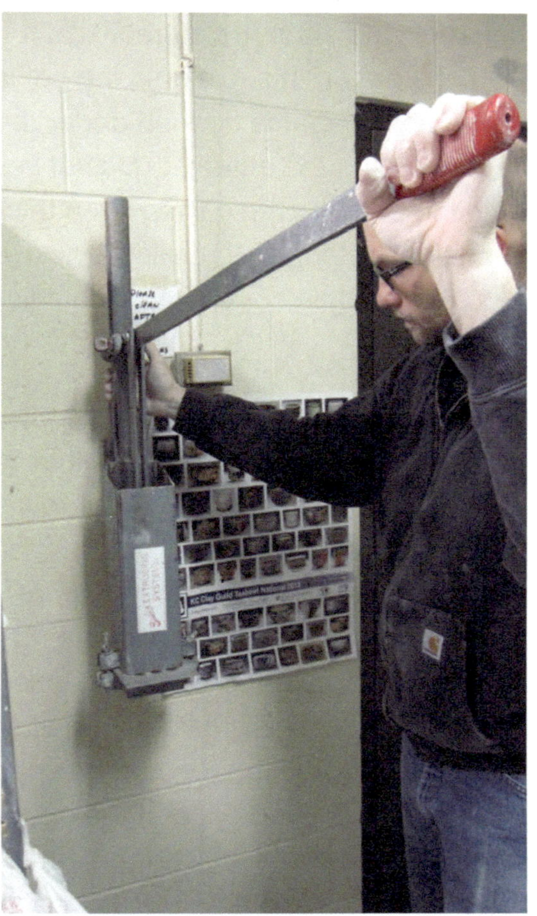

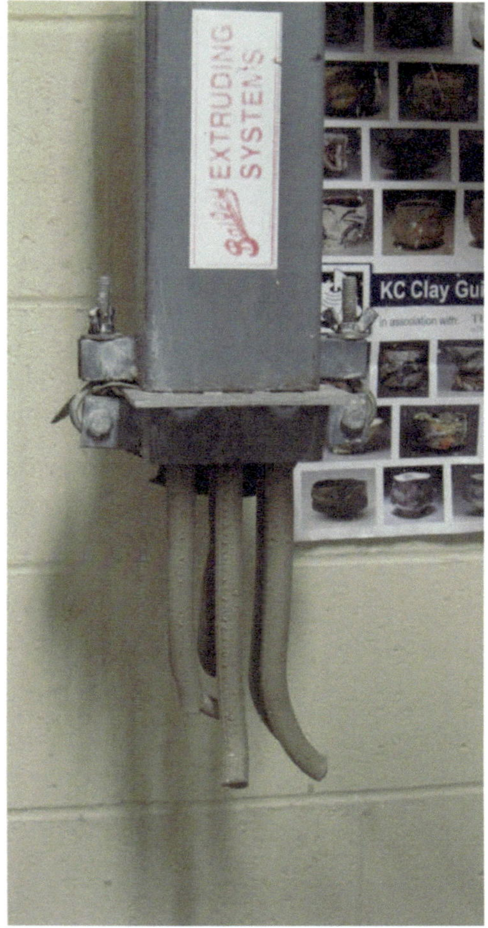

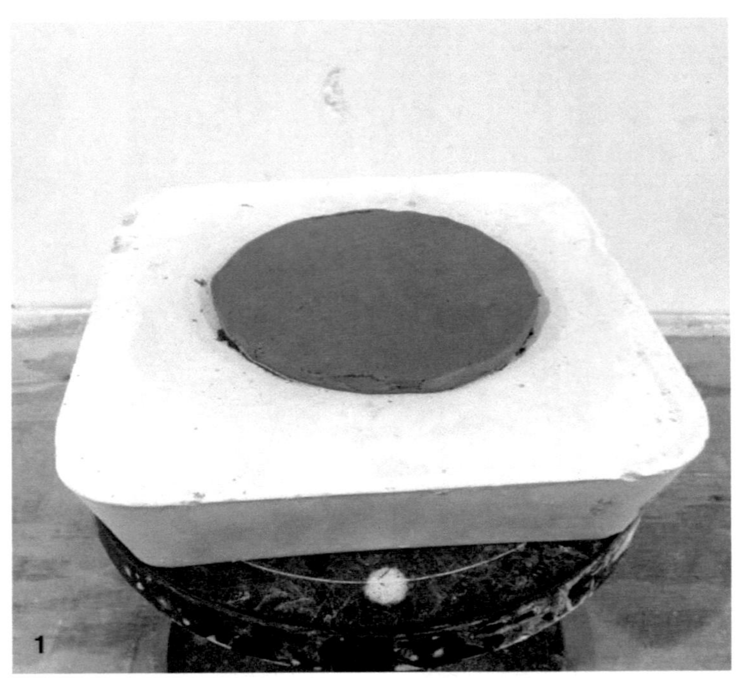

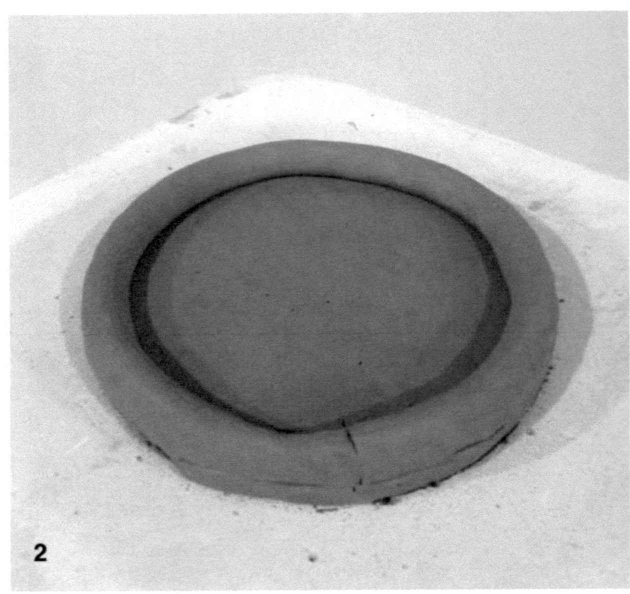

BUILDING WITH COILS

To start, make a solid sheet of clay (a slab) the correct size for the base (image 1). Build on top of a bat, in this example the pot is being built on a plaster bat so no newspaper is needed under the slab. Next, roll coils on the table using the entire surface of your hands (palms and fingers) trying to make the coil an even thickness and round shape over its entire length. If available, you should use an extruder to create multiple coils of identical thickness all at the same time.

Begin by stacking the first coil on the slab base (2). Pinch this coil down to the base. Continue to stack coils on top each other and pinch together to create the shape (3). After three or four rows, begin to blend all the coils together to make a strong, stable shape (4). A great tool to use for surface and shape refinement is a toothed rib. Work over the inside and outside of the shape (5), these marks will be removed later in the process. Continue to add coils as needed. If the form desired is a straight vertical wall, stack the next coils directly top of the ones below it. If the shape moves out, build the next coil on the outside edge of the one below (6). Stack, pinch, and join each row to develop the shape desired (7). If the shape needs to move in, build on the inner edge of

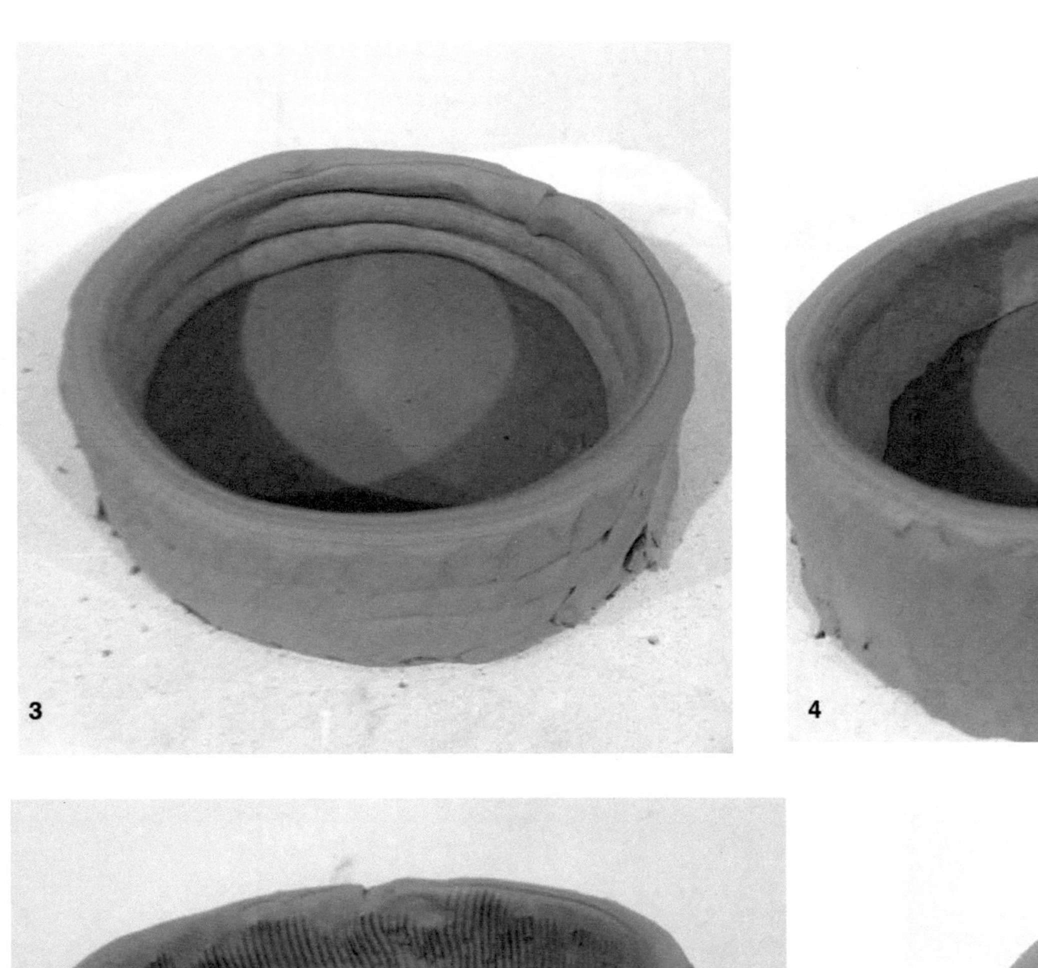

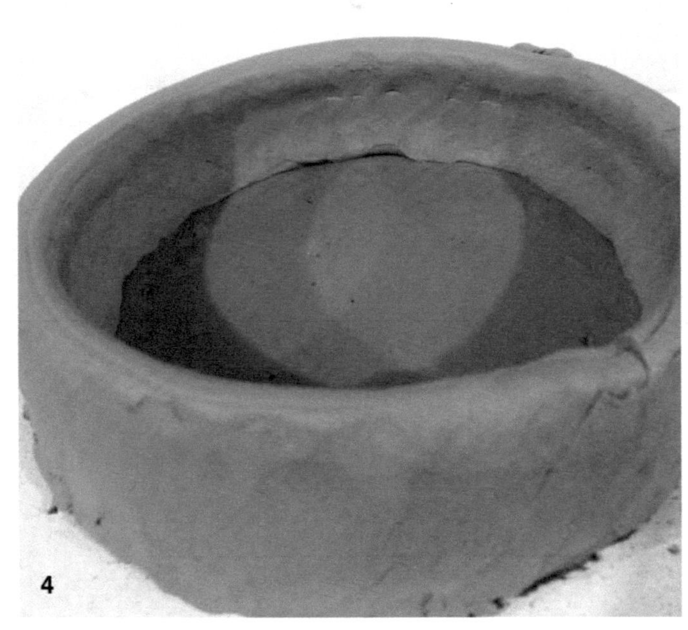

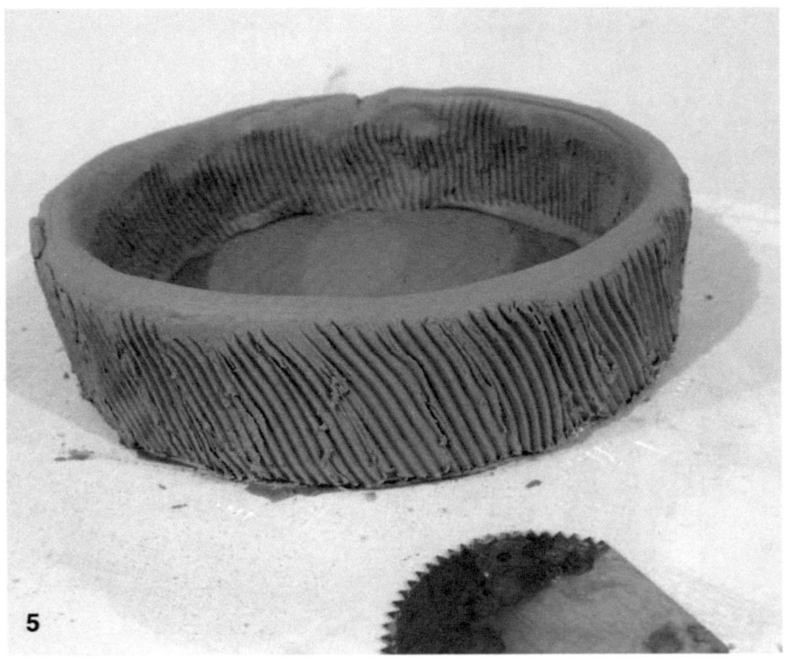

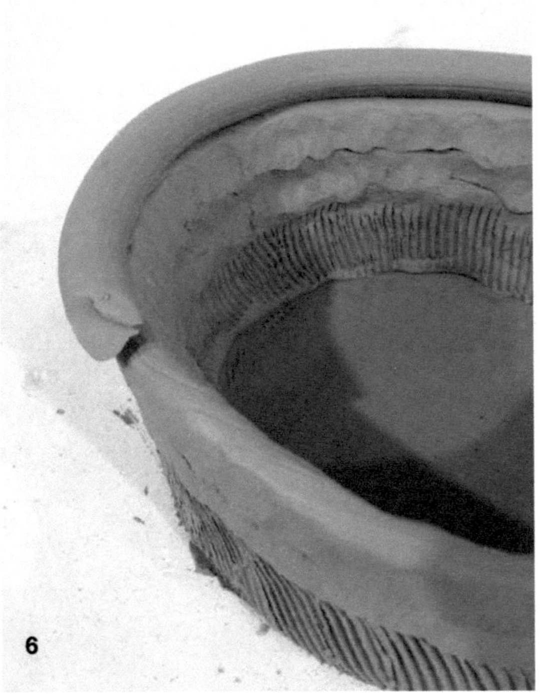

the coil below (8). Continue to build and blend coils together on the inside and outside (9). Make sure to check the shape and symmetry by spinning the piece on a turn-table and stepping away from it often. Begin to refine the overall shape by smoothing the toothed rib marks away from the inside and outside (10). As you finish the shape, make sure to cut a bevel on the bottom edge of the piece and also smooth out the top edge to create a fully refined shape.

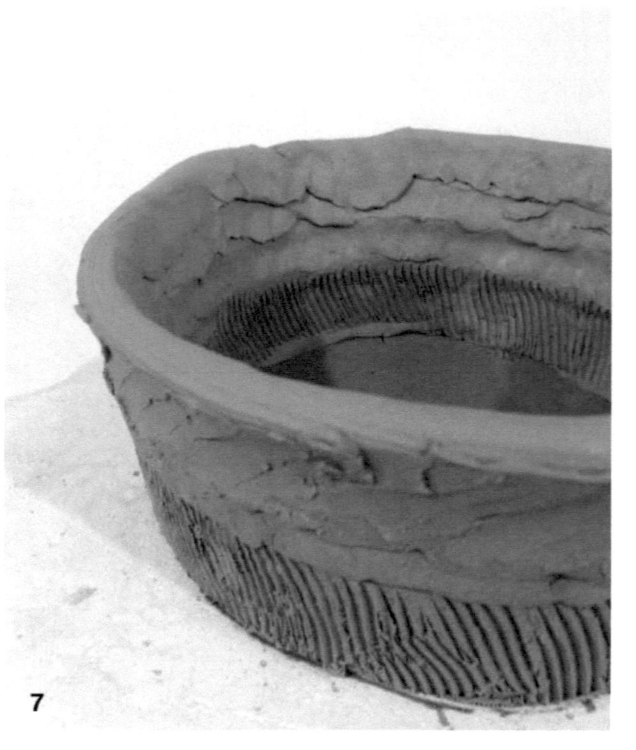

7

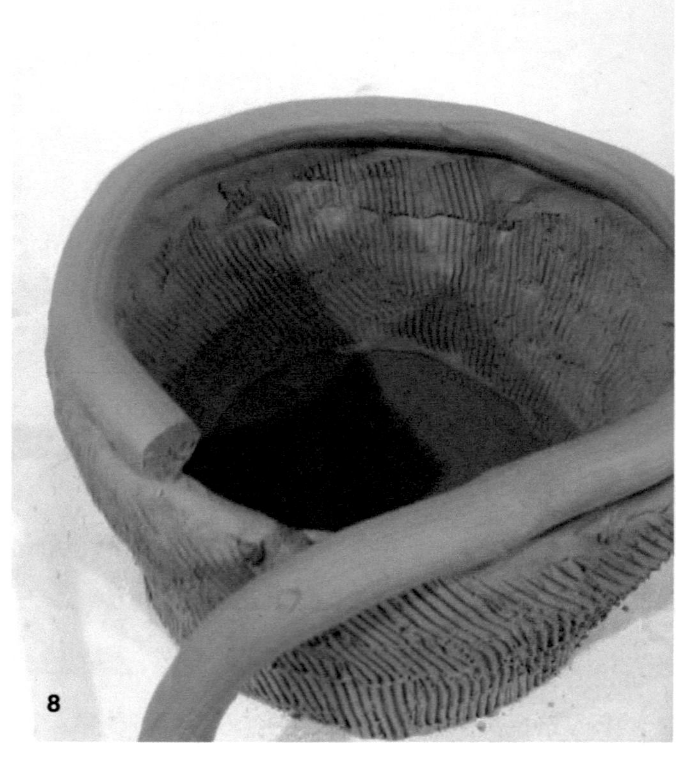

8

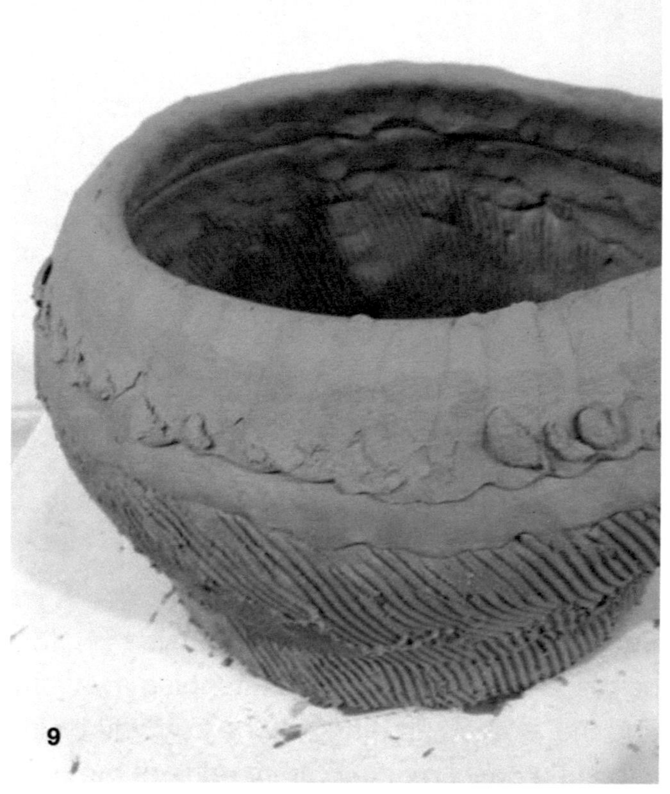

9

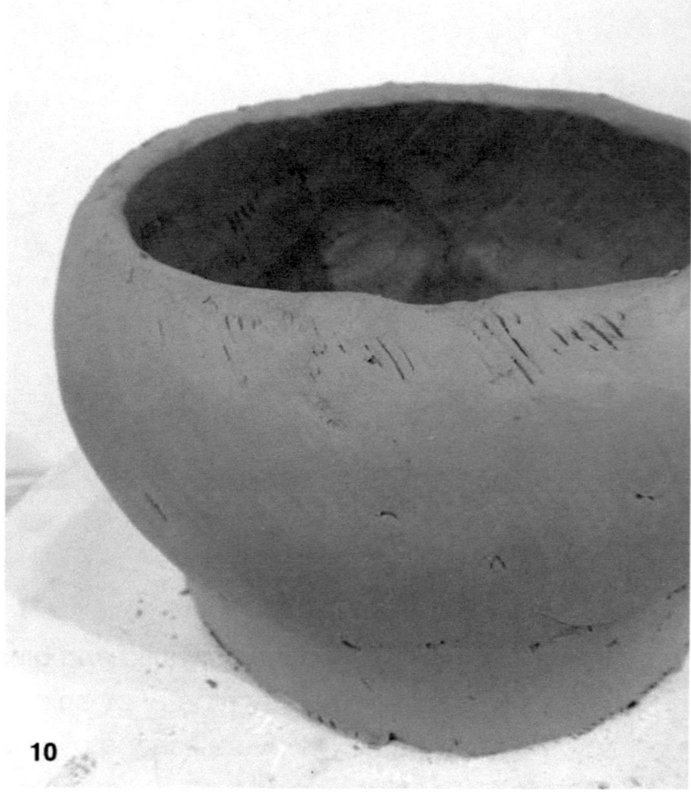

10

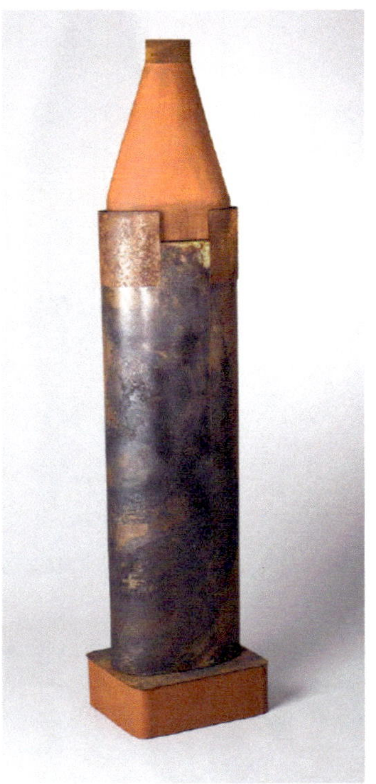

Lynn Duryea, "WRAP", slab earthenware and metal[3]

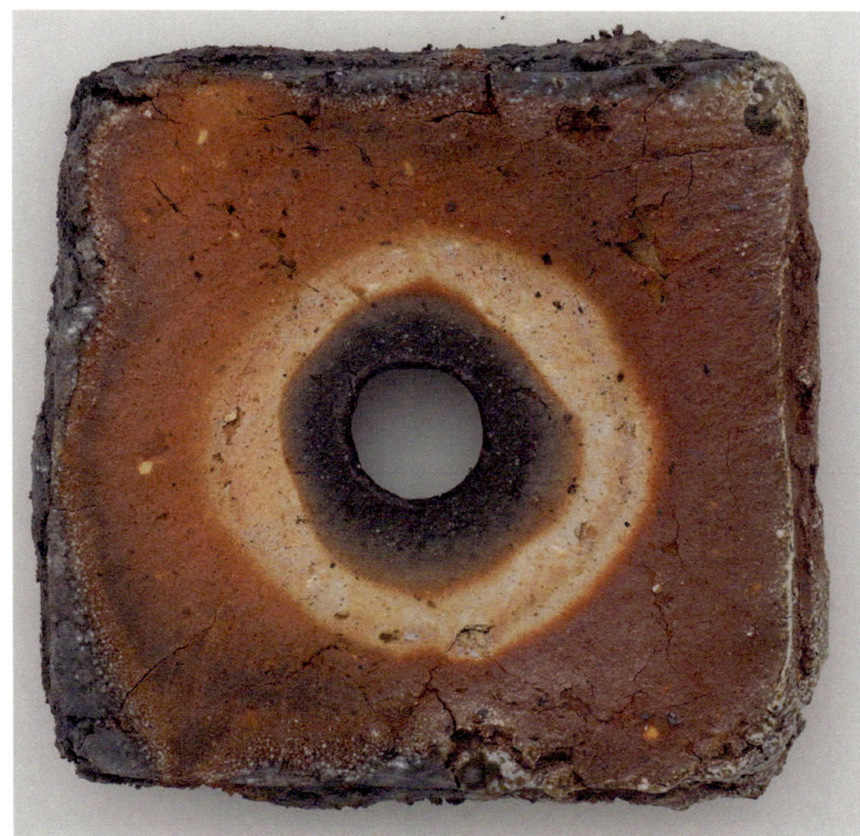

Jordan Taylor. "Square", slab woodfired stoneware[3]

SLAB

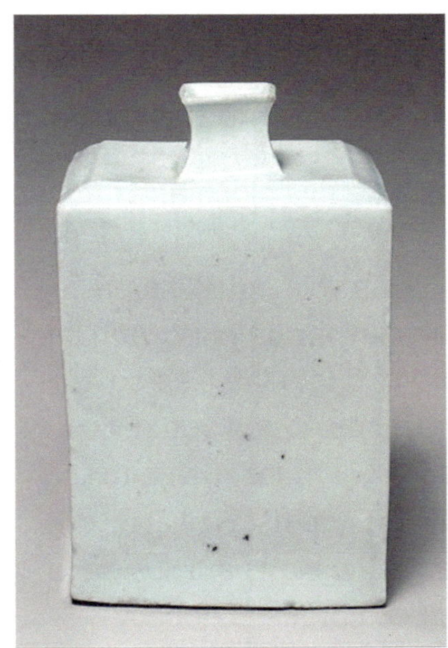

Korean slab porcelain bottle[4]

Slab building can be useful for making geometric forms or flat shapes. Slabs can also be used in conjunction with molds to create a variety of shapes. Slabs are most often made by using a slab roller machine, rolling pins, or throwing the slab out on a table like pizza dough. The process of creating the slab compresses the clay particles but it is a good idea to roll or stretch the slab in multiple directions to prevent any problems with cracking or warping.

There are two main slab construction approaches depending on when you use slabs and what your design requires. For "soft slab" construction and gestural/organic shapes, you will use the slabs soon after rolling them out. This approach is more useful for organic shapes but requires some type of support (molds, newspaper, tar paper, cardboard tubes) to hold the slabs in place as they dry.

The "stiff slab" method uses slabs that were rolled out and then allowed to dry to the near leatherhard stage. This approach is similar to building with wood or cardboard and allows for crisp geometric forms. It is very critical that when leatherhard slabs are joined, you carefully score and add slip to the seam. If this is not done well, the piece will crack apart during drying and/or firing. If possible, add a small coil into the seam to reinforce the connection.

One common and invaluable step is to make a paper or cardboard model of the object you plan to build. Tape this model together to get a sense of the overall shape and proportion. You can then take the model apart and use that as a patten to cut out your slabs.

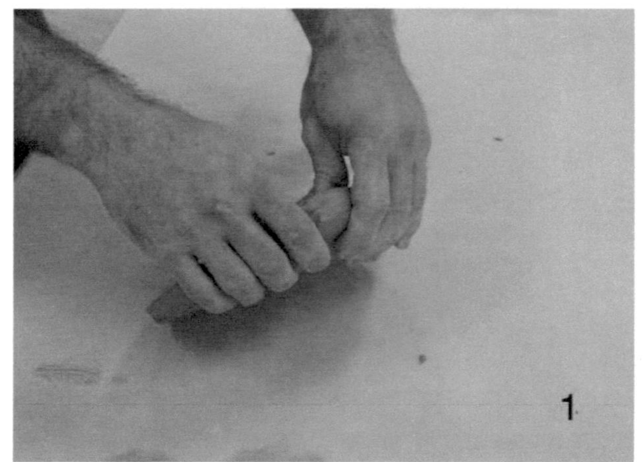

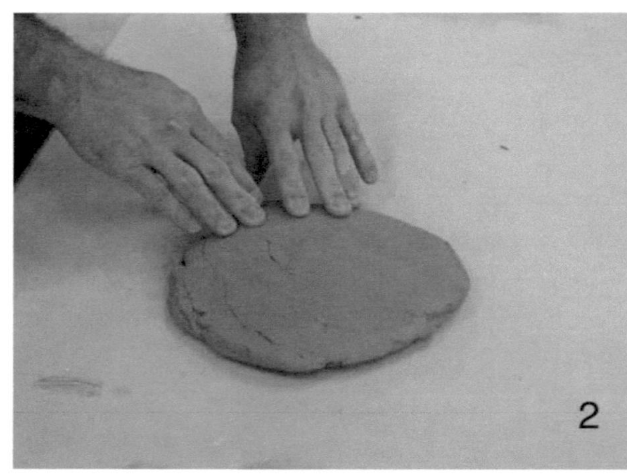

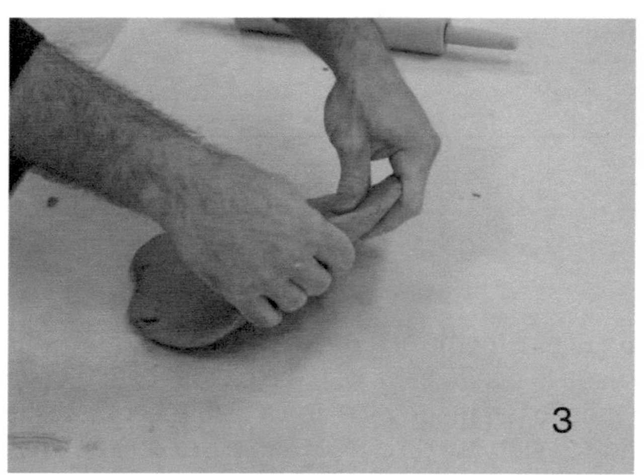

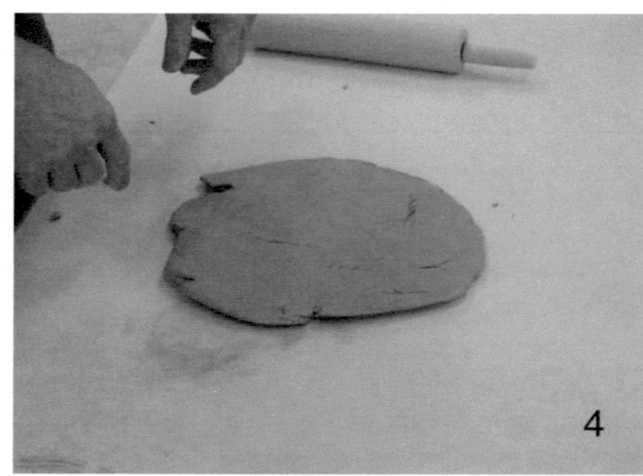

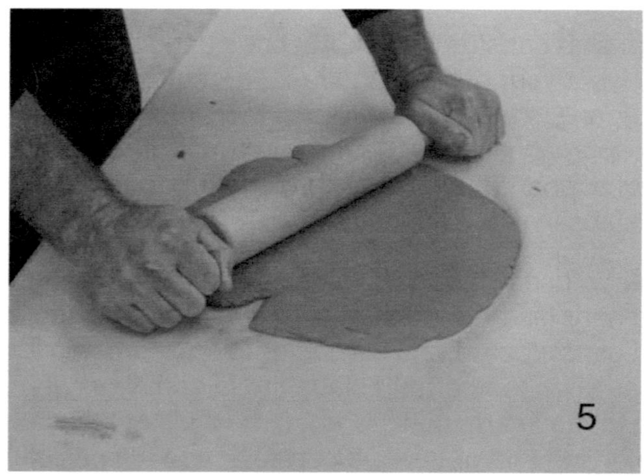

One way to make a slab is to press out a chunk of clay. Then take this piece and throw it down on the table at an angle. Continue to pick up the slab and throw is out like a piece of pizza dough. The clay is stretching and thinning out. Make sure to rotate the slab so it is stretching in all directions. When you get close to the thickness you need, use a rolling pin to even out any thick spots. Roll in all directions to make sure the clay particles have been stretched and compressed equally.

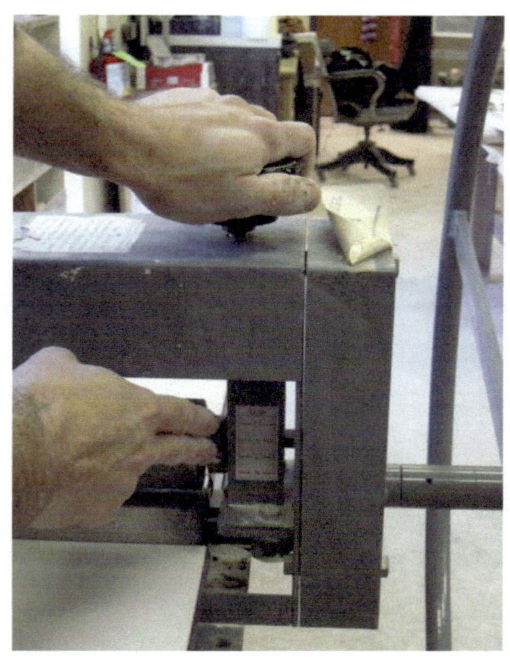

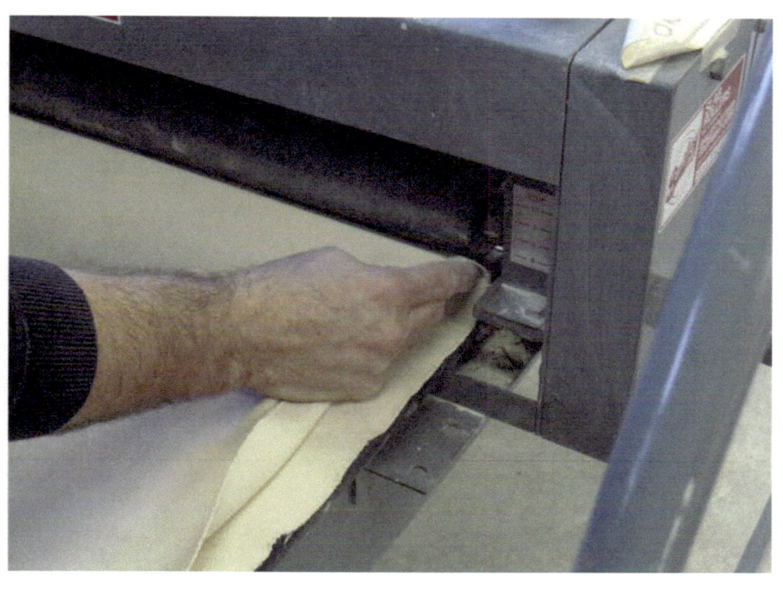

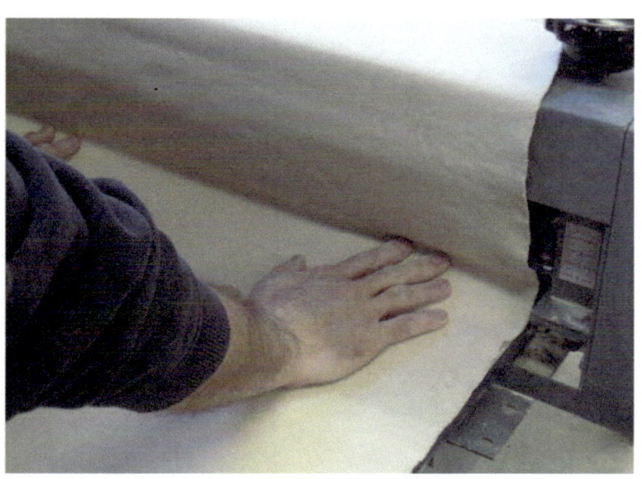

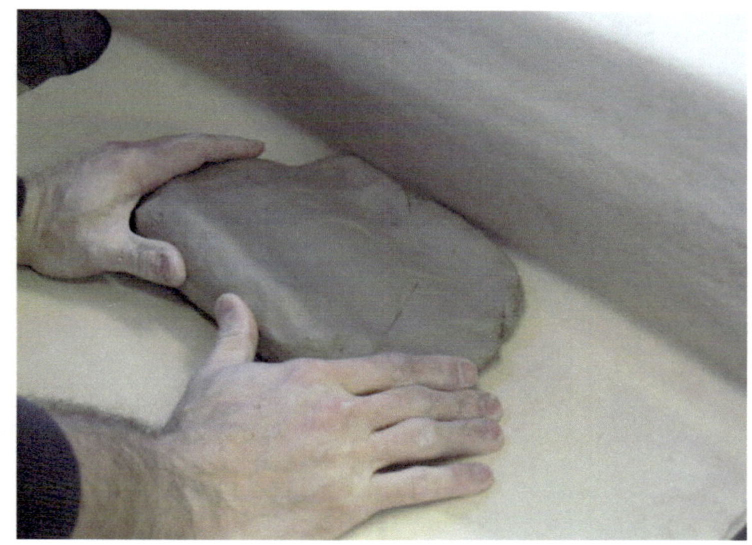

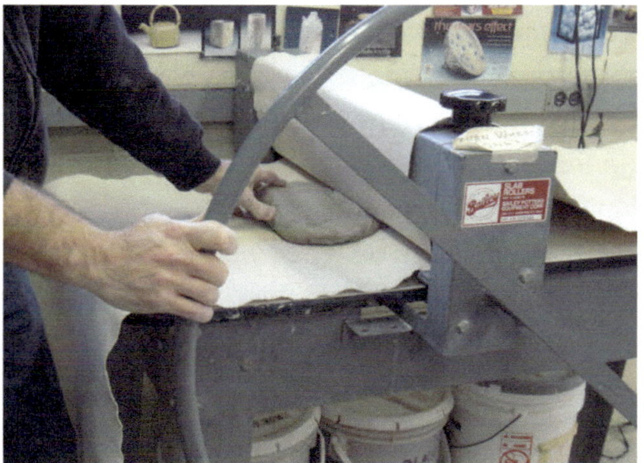

Another way of making slabs is by using the slab roller. The pictures on this page show the beginning of the process. First check and adjust (if needed) the thickness of the slab. For most things you need a slab around a 1/4" thick. Then fold the canvas in half and place the fold where the 2 rollers come together. NO CLAY should ever touch the rollers, only canvas should be in contact with the rollers. Next, take your lump of clay that is shaped into a rough wedge and place it up to the fold/rollers. Turn the gear wheel toward yourself to start the process.

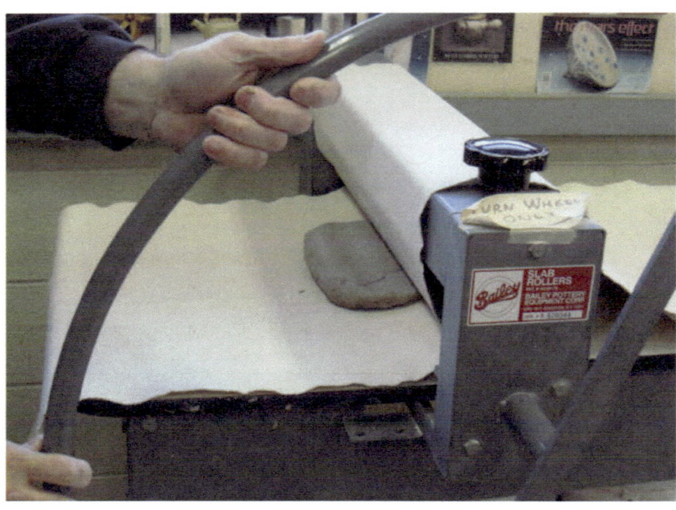

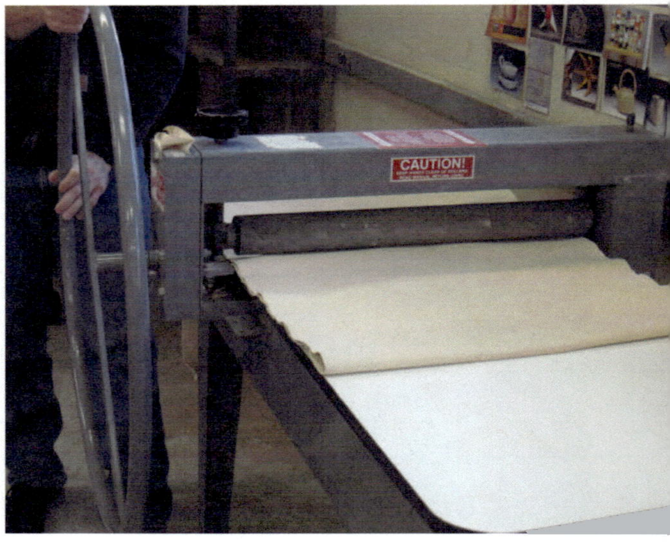

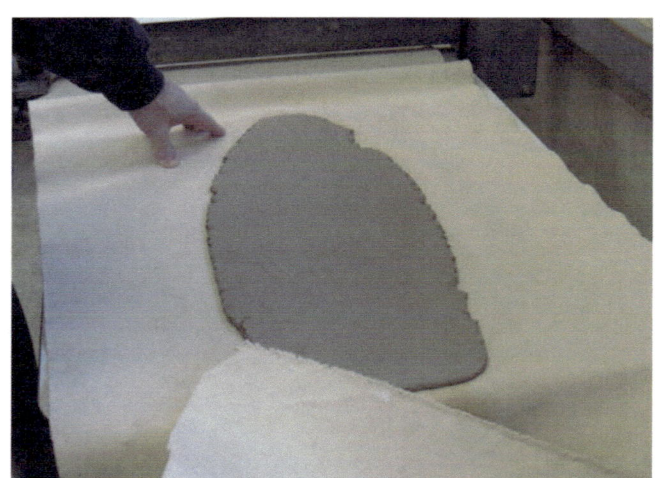

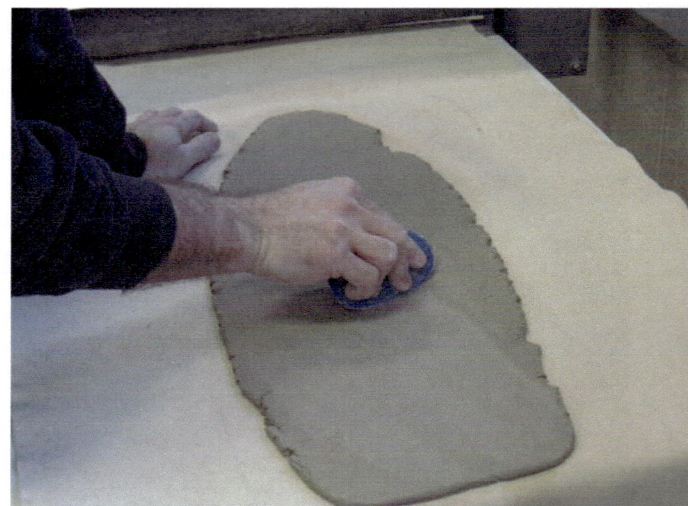

Continue to turn the wheel toward yourself to pull the clay into the rollers. The new slab will push out onto the table surface. Once all the clay has been pulled through, carefully pull the upper canvas layer off the slab. Use a soft rib to remove the canvas texture from the slab. You can use the canvas to move your slab over to the table to continue working. There is one major point to note about how this machine works. The slab is being compressed mostly lengthwise but not much in width. The best thing to do is make sure the block of clay you start with is wide enough for your needs before you begin to roll it through the machine.

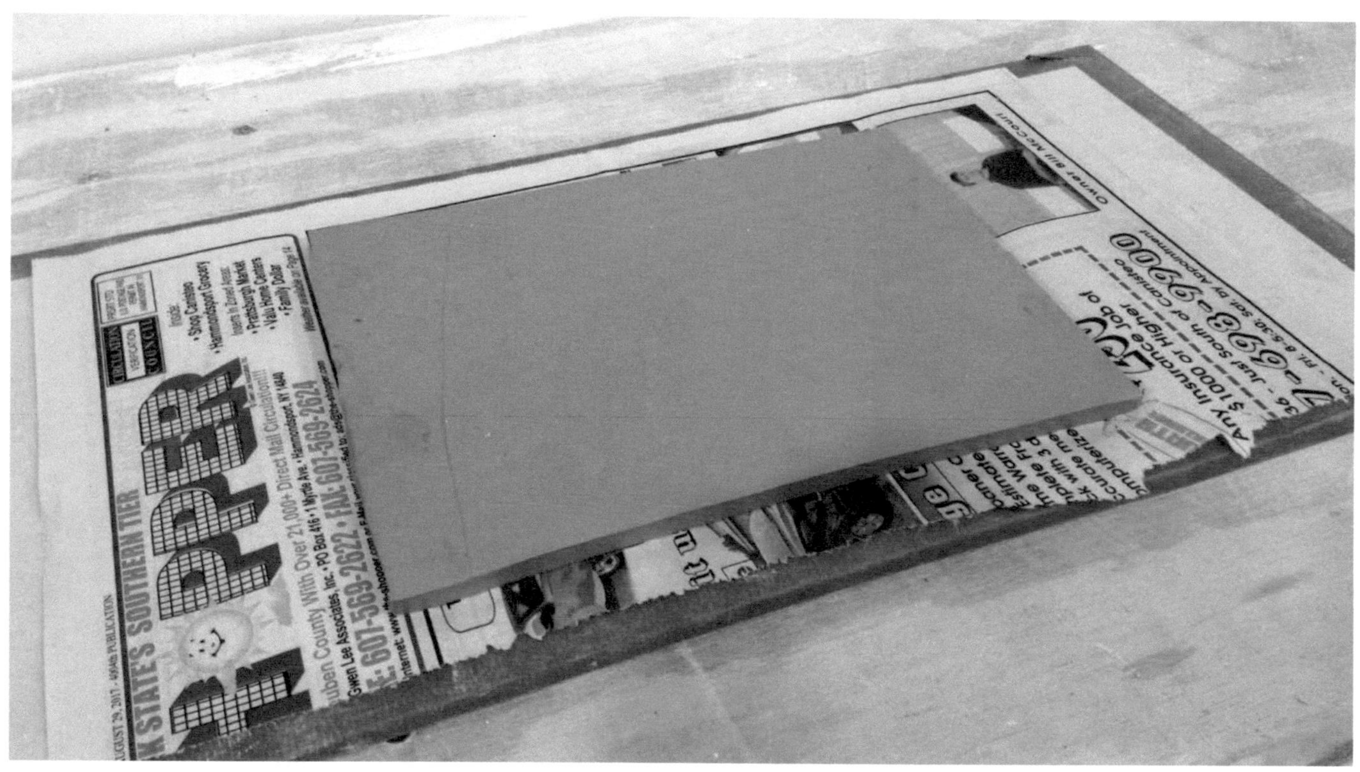

1

BUILDING WITH SLABS

Start with the base slab on a board with newspaper underneath. This example (a rectangular dish) is being built on a scrap piece of drywall (image 1). This material is used by many ceramic artists because moisture will be absorbed off the bottom of the object as it sits on the board. Scrap drywall pieces should have the edges taped so that the drywall powder does not get mixed into the clay.

This pot is being built with slightly dried slabs so that they have some flexibility but at the same time, will stand up well. Once the base is set, begin assembling the sides by scoring and slipping the seams and edges of the slabs (2). As you create corners, roll thin coils and blend them into the seams between slabs to serve as reinforcement (3). Complete the construction by attaching all the necessary sides making sure to blend and compress all the corners and seams between slabs (4). Continue to refine the sides, angles, and corners with ribs and other tools (5). Make sure to finish the top and bottom edges so that all elements of the object are well made.

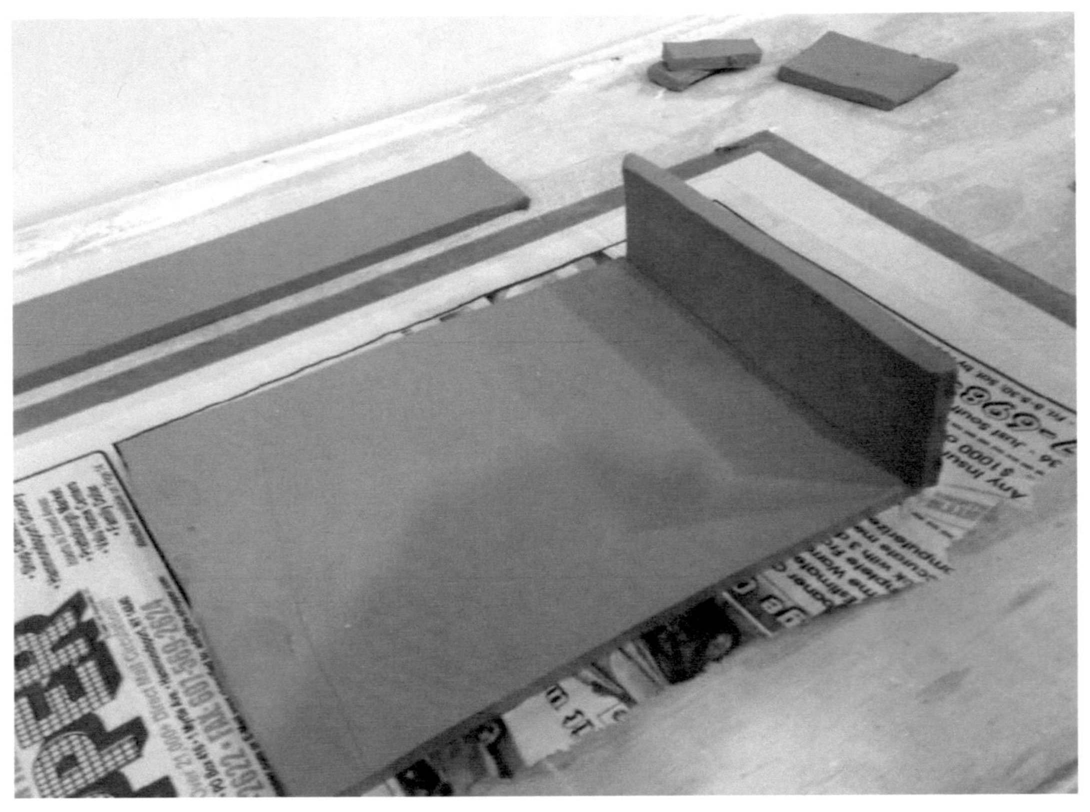

2

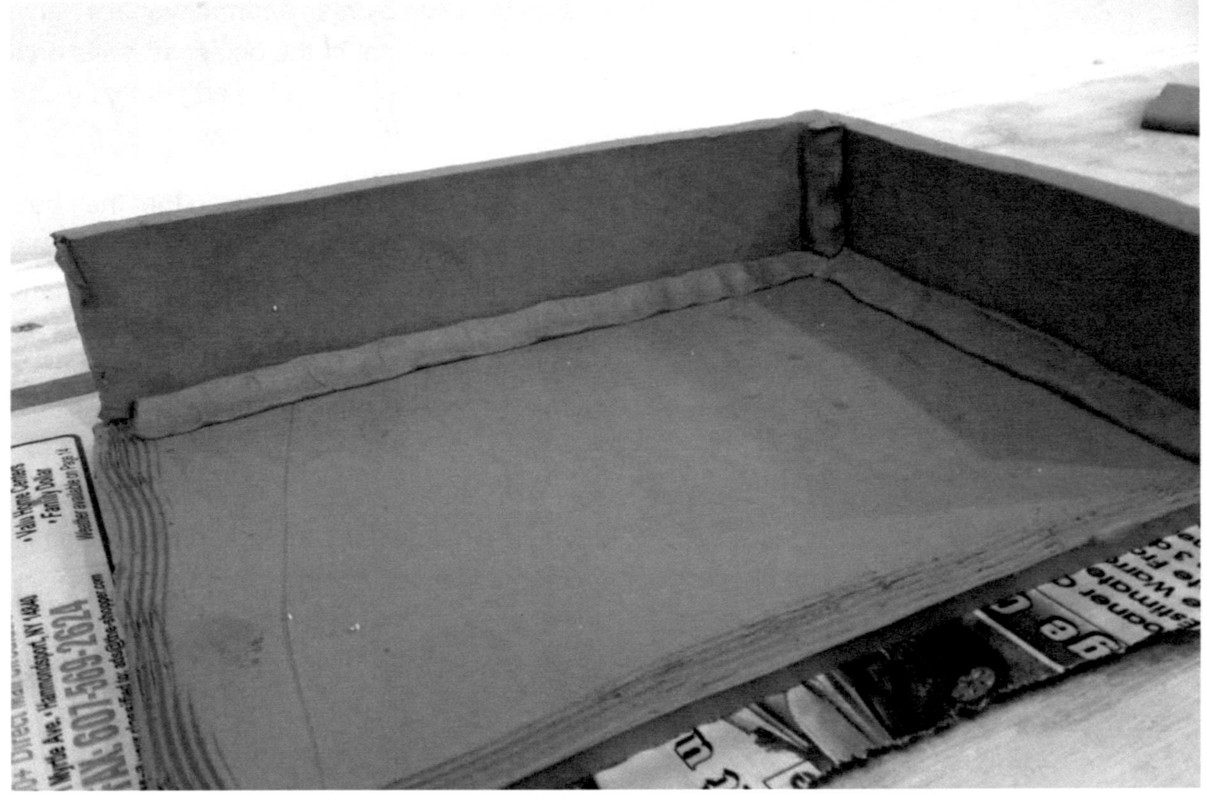

3

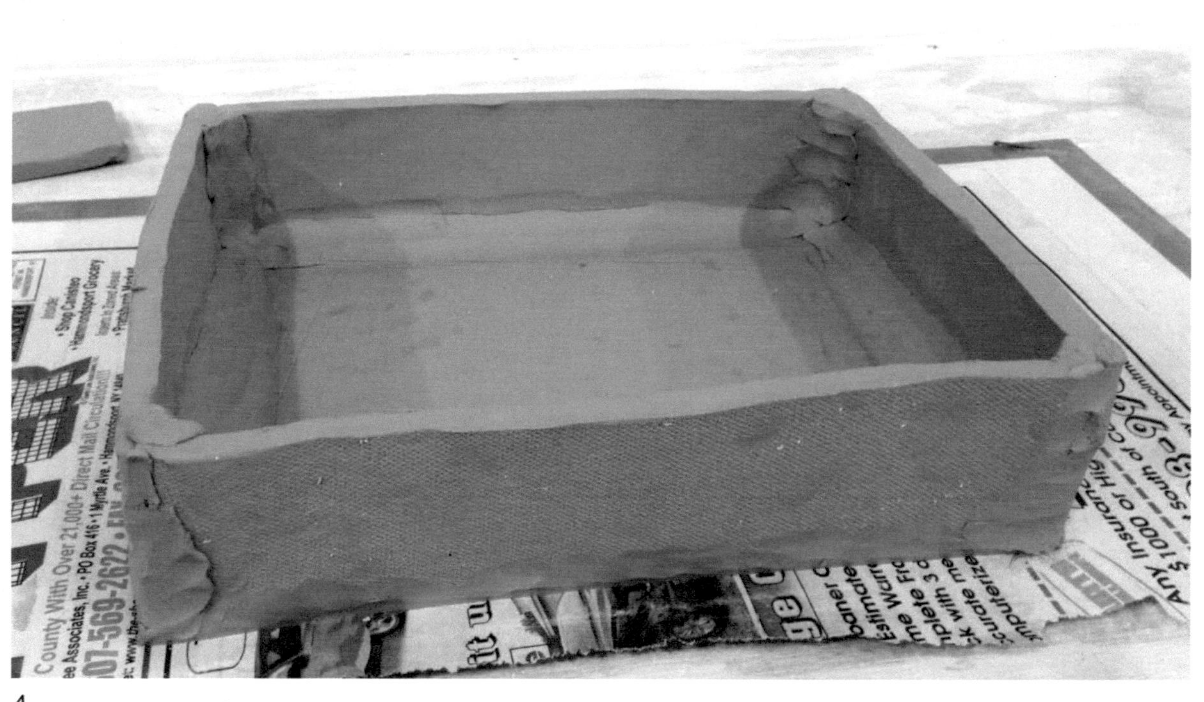

4

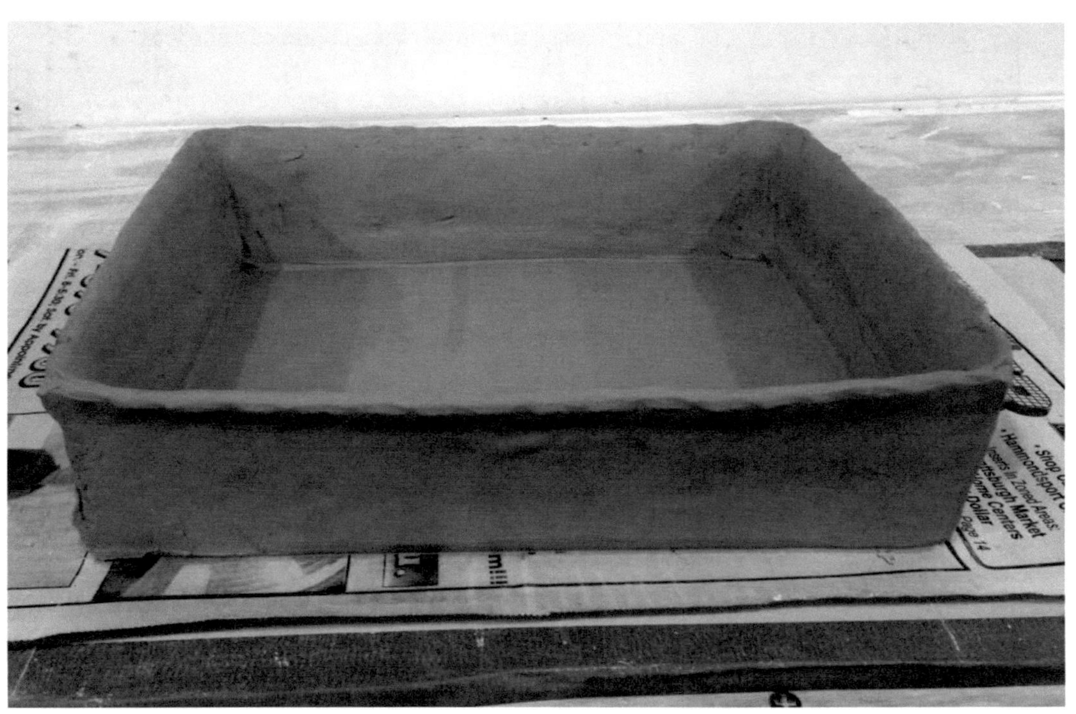

5

One of the best books on the plaster mold making process for ceramics. This book by Andrew Martin is available in the CCC Library.

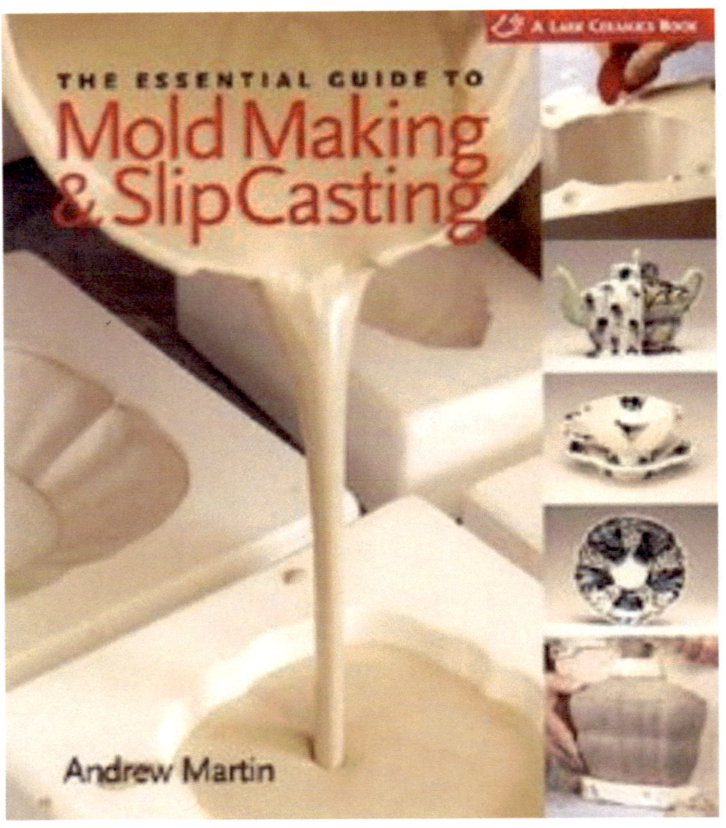

PLASTER
PLASTER MIXING

Plaster is made from naturally occurring gypsum which has been ground up, heated, and processed to become a very useful material for many industries. There are a variety of types and brands of plaster available for the ceramics artist but the most useful is called #1 Pottery Plaster. It is the best for general studio use and is easily purchased from ceramics suppliers.

Plaster has many advantages for ceramics production. The main being that you can create a liquid and pour that material to create molds and other shapes. Once mixed it will go through a chemical change that will harden the liquid into a solid block. This solid, cured piece of plaster will absorb moisture from the clay surface or liquid casting slip. Plaster can also be cast in solid blocks to sculpt into shapes that then can have a mold made of that shape.

There are some important tips to remember about mixing and using plaster in the studio.

1- Always add plaster powder to the required amount of cold water. Never use hot water and never add water to an amount of dry powder.

2- Keep your plaster powder in a dry place inside a sealed plastic container. Old plaster powder will absorb excess moisture from the air and start to solidify and forms lumps. Rotate your supply so that you are always using up powder so it doesn't sit too long.

3- Never wash mixed plaster, powder, or plaster chips down the drain. This will solidify and permanently block pipes. Pour excess material into the trash and keep a rinse bucket to wash your hands and tools. This bucket can then be dumped outside.

4- If possible, keep clay working space and plaster separated. In large studios, there is often a plaster room that prevents problems. If solid plaster chips get into wet clay and then are fired with the piece, the plaster will swell after firing and break your piece.

5- Liquid plaster will stick to almost everything except wet clay! If you are using wooden mold forms (called cottles), making molds of porous materials, or pouring liquid plaster on solid plaster, you MUST use a release agent applied (brushed on) to the porous surface to keep the new plaster from sticking. One of the cheapest and easy to find mold releases is Murphy's Oil Soap. Other releases include vaseline, cooking spray, or commercially produced sculpture mold releases.

6- Wet clay can be used to sculpt your original shape, as containment walls, or to seal wooden cottles. This clay should never be reclaimed with normal clay since it will contain plaster chips. Keep this clay wrapped up and you can reuse it for additional mold making.

7- Make sure to use the correct amount of powder for the water volume needed. Plaster mixed with less than the powder required will never set strong and be "punky" or extra weak.

8- During the chemical reaction that sets the solid plaster, it will heat up. Do not move your mold until it has gone through this change and starts to cool off. After the setting process, you can disassemble the walls and take any clay out. Scrape down any sharp edges and allow the mold to dry. Thick molds can take days for the moisture inside the plaster walls to come out. Plaster molds work best when dried and this can be sped up by setting the molds in front of a fan. DO NOT heat molds as this will break down the strength of the plaster wall.

Steps for plaster mixing:
1- Make sure to have your piece ready before you begin mixing plaster. Have your mold release applied if needed and the cottle forms sealed to the bottom board. The worst "plaster disaster" is when the pressure of the liquid plaster blows out your seal or clay containment wall. Overbuild your reinforcements.

2- Either calculate the overall mold volume needed or do a rough estimate of the water needed. The unscientific method will be using the "floating islands" method of mixing that uses observation and experience. The official manufacturers method will use specified amounts of water and plaster powder in order to get the correct volume.

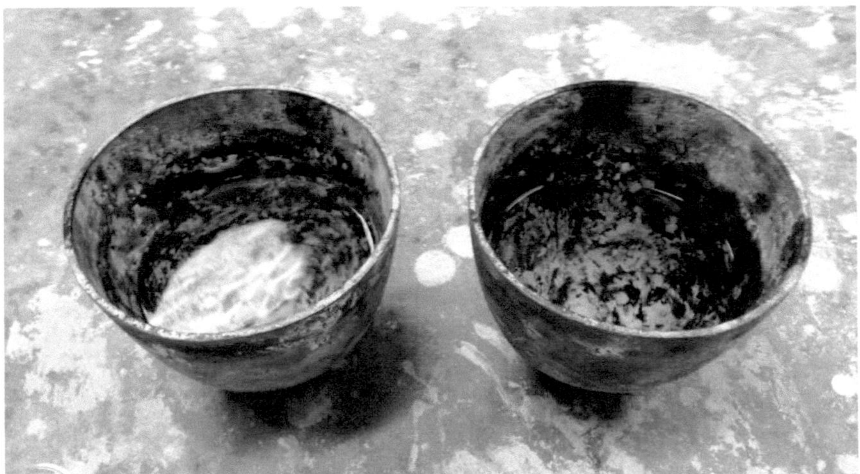
Flexible rubber bowls used for mixing plaster. These are filled 1/2 way for a small batch.

3- Fill mixing container with cold water about 1/2 the needed volume for floating islands or the correct amount for official method

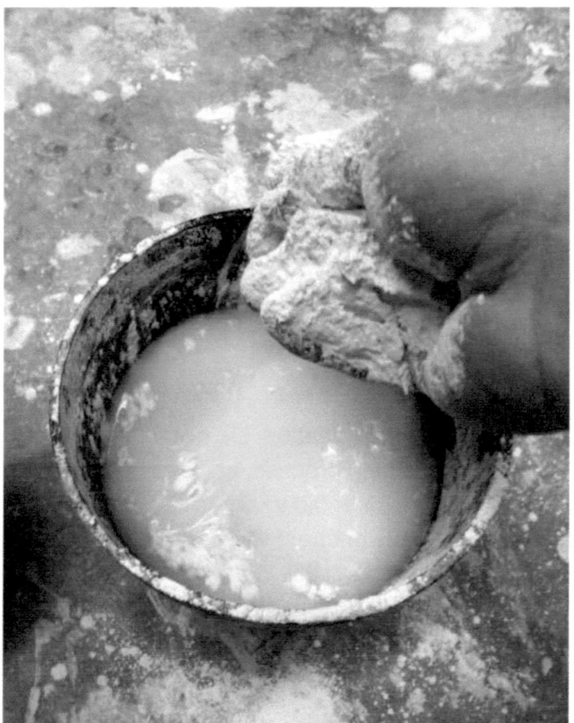
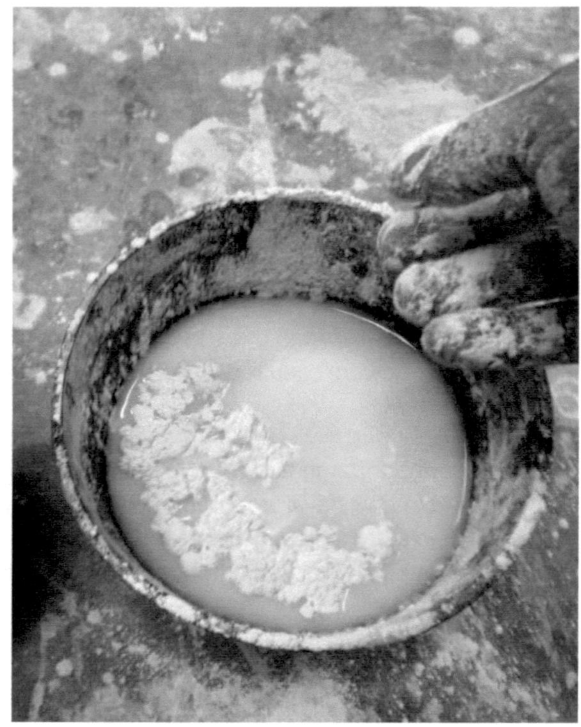

4-Carefully sift plaster powder into the water making sure to go all the way around the water surface. If all the powder is dropped into the middle of the container, the floating islands method will not work and the powder will not mix well.

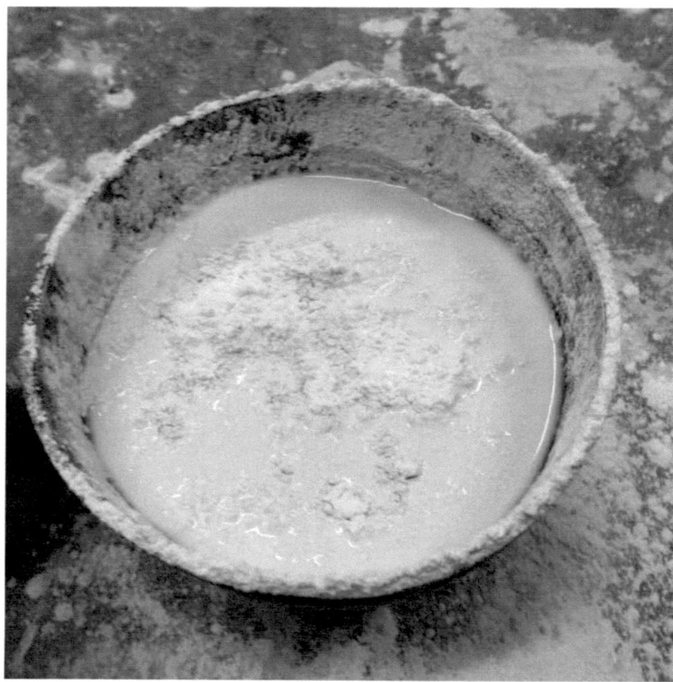

Correct amount of powder added for water volume= "floating islands".

5- If using the floating islands approach, watch the surface as the powder is added. When the correct amount of powder is reached, it will not drop into the water as quickly.

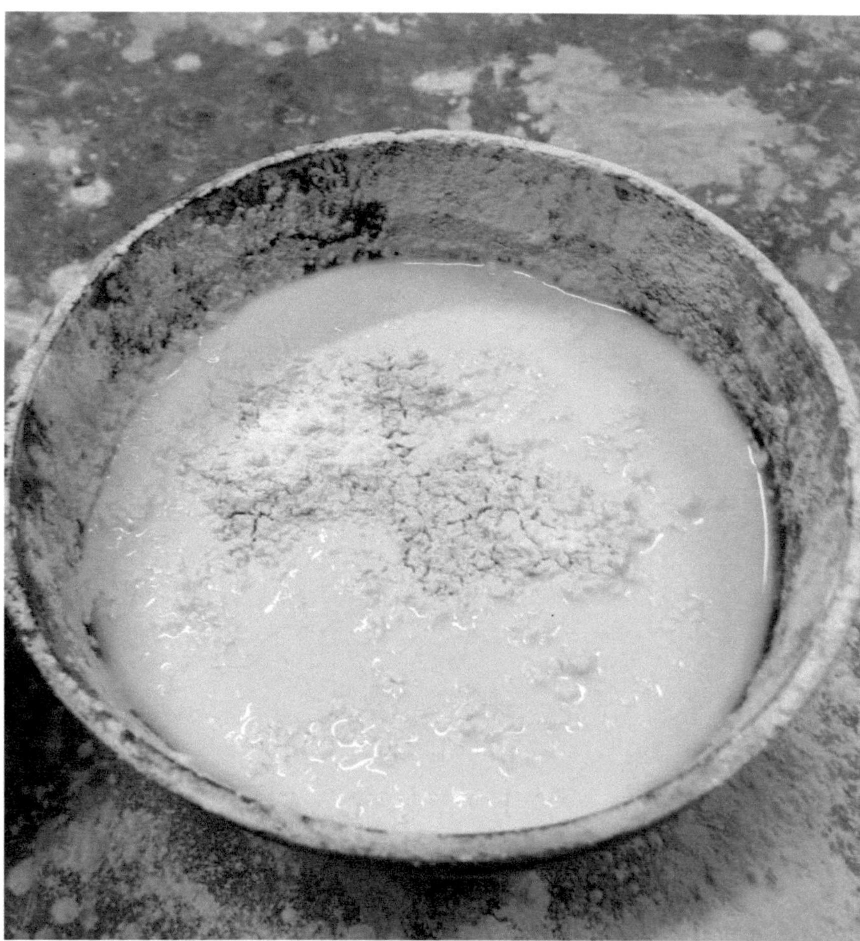

Allow powder to fully soak into the water. This creates less lumps in the mix.

6- Once all the powder is added, allow it to soak for 3-5 minutes or until all the dry powder at the top is wet.

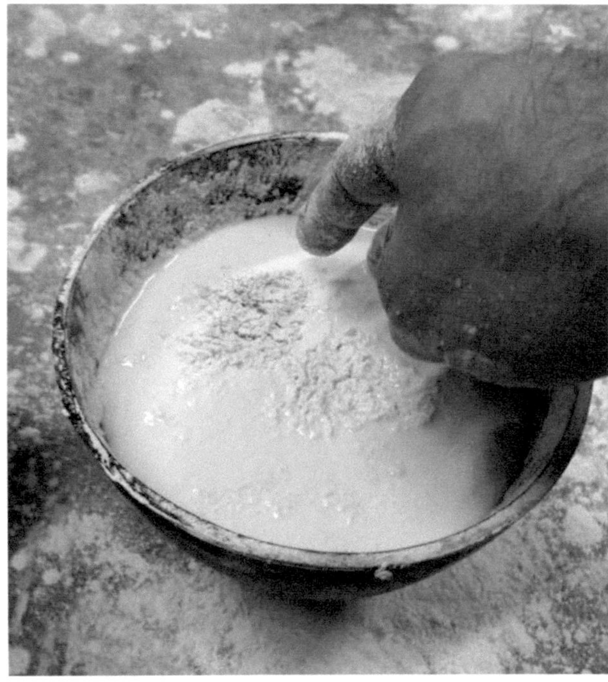

7- Carefully push your hand into the plaster, stir, and squeeze any lumps in order to mix the liquid to an even consistency. For larger amounts, you can use a drill mixer to thoroughly mix the plaster. Once you have mixed and agitated the liquid, the timer begins as the chemical reaction has started. You will have about 2 or 3 minutes to pour your molds before the mix starts to thicken. It will go from cream consistency to solid is about 8 to 10 minutes.

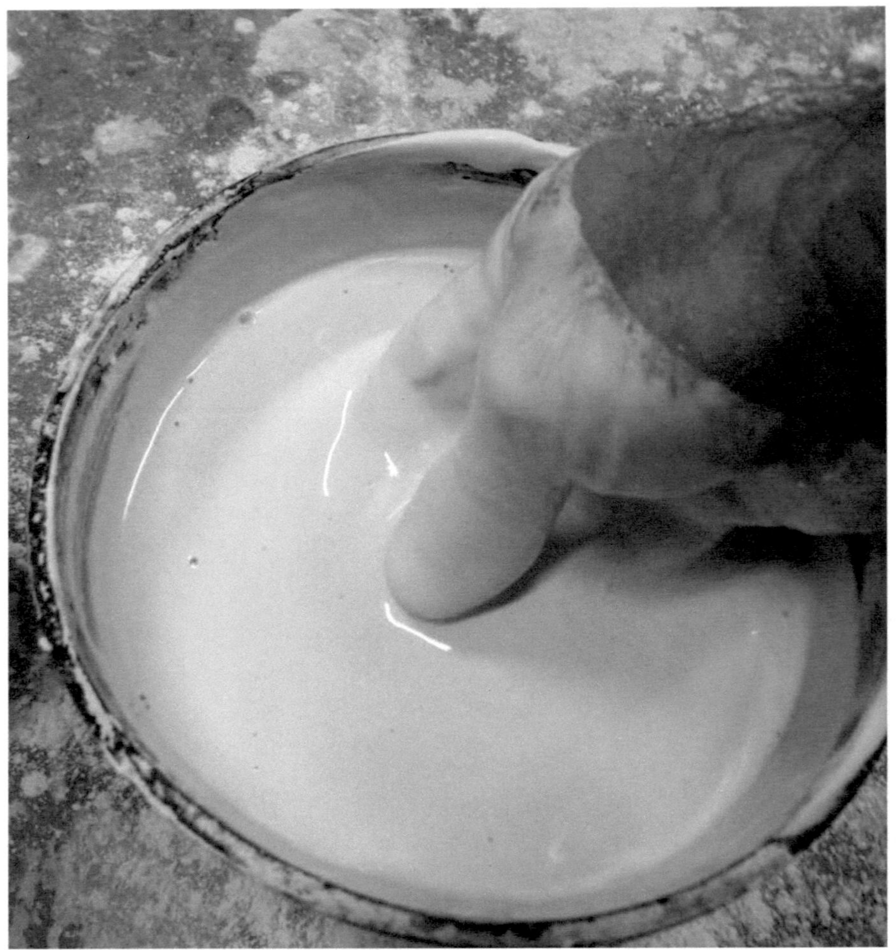

8- After the liquid is poured, make sure there are no mold blowouts that need plugging. Dump extra plaster into the trash and use rinse bucket to clean your hands and the mixing container.

9- Wait until the plaster has heated and cooled (usually about 30-45 minutes total) before you move and disassemble your new molds.

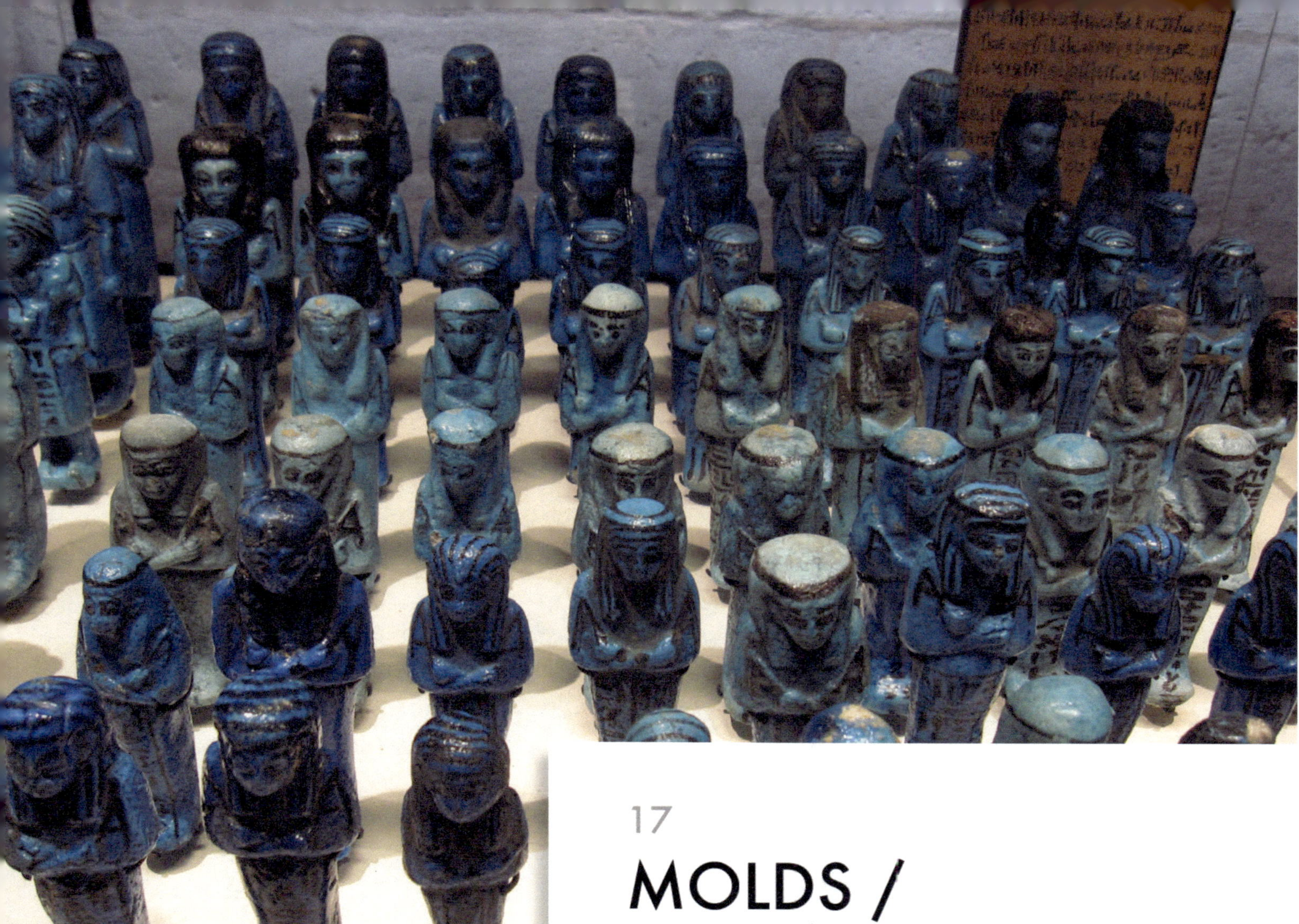

Ancient Egyptian press-molded ushabti tomb figures[1]

17

MOLDS / SLIPCASTING

Molds have been used in the production of ceramics since ancient times. The main advantage in the use of a mold is the ability to create a large number of identical pieces quickly. A variety of materials can be used to create molds, the most common being plaster, bisque fired ceramics, and wood. A common industrial production mold process called slip casting, has been in use for hundreds of years. Contemporary studio artists have taken the process and ideas of slip casting to new extremes in the production of their work.

One of the most useful materials for the production of molds is plaster. Plaster and clay will never stick together and the porous nature of plaster allows it to remove moisture from the clay surface.

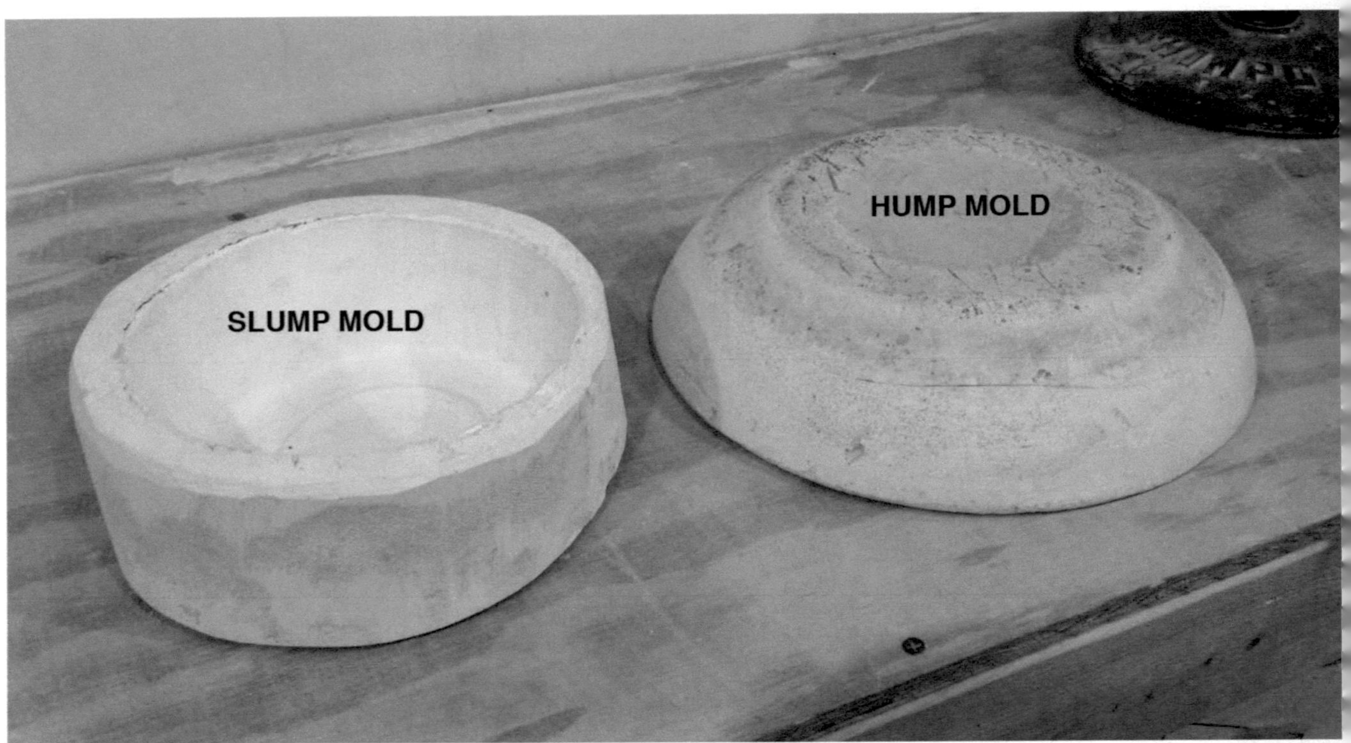

Types of simple one piece molds:

One of the most important concepts behind the use of molds is that it allows the repetition of shapes quickly and easily. This doesn't mean that you can mindlessly slap clay on a mold and expect success. Remember, clay is shrinking as it dries and this fact determines how you work with a mold. Some basic mold shapes in common usage are hump molds and slump (or press) molds.

Hump molds are used by draping a clay slab over the mold shape. If the mold has a hard surface (like plaster), the clay must be removed when it firms up but before it shrinks too much. If the clay is trapped on the form, it will crack apart as it continues to dry and shrink.

Slump molds are essentially the opposite of hump molds. In order to use a slump mold, you drape (slump) or press the clay into the mold. As the clay dries and shrinks, it will pull away from the mold on its own.

The type of mold you use is determined by what part of the shape (the inside or outside) you are trying to copy.

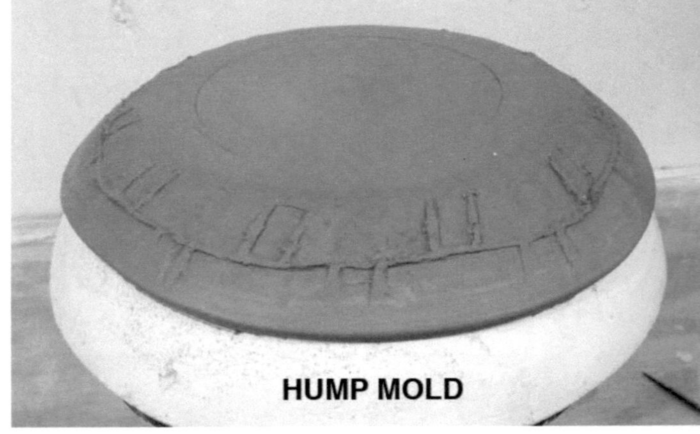

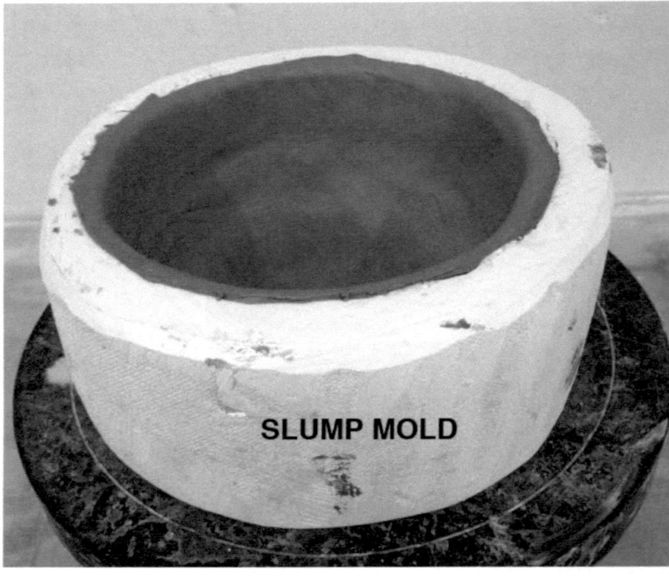

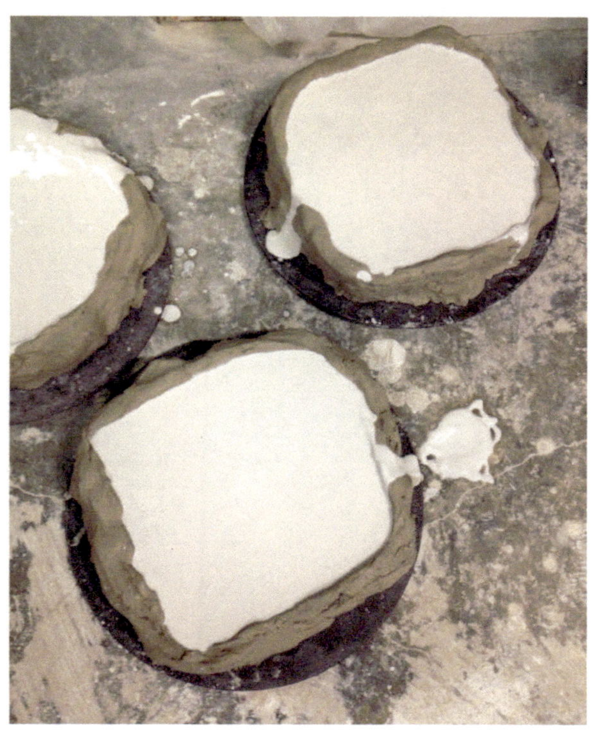

1

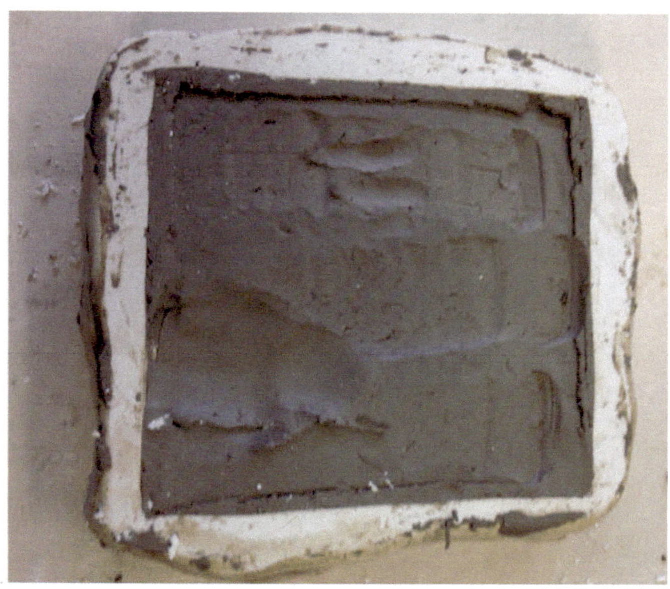

2

Making and using a one piece tile mold:

A common introductory experience with mold making is the production of a one piece tile mold. The first step is to sculpt the original in clay at slightly larger than the final size needed. This is done since the clay will be shrinking during the process when drying and firing. Once the original object is finished, a clay wall is built approximately 1" away from and 1" higher than the original. Plaster is mixed and poured into the "fenced" off area and allowed to solidify (image 1). After the plaster has hardened, the mold is flipped and the original sculpted clay object is removed from the mold (2). The empty mold is then cleaned, sharp edges scraped off, and allowed to fully cure and dry (3). New clay is pressed into the mold. This will start shrinking away from the mold walls and should drop out of the mold as it is turned upside down. The finished mold can now be used to make a large number of identical copies of the original shape (4).

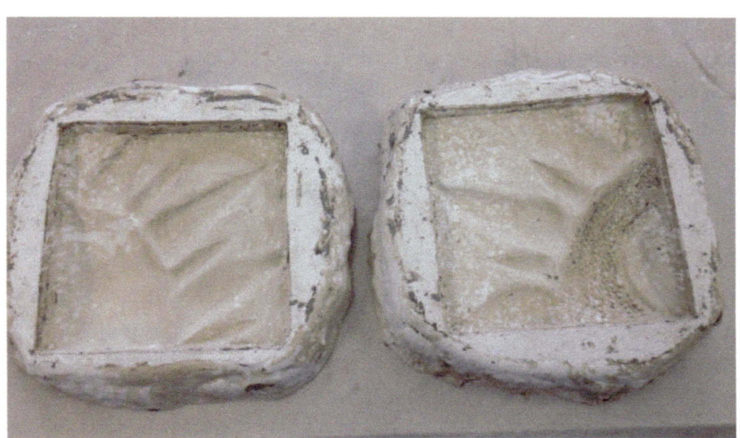

3

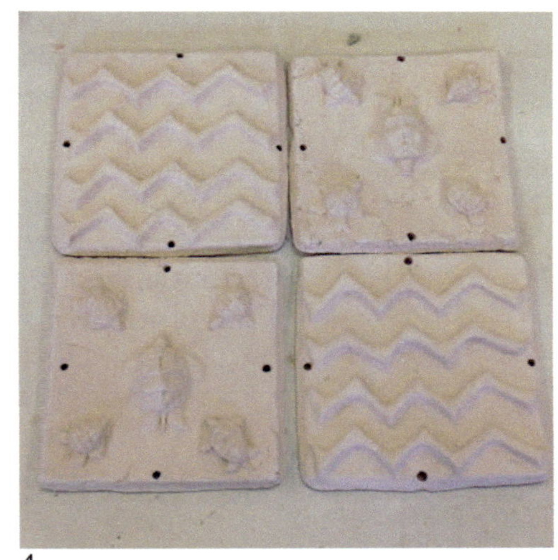

4

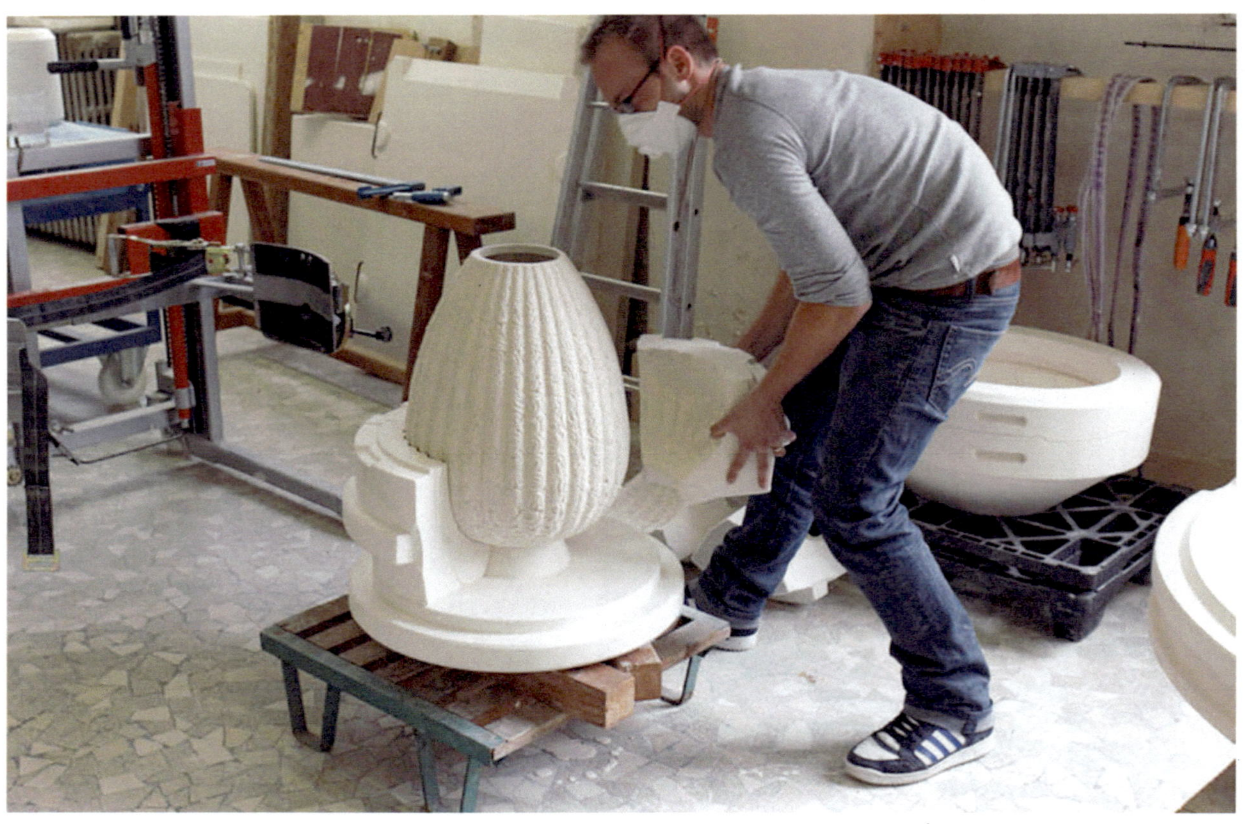

A small-scale slipcasting workshop of the Manufacture Nationale de Sèvres in France. The artist is removing plaster mold parts from a cast porcelain vessel. [12]

SLIP CASTING

Slip casting is a very important industrial process for making ceramics of all types. Most of the commercially made pottery and sanitary ceramics (sinks, toilets, urinals) we use everyday has been made using this process. Plaster molds (often with multiple complex parts) are assembled and a specially altered liquid clay slip is poured into the mold. The slip is left in the mold for an amount of time. The plaster mold starts to suck water out of the slip creating a sedimentary shell of clay against the mold wall. After the desired wall thickness is achieved, the excess slip is poured out of the mold and the object begins to dry. When the piece is stable enough to remove, the mold is disassembled and the object taken out. The mold is dried and can be used to cast a large number of repeat shapes. Complex objects can be cast in separate molds and then easily assembled later, for example teapot spouts cast in a small spout mold and then attached to the teapot body.

The clay slip used for this process is not just normal clay made more liquid. Casting slip has a special material added called a deflocculant. Normal clay particles want to stick together or flocculate (think of them as "flocks" of sheep) By adding a deflocculant, the electrical charge of the clay particles is changed and they begin to repel each other. This action allows the slip to stay fluid without using an excess amount of water. The correct consistency of this mixture is critical to having a strong cast object. The other vital part of this process is a skillful mold making practice and understanding of how to make complex, multipart molds.

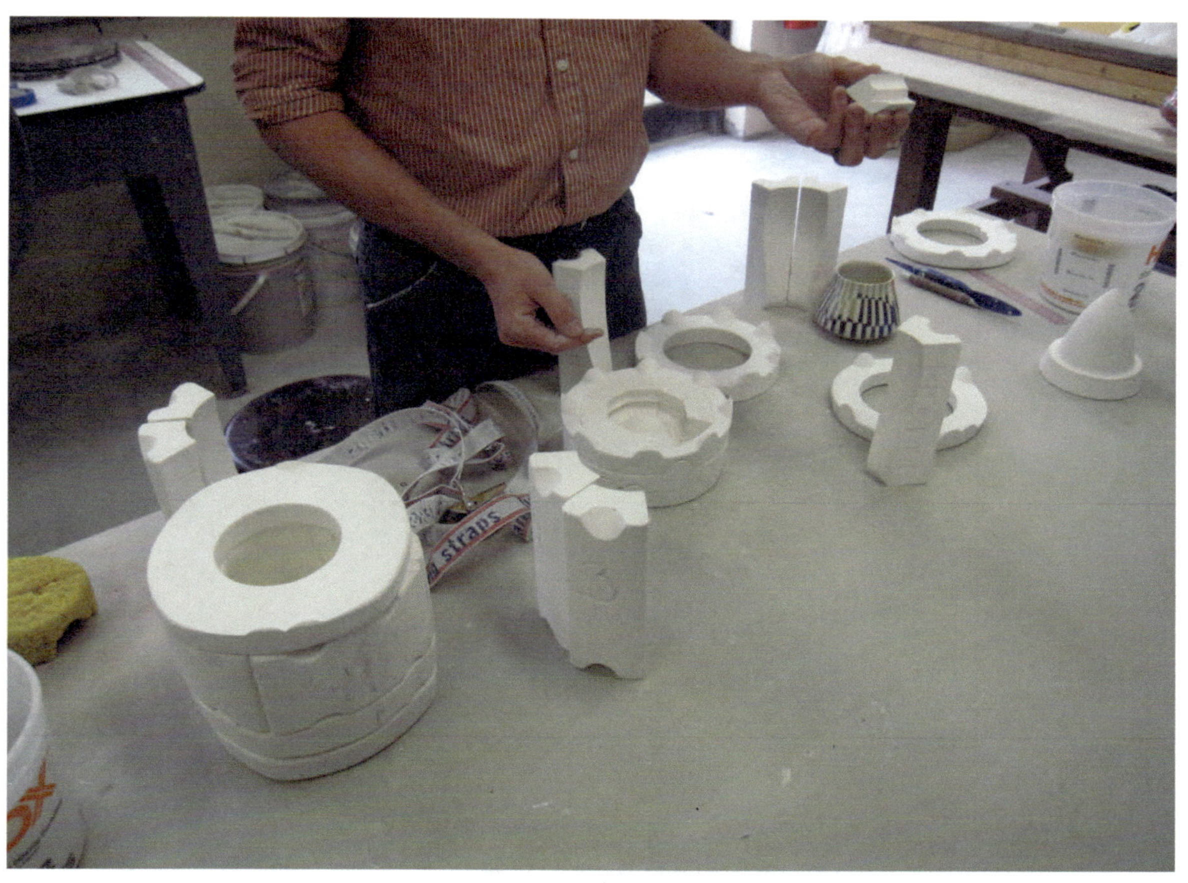

Visiting artist and RIT Ceramics professor Peter Pincus demonstrating his unique slip casting method at the CCC studio[1]

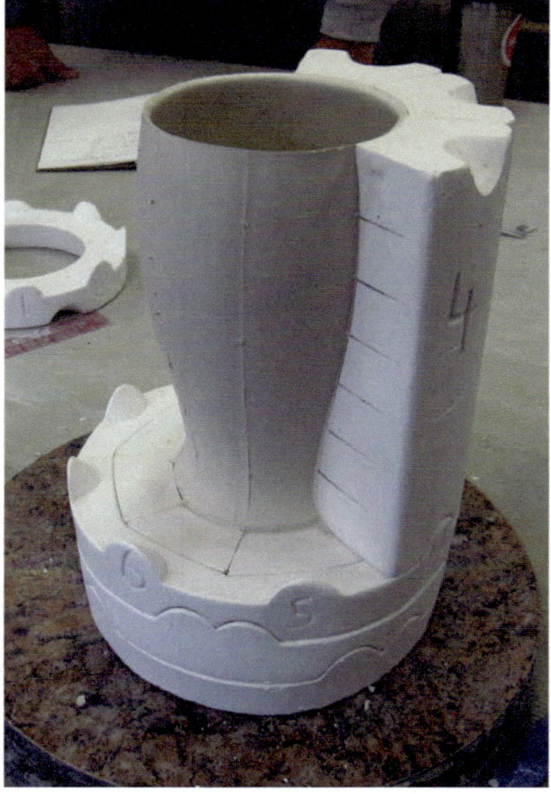

A finished cast form coming out of the multi-piece mold used by Pincus[1]

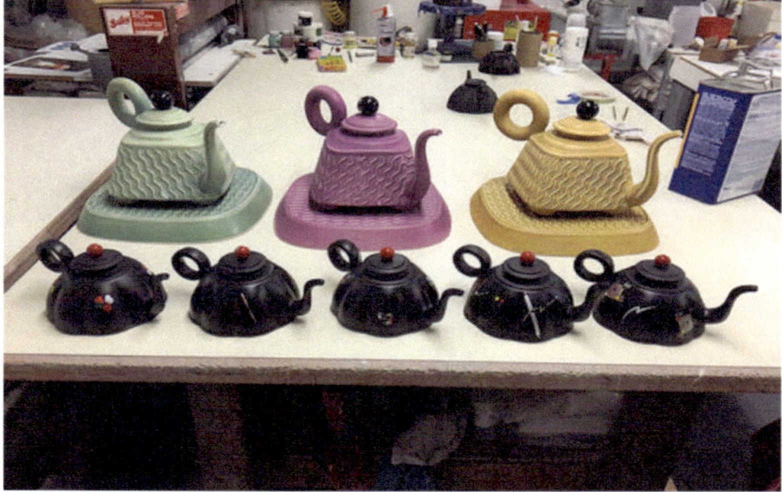

View of Jonathan Kaplan's studio with slip cast teapots[3]

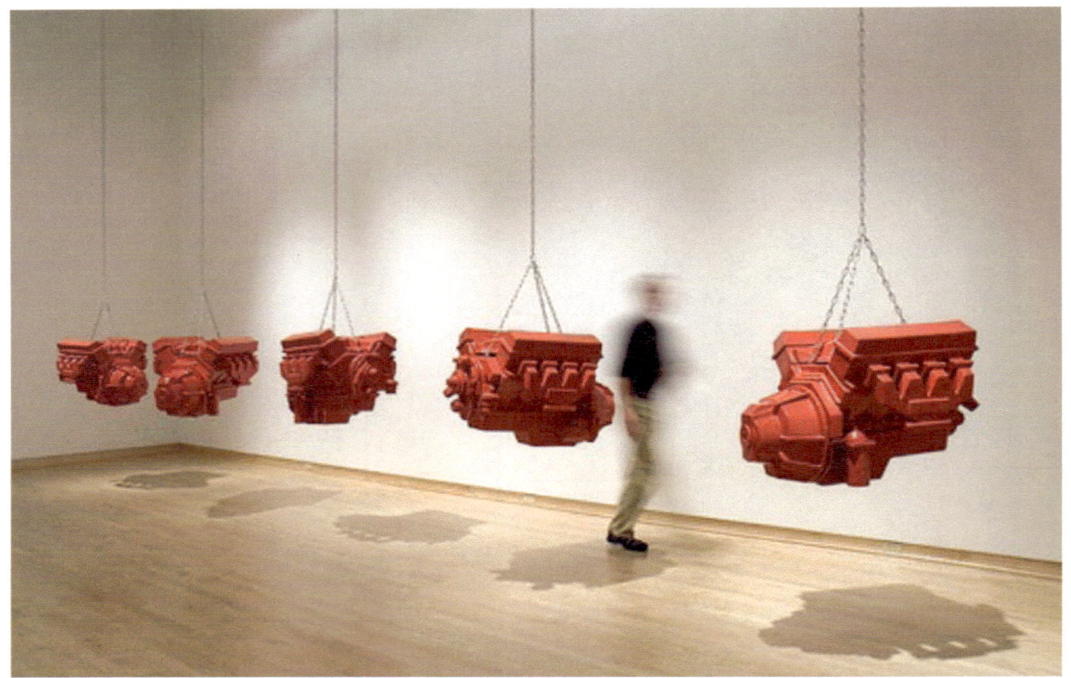

David Packer, "The Last of the V8's" slip cast porcelain[2]

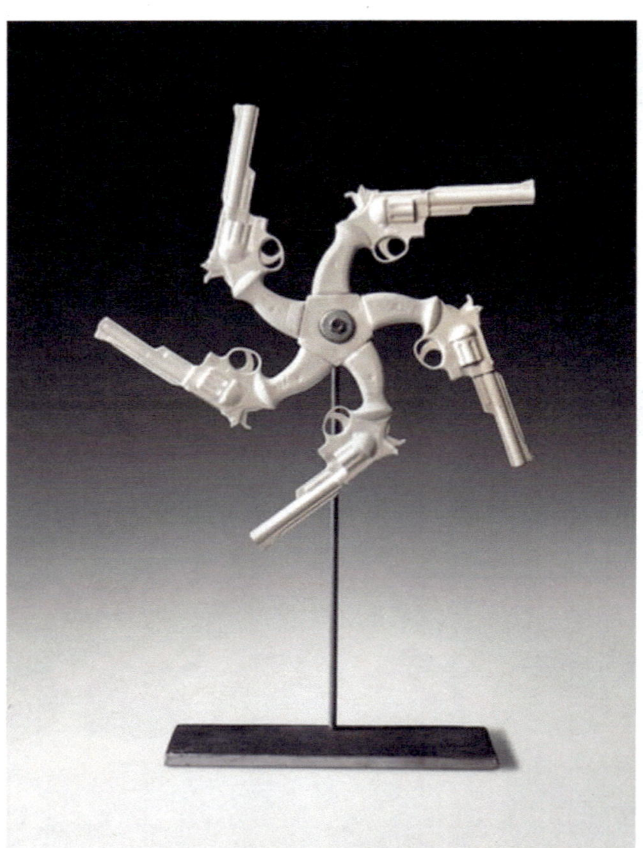

Linda Lighton "44 Magnum Mandala", slip cast earthenware[3]

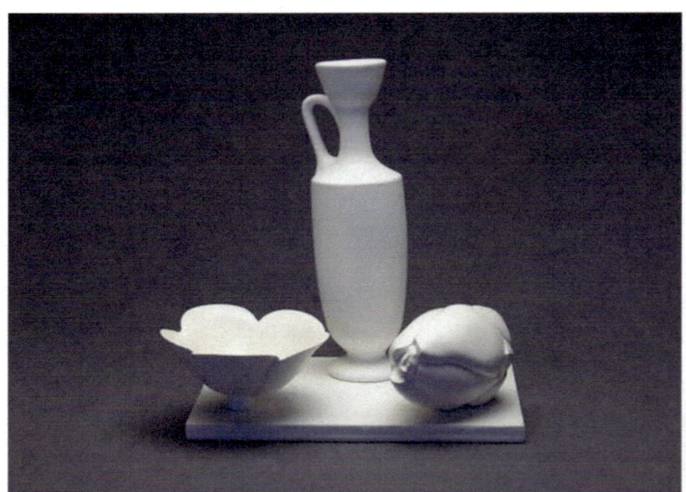

Anat Shiftan, "Still Life with Bowl, Bud, and Lekythos", slip cast porcelain[5]

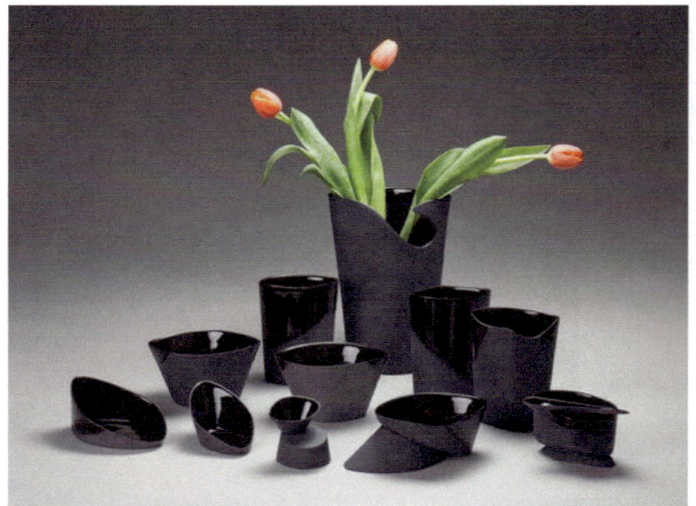

Heather Mae Erickson, "The Industrial Hand Collection", slip cast porcelain[3]

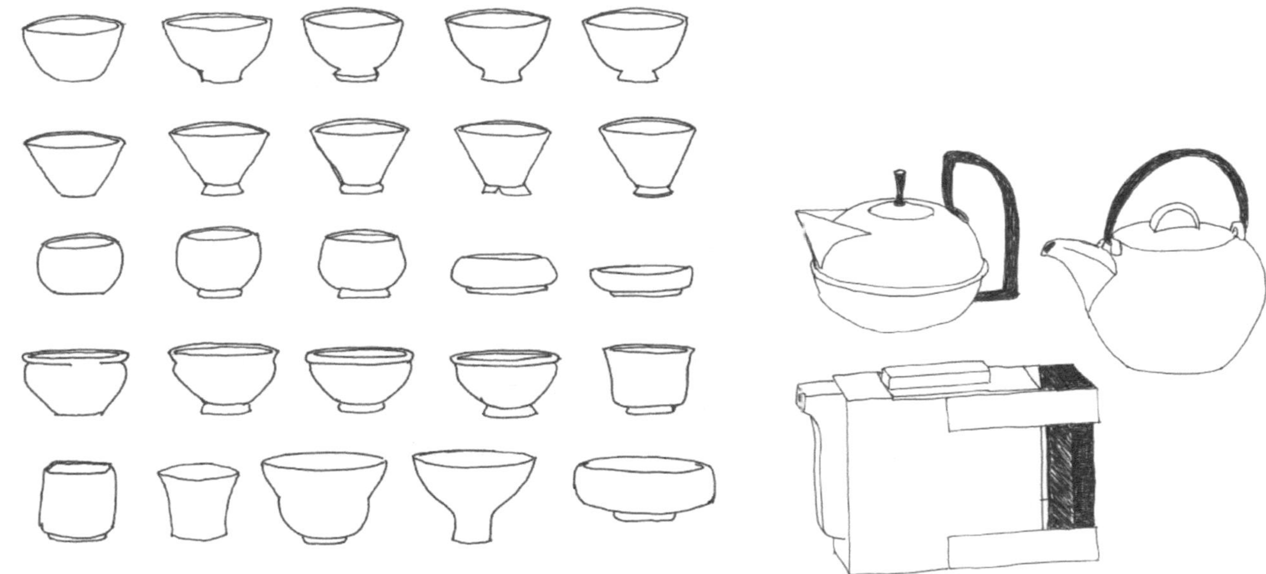

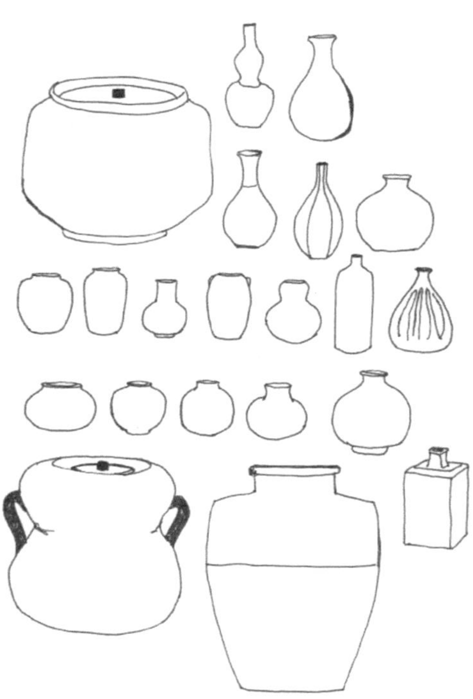

18

SKETCHBOOK / PICTURES

The artist's sketchbook is a critical tool in the development of their work. It is the location to sketch ideas, take notes, and plan the next steps in the production of work. Most artists carry a sketchbook (or something that functions like it) in their daily life in order to capture ideas before they are forgotten. In studio classes, professors will ask you to make sketches of your ideas for projects before you begin. This will allow both you and the professor a chance to look at the idea and discuss any issues that may come up with design or construction. Having something on paper to share makes this process possible and the most effective. In addition, this section of the handbook can be used to paste required pictures.

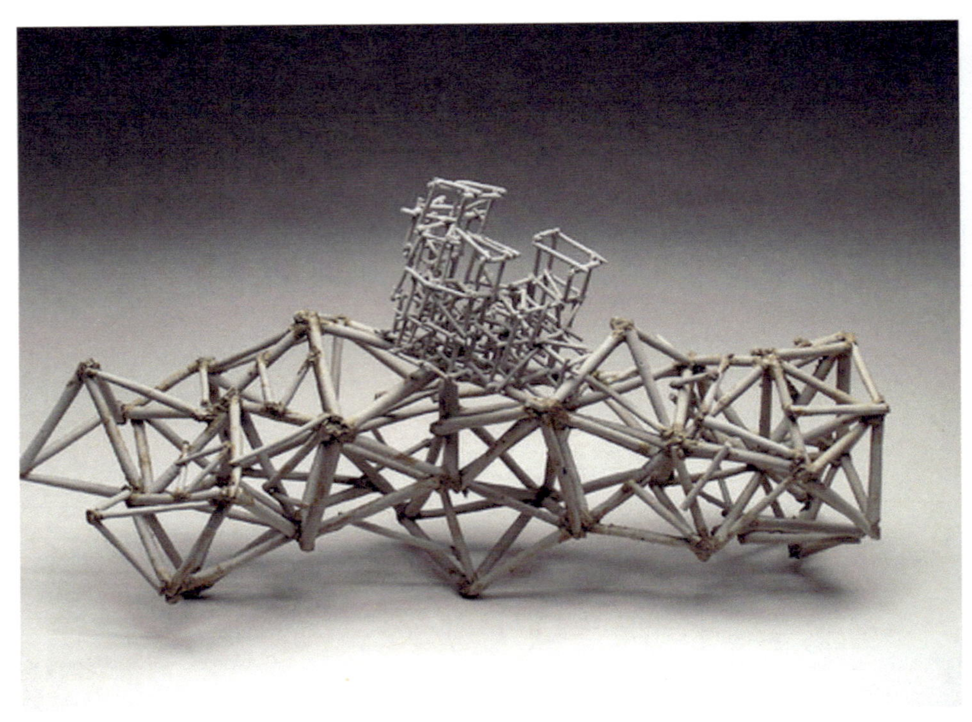

"Migration Grid #1", Stanton Hunter[5]

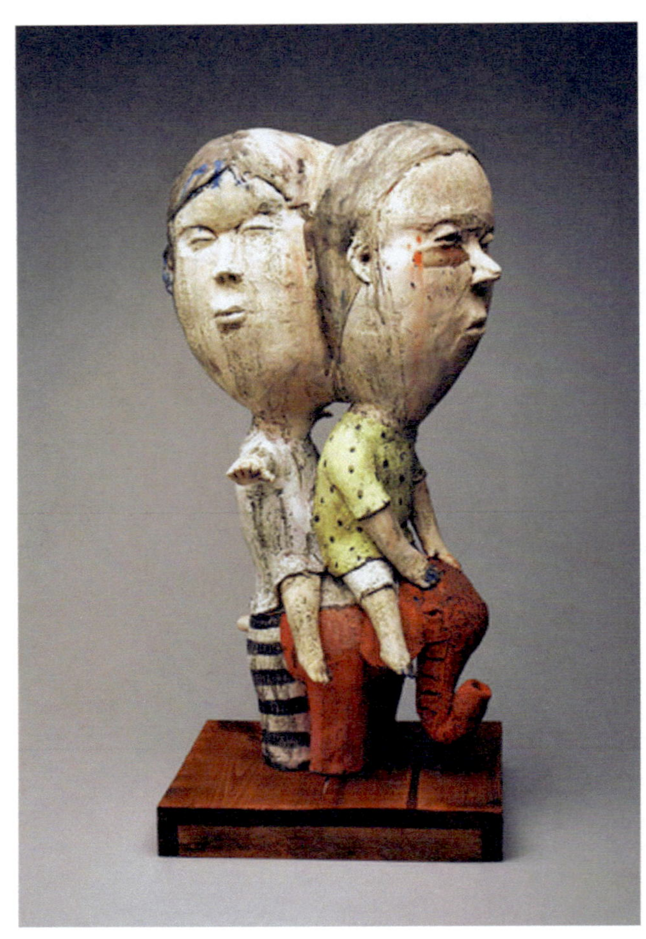

"Elephant Rider", Kensuke Yamada[3]

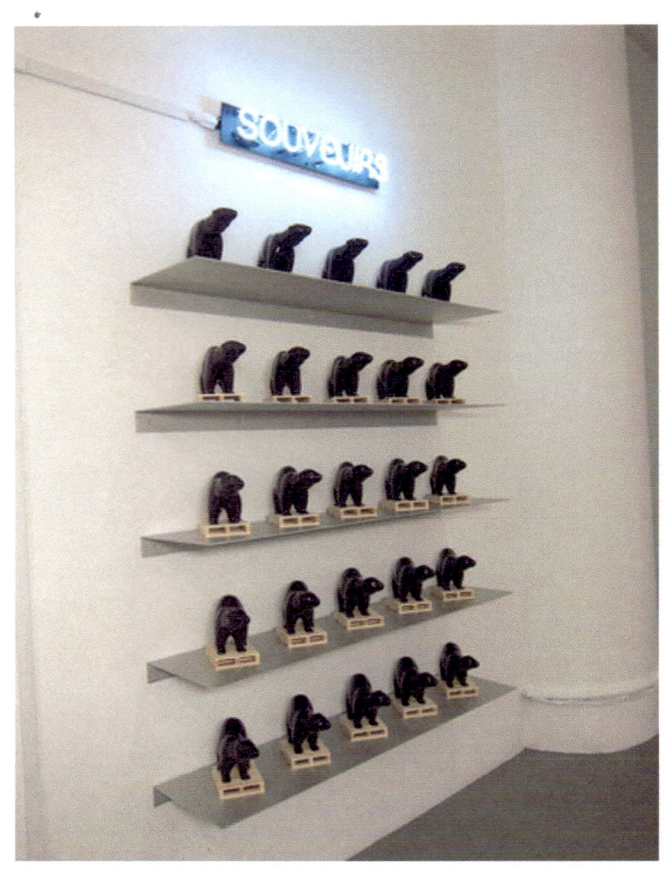

"Against the Tide, Souvenirs", Tim Berg and Rebekah Myers[3]

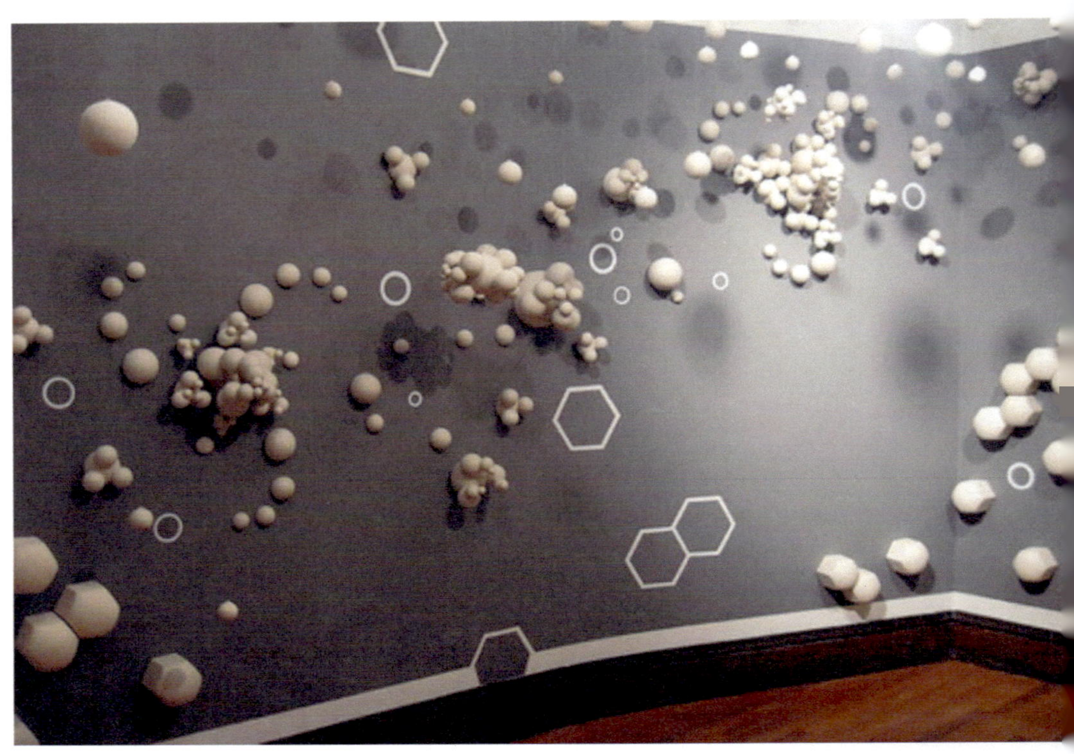

"A Stochastic System", Sarah House[3]

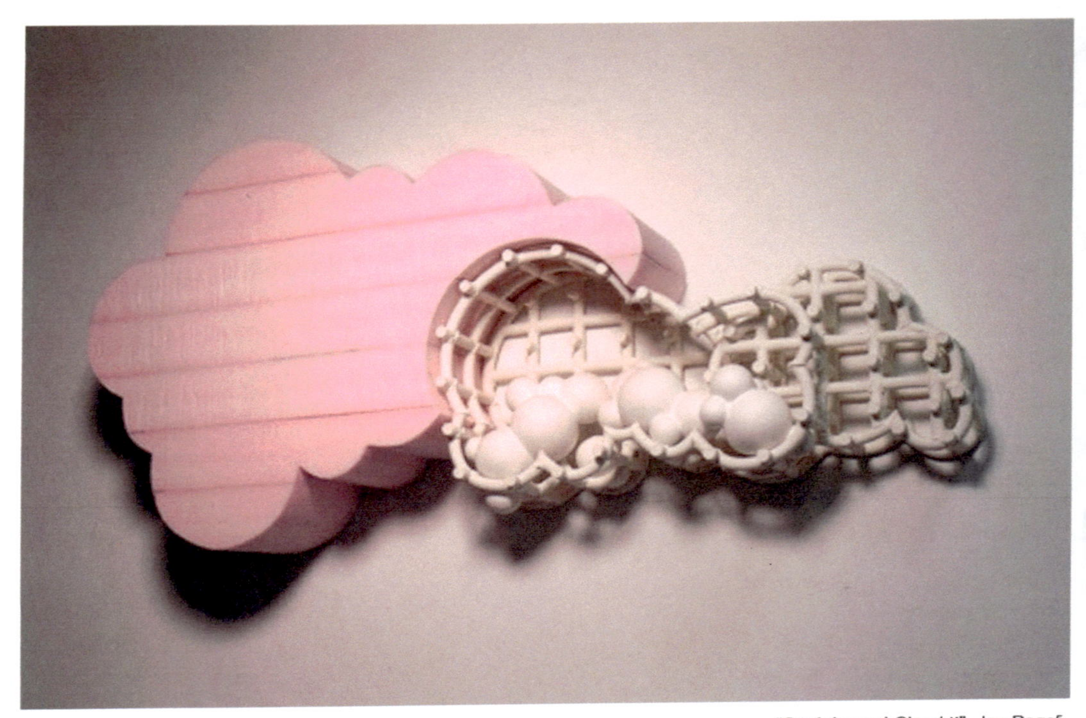

"Containment Cloud II", Joe Page[5]

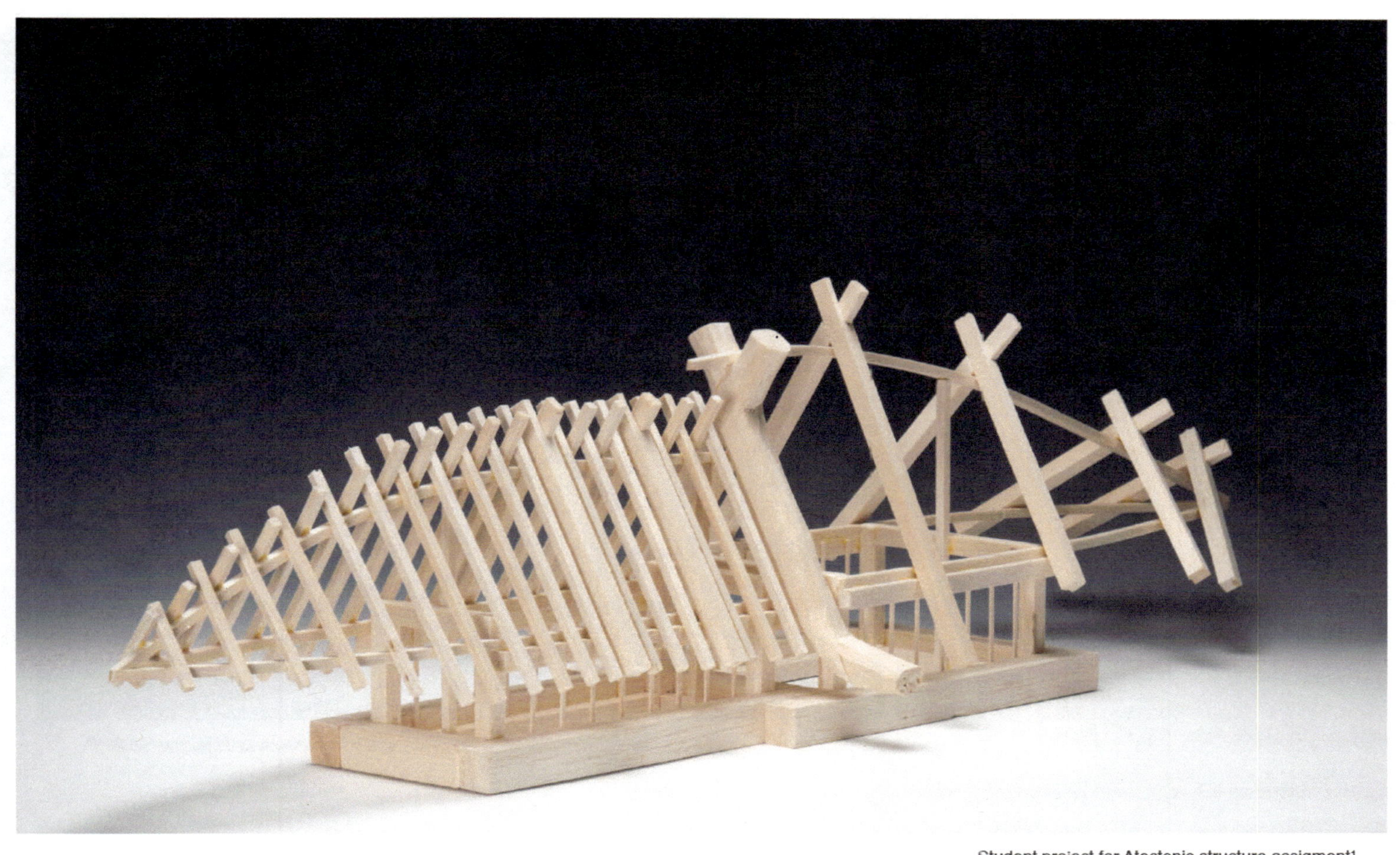

Student project for Atectonic structure assigment[1]

19

ASSIGNMENTS

This section contains potential assignments for ARTS 1420. Please double check
with the instructor as some criteria change semester to semester.

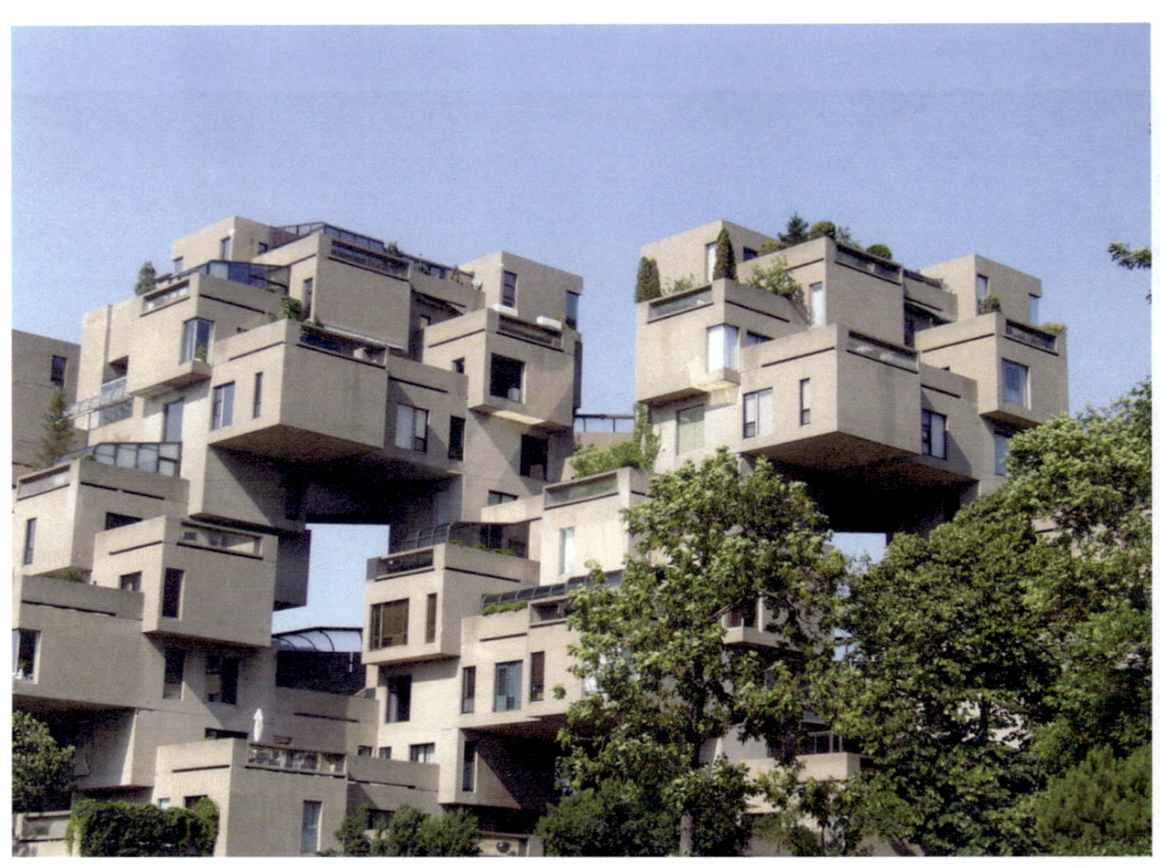

"Habitat 67" in Montreal, Canada by Moshe Safdie [32]

TECTONIC MODULAR COMPOSITION

OBJECTIVE: to explore making three dimensional shapes from a flat stock material. Tectonic modules (also called Platonic solids) will be produced and then combined to create a larger work. The finished piece may or may not be tectonic.

MATERIALS: pencil, sketchbook, TinkerCAD, steel ruler, cutting mat, Exacto knife, cardstock, white glue

1. Using the worksheets provided as a pattern, trace five patterns (called nets) each for the tetrahedron, cube and octahedron on white cardstock. (15 shapes total, 5 of each type)

2. Cut out the patterns with your Exacto knife and steel ruler.

3. Score and fold at the dotted lines. Use the back of a tool (like your knife) to make the folds crisp. Then assemble with glue on the tabs- tabs go inside the shape. Make sure that pencil lines are inside the shape for better craftsmanship. Make sure to keep seams/folds crisp and keep the shapes clean.

4. Next in your handbook or on TinkerCAD, draw at least 5 thumbnail sketches of possible combinations of all 15 shapes to create a freestanding construction. Choose the most visually dynamic solution and glue the 15 modules together. Do not use any other supports or binding materials other than glue. Craftsmanship will be graded.

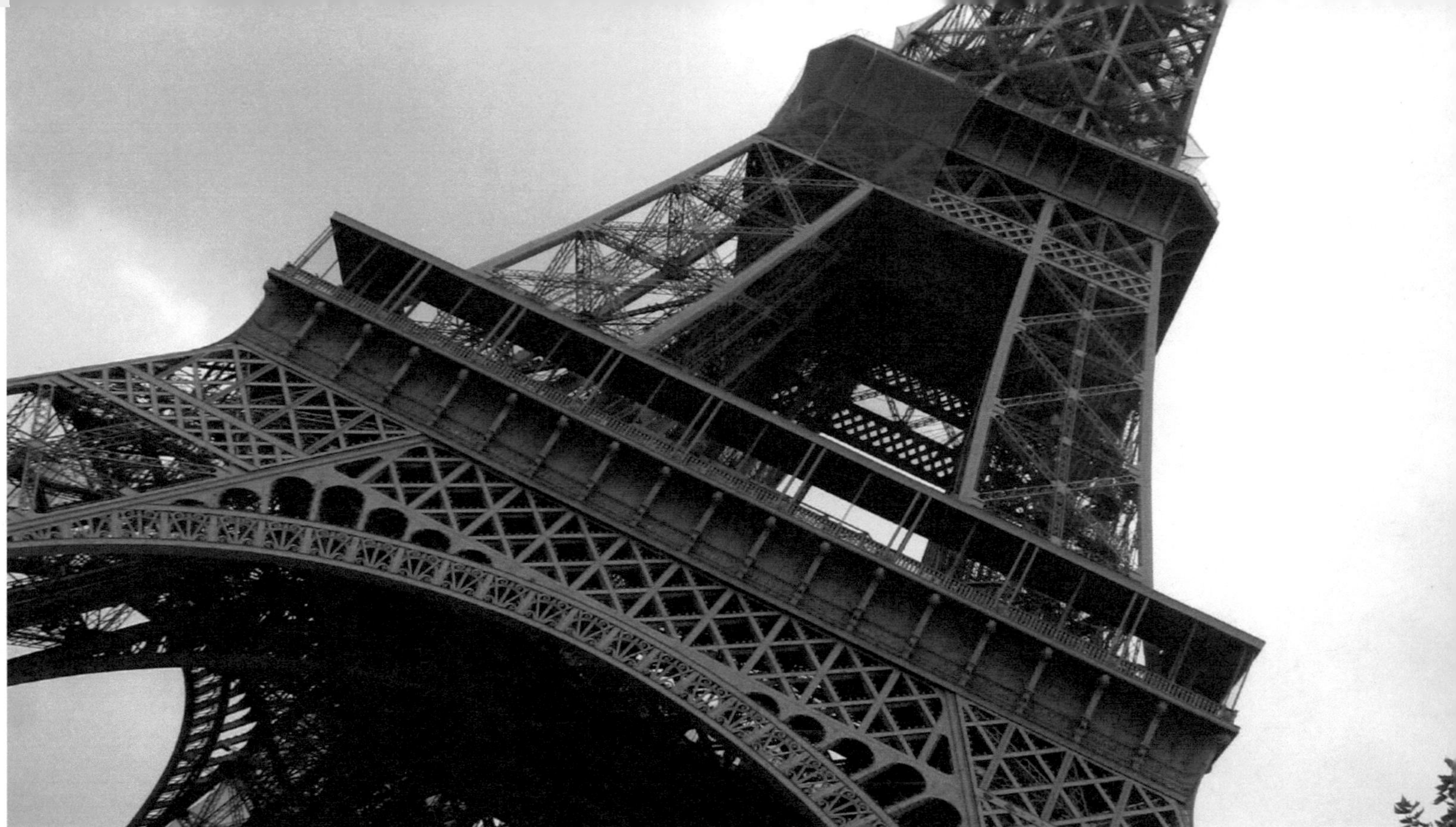

Eiffel Tower, Paris, France[1]

ATECTONIC STRUCTURE

OBJECTIVE: explore three-dimensional line, shape and space by creating an atectonic structure.

MATERIALS: sketchbook / exacto knife / wood glue / balsa wood / sandpaper, cutting mat

METHOD:

Research Phase:
1. Using architectural, airplane, bridge, and boat hull forms (or combinations) as inspiration: research, print out, and glue into your handbook at least 5 pictures that can serve as inspiration for your piece. Explore possible structures with at least 5 sketched concepts for your larger piece.
2. Using the best concept, establish a basic concept / shape. Explore different types of connections for the elements of the piece.

Building Phase:
1. Create a structure that is at least 12" in one direction. The final piece will be freestanding. Begin construction by building the main support elements. Use pins to tack balsa wood in place while gluing (if necessary). Proceed to smaller detail areas.
3. Continue to increase interior structure and detail.
4. Good craftsmanship is essential.

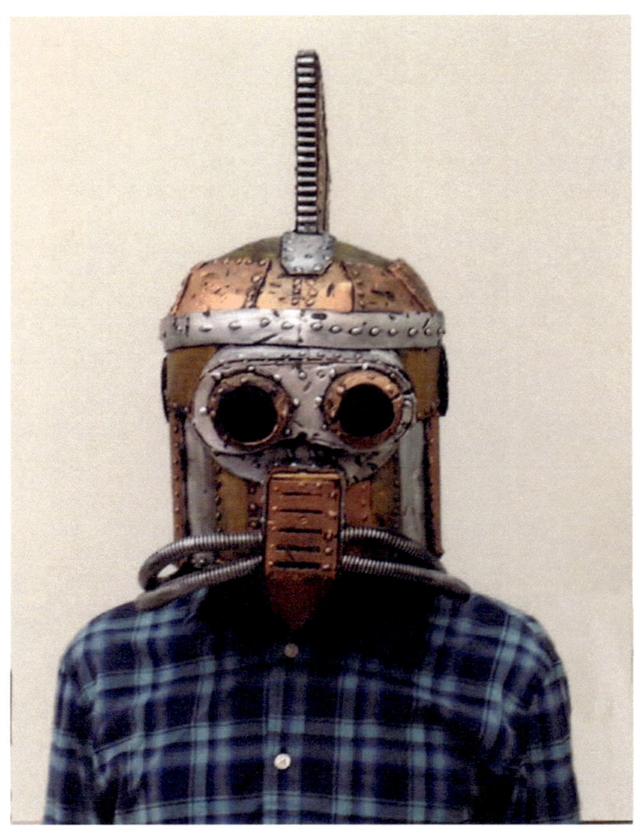
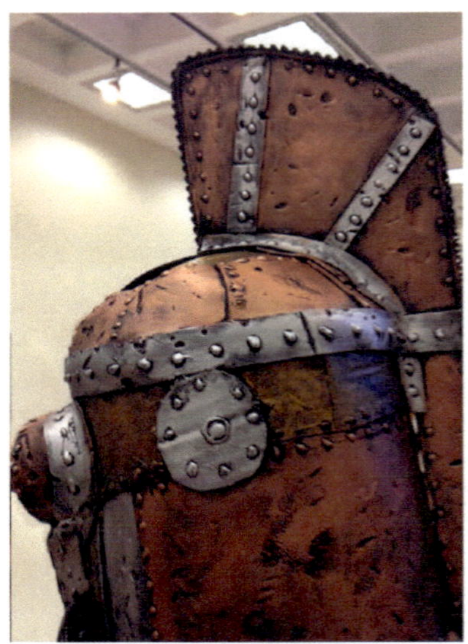

Student example [1]

CARDBOARD WEARABLE

OBJECTIVE: explore three dimensional line, shape and space to create a wearable sculpture made from cardboard as the base material

MATERIALS: sketchbook, utility knife, glue, cardboard, other materials as needed

METHOD:

Research Phase:

1. Research existing historical, sport, fantasy, and science fiction examples as inspiration: print out, and glue into your handbook at least 5 pictures that can serve as inspiration for your helmet design. Explore possible prototypes with at least 5 sketched concepts for your larger piece.
2. Using the best concept, establish a basic concept / shape. The final design must not interfere with vision or speech of the wearer.

Building Phase:
1. Create a sculpture that will be worn on your body at the critique. The final piece must fit you and must touch your head and at least 1 other area of your body (shoulder, arm, feet…). Begin construction by building the main elements and system to stabilize the sculpture.
2. Continue to increase details and finish the surface to fit your design.
3. Good fit and craftsmanship are essential.

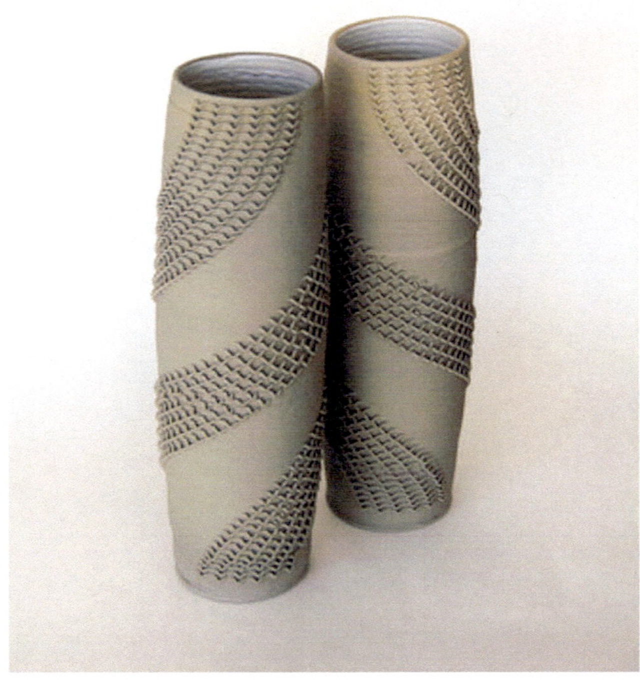

3d printed ceramic vases by Sanver Özgüven[3]

CAD AND 3D PRINTING

OBJECTIVE: to explore three dimensional line, shape, space, volume (both open and enclosed); to create a visually dynamic structure that is extremely small in scale using the tools of Computer Aided Design (CAD) modeling software and 3-d printing. The piece should include details that will provide interest within the structure as well as on the surface.

MATERIALS: TinkerCAD software, laptop, 3-d printer

METHOD:

1. Explore the TinkerCAD software tools and create possible structures through at least 3 prototype designs. The object should be no larger than 3" to 4" in any direction and should explore enclosed and open volume and the new possibilities of the 3-d printer. Surface texture can also be a consideration to increase visual and tactile interest. Prototypes will be projected on screen for discussion, critique, and selection for printing.

2. Email the final TinkerCAD file in STL file format to be printed using your full name was the file name. Objects will be returned once printing is complete.

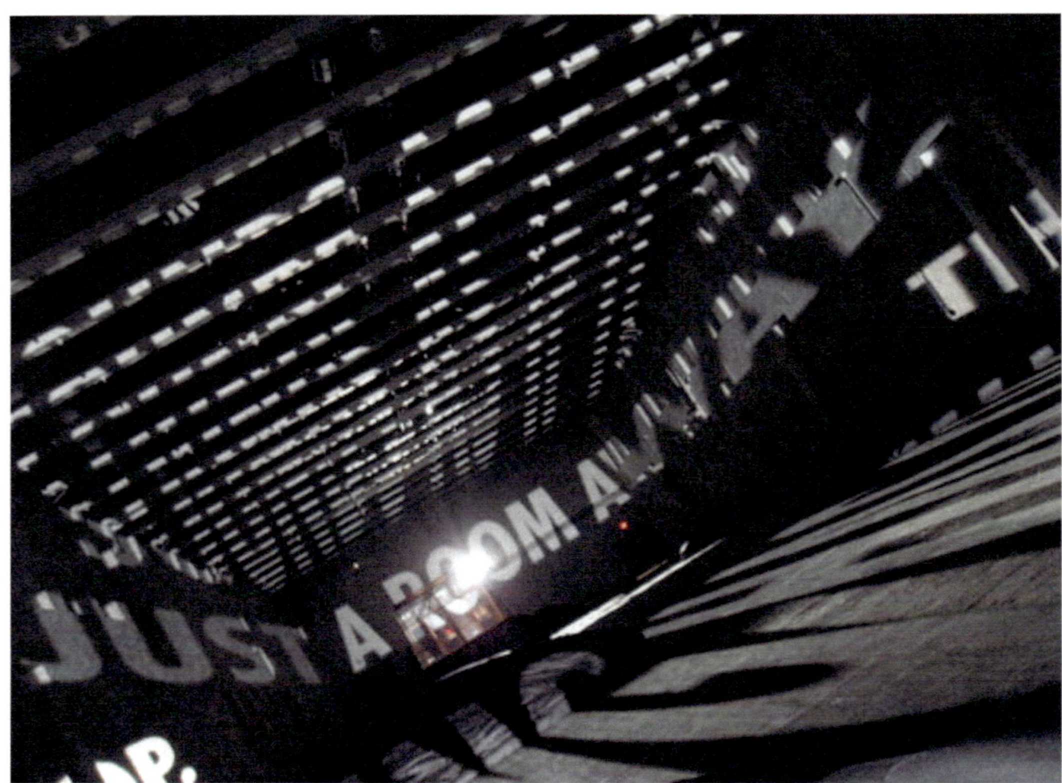

Jenny Holzer projection piece "Just a Room..."[34]

VIDEO

OBJECTIVE: to explore four-dimensional elements of light, movement, time, sound and the principles of duration, intensity, tempo, and transition.

We are surrounded by video / film on TV, YouTube, and social media video sharing. A number of artists are utilizing these tools and ideas to create powerful works of art. This project will help you understand and get basic experience with creating a video work. Your video will deal specifically with the critically important 4d art approach dealing with time.

MATERIALS: phone or camera capable of recording video, video editing software if needed

METHOD:

1. Create a plan for the overall idea and makeup of your video. Storyboarding ideas in your sketchbook will be helpful in executing the work. The theme must address recording TIME in some manner. Some basic ways to approach this could be through showing transformations, consumption, flow, duration, passage, light change....

Keep this in mind as you develop your idea— NO CLOCKS- analog or digital should be used to show time passing.

2. Record the video clips needed. If you would like to use basic video editing software (like iMovie) you may do this but it is not required. Your piece needs to have at least a 1 minute duration but last not more than 3 minutes.

3. Video pieces may be viewed at the critique on your phone, projected from computer onto the screen, or shared on video services like YouTube or Vimeo. The way you display your work needs to be taken into consideration and could improve or take away from the effectiveness of your work.

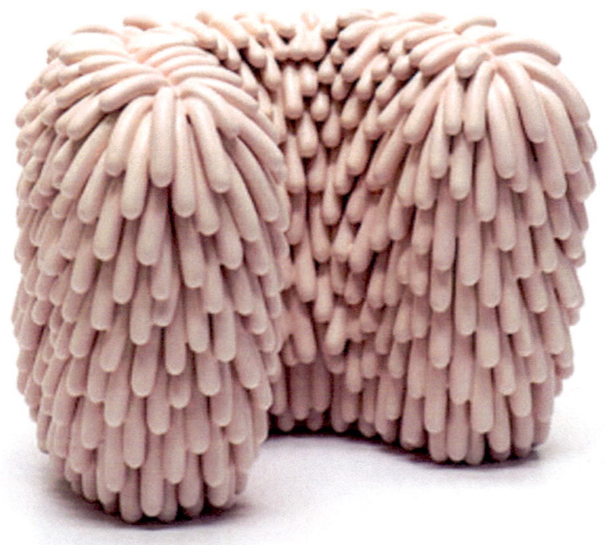

"Untitled (Pink Horseshoe)", handbuilt earthenware by Linda Lopez[3]

CERAMIC CONSTRUCTION

OBJECTIVE: to explore three dimensional line, shape, space, volume (both open and enclosed) and texture. The piece should include details to provide interest within the structure as well as on the surface. The work should be freestanding and structurally sound and must be at least 12" in at least one direction.

MATERIALS: clay, slip, glaze

Note we will be working in the Ceramics studio for this project, meet there at the beginning of class

METHOD:

1. Do research (text and visual) on the words/ideas you are assigned from the Richard Serra "Verb List Compilation: Actions to Relate to Oneself."

2. Explore possible sculptures that directly relate to your assigned words/ideas through a series of sketches. Establish a basic concept / shape. Explore the clay material, and investigate different types of supports, connections and joints for the piece. Surface texture should also be a consideration to increase visual interest. Be aware that if the clay dries too much, you will not be able to continue to add new elements.

Richard Serra, "Verb List Compilation: Actions to Relate to Oneself" (1967-1968)

to roll
to crease
to fold
to store
to bend
to shorten
to twist
to dapple
to crumple
to shave
to tear
to chip
to split
to cut
to sever
to drop
to remove
to simplify
to differ
to disarrange
to open
to mix
to splash
to knot
to spill
to droop
to flow

to curve
to lift
to inlay
to impress
to fire
to flood
to smear
to rotate
to swirl
to support
to hook
to suspend
to spread
to hang
to collect
of tension
of gravity
of entropy
of nature
of grouping
of layering
of felting
to grasp
to tighten
to bundle
to heap
to gather

to scatter
to arrange
to repair
to discard
to pair
to distribute
to surfeit
to compliment
to enclose
to surround
to encircle
to hole
to cover
to wrap
to dig
to tie
to bind
to weave
to join
to match
to laminate
to bond
to hinge
to mark
to expand
to dilute
to light

to modulate
to distill
of waves
of electromagnetic
of inertia
of ionization
of polarization
of refraction
of tides
of reflection
of equilibrium
of symmetry
of friction
to stretch
to bounce
to erase
to spray
to systematize
to refer
to force
of mapping
of location
of context
of time
of cabonization
to continue

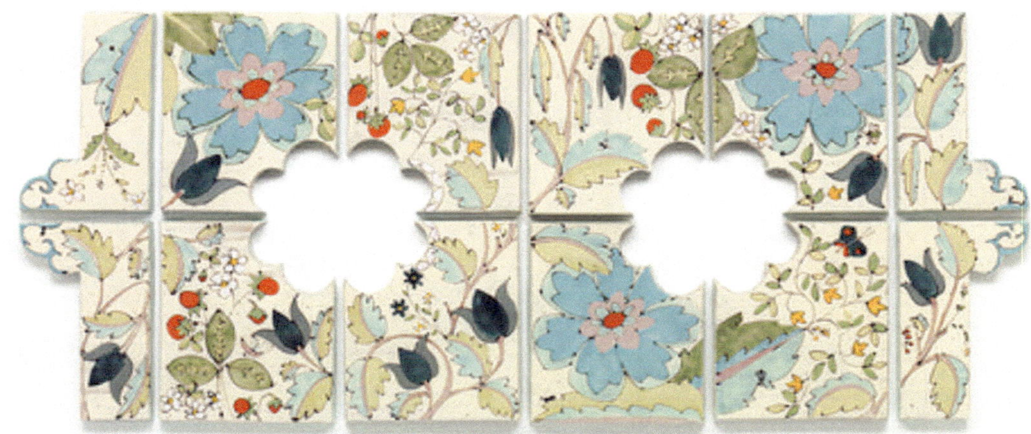

PLASTER MOLDS

OBJECTIVE: to explore three dimensional line, shape, space, volume (both open and enclosed) and texture through the process of mold making. The overall composition will be made up of 2 different master shapes that will have plaster press-molds created for the production of at least 4 total elements. The work should be designed to hang on a wall and should take up at least 12" in height and width.

MATERIALS: clay and plaster

METHOD:

1. Design 2 different shapes that have 6" square flat backs and that should fit together to create a larger composition. Create the 2 shapes in clay.

2. Both shapes will be used to create simple 1 piece plaster molds. Once the plaster molds are dry, remove the clay, clean them off, and allow them to dry fully.

3. Use the molds to press in new clay and create a total of 6 different shapes that will make up the larger piece. Make sure to deal with a hanging method on the back of the shapes.

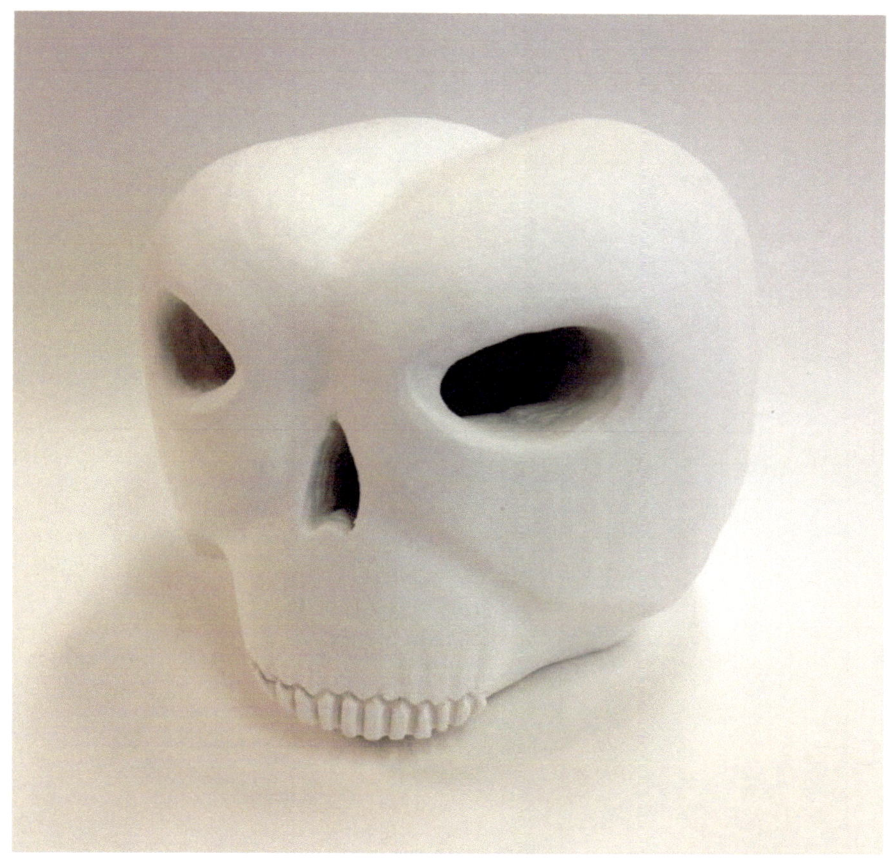

Student example [1]

CARVING

OBJECTIVE: to explore three dimensional line, shape, space, volume (both open and enclosed) and texture through subtractive carving. The piece should include details to provide interest within the shape as well as on the surface. The work should be freestanding and structurally sound. No original contours of the container used to cast the plaster block should remain in the final piece.

MATERIALS: plaster and carving tools

METHOD:

1. Assess the overall scale and shape of the solid block.

2. Sketch possible sculptures in your handbook that utilize the elements of 3-d design you have learned this semester. Begin by roughing out the major contours of the shape and then progress to smaller details like surface texture. Your finished piece must have at least 1 negative space that cuts through the entire mass of plaster.

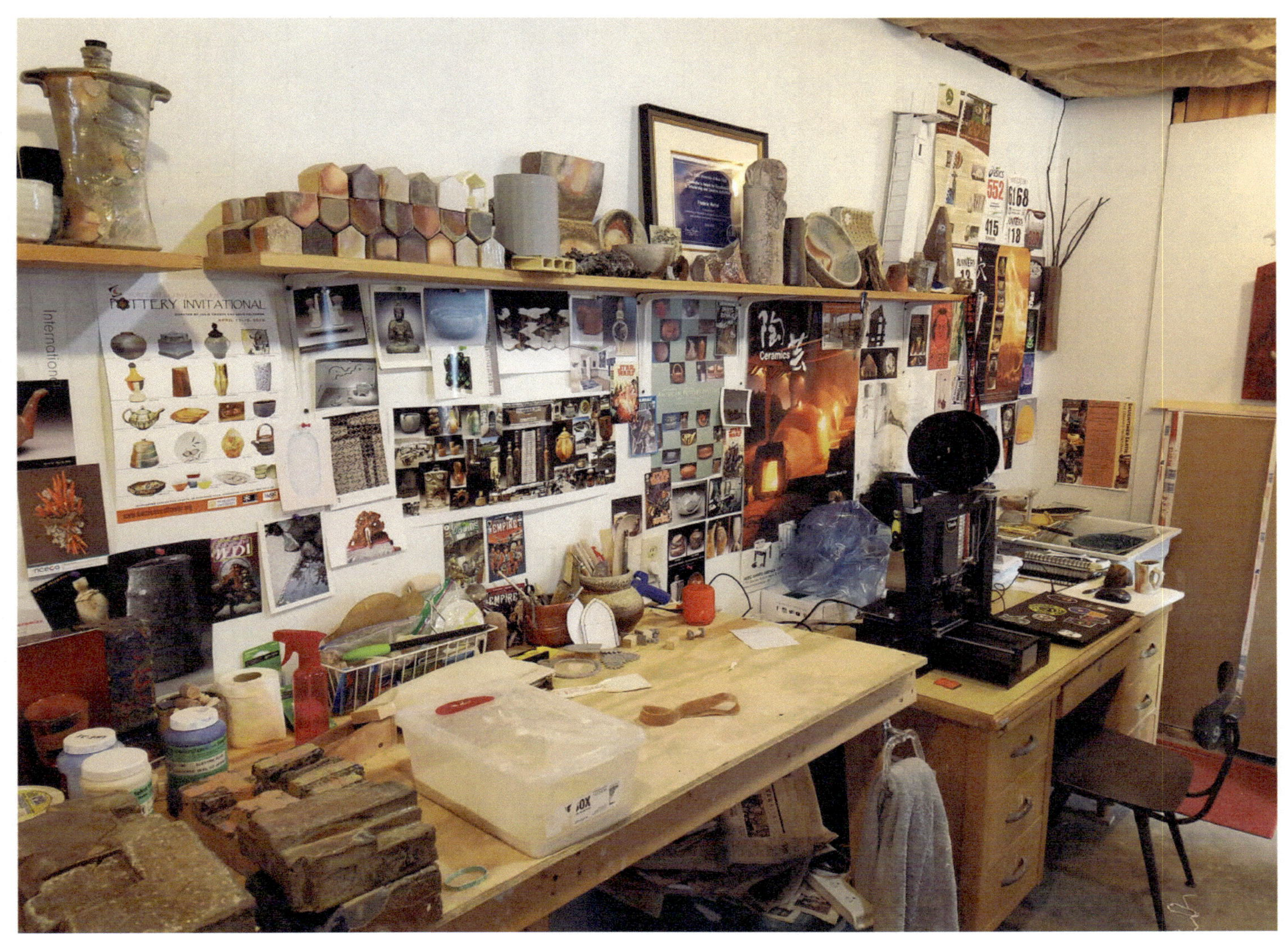

A studio in action [1]

20
RESOURCES

RESOURCES

Recommended Art and Design transfer schools for a focus in 3d materials:

SUNY / Public
New York State College of Ceramics at Alfred University
SUNY - New Paltz
SUNY-Purchase
Penn State
Tyler School of Art at Temple University

Private
Syracuse University
RIT

Ceramics Suppliers
Bailey Ceramic Supply - Kingston, NY
Clayscapes Pottery, Inc. - Syracuse, NY
Studio Sales Pottery Supply Co. - Avon, NY

Books and Magazines
Art books in the N, TP, and TT sections in the SUNY-CCC library
Art related magazines at the CCC Library: *Art in America, Ceramics Monthly, American Craft, Pottery Making Illustrated*

Web Resources
Art Axis- artaxis.org
CFile Online- cfileonline.org
NCECA - nceca.net
Access Ceramics- accessceramics.org/
Ceramic Arts Network - ceramicartsnetwork.org
Julia Galloway's Field Guide for Ceramic Artisans- ceramicsfieldguide.org/
Colossal blog- www.thisiscolossal.com

IMAGE ATTRIBUTIONS

Images in the Studio Handbook were used under a variety of Creative Commons licenses. The main sources were from the Access Ceramics database, the Metropolitan Museum of Art, and images taken by Fred Herbst. Number notations below correspond to the Supersript Number in each caption and also indicate the source and type of Creative Commons license of each image.

Any image not noted with a caption was taken by Fred Herbst and may be used under the Creative Commons license: Attribution-ShareAlike 3.0 Unported (CC BY-SA 3.0)

1- image by Fred Herbst, Attribution-ShareAlike 3.0 Unported (CC BY-SA 3.0)

Images from Access Ceramics Database - http://accessceramics.org

2- Attribution- 2.0 Generic (CC BY 2.0)
3- Attribution-NonCommercial-NoDerivs 2.0 Generic (CC BY-NC-ND 2.0)
5- Attribution-NoDerivs 2.0 Generic (CC BY-ND 2.0)
9- Attribution-ShareAlike 3.0 (CC BY-SA 3.0)
13- Attribution-NonCommercial-ShareAlike 2.0 Generic (CC BY-NC-SA 2.0)
14- Attribution-NonCommercial 2.0 Generic (CC BY-NC 2.0)

Online Collection of the Metropolitan Museum of Art
https://www.metmuseum.org/

4- Attribution- CC0 1.0 Universal (CC0 1.0) Public Domain Dedication

Other Images
6- Wikimedia Commons - This work is in the public domain in its country of origin and other countries and areas where the copyright term is the author's life plus 100 years or less. This work is in the public domain in the United States because it was published (or registered with the U.S. Copyright Office) before January 1, 1923.

7- Drawn by Dick Lyon and posted to Wikimedia Commons. I, the copyright holder of this work, release this work into the public domain. This applies worldwide.

8- By unknown - http://libraryphoto.cr.usgs.gov/cgi-bin/show_picture.cgi?ID=ID.%20Bartsch-Winkler,%20S,%20%20%20%20%20%20%20%208, Public Domain, https://commons.wikimedia.org/w/index.php?curid=26512534

12- Coyau / Wikimedia Commons / CC BY-SA 3.0

15- image by angs school/ CC BY-NC-ND 2.0

16- image by ShellyS/ CC BY-NC-SA 2.0

Online Collection of the Art Institute of Chicago

www.artic.edu/collection

17- Attribution- CC0 1.0 Universal (CC0 1.0) Public Domain Dedication

Images from Creative Commons Image Search

18- image by Marc Wathieu / CC BY-NC-ND 2.0

19- image by mira66 / CC BY-NC-SA 2.0

20- image by yrpopqueen / CC BY-NC-ND 2.0

21- image by profzucker / CC BY-NC-SA 2.0

22- image by Brandon Morse / CC BY 2.0

23- image by M D Schilling / CC BY-NC-ND 2.0

24- image by Mark Nazimova / CC BY-NC 2.0

25- image by sansumbrella / CC BY-NC-ND 2.0

26- image by James Beardmore / CC BY-NC 4.0

27- images by Alejandro Palandjoglou / CC BY-NC 4.0

28- image by Johnson Trading Gallery / CC BY 2.0

29- image by Atelier Teee / CC BY-NC-ND 2.0

30- image by kellan / CC BY-SA 2.0

31- image by nicmcc / CC BY-NC-SA 2.0

32- image by Moise sauvé des Eaux / CC BY-NC-SA 2.0

33- image by smallcurio / CC BY 2.0

34-image by bgblogging / CC BY-NC-SA 2.0